W9-BXM-373

Tragedy,

Myth, and

Mystery

RICHMOND Y.
HATHORN

Indiana University Press
Bloomington

Tragedy,

Myth, and

Mystery

46322

*This book has been published with the assistance
of a grant from the Ford Foundation.*

Contents

Acknowledgments

CHAPTERS 3, 4, and 5 are developments of articles which appeared in *The Classical Journal;* Chapter 8 appeared in substantially its present form in *The Centennial Review:* my thanks to the respective editors, Professors Norman T. Pratt, Jr., and Herbert Weisinger, for permission to use this material.

Chapter 6 was developed from a public lecture delivered in the spring of 1959 at the University of Notre Dame and the University of Michigan, thanks to the kindness of Dean Charles E. Sheedy, Professors John Edward Hardy, Gerald F. Else, and Warner G. Rice.

Grateful acknowledgment is especially due to the American Council of Learned Societies, whose grant-in-aid for 1958–59 made possible much necessary research.

The quotations from the following works of T. S. Eliot are reprinted by permission of Harcourt, Brace and Company, Inc.: *Murder in the Cathedral,* copyright, 1935, by Harcourt, Brace and Company, Inc.; "Ash Wednesday" from *Collected Poems 1909–1935,* copyright, 1936, by Harcourt, Brace and Company, Inc.; "Burnt Norton," "Little Gidding," and "East

Coker" from *Four Quartets*, copyright, 1943, by T. S. Eliot.

The following publishers and copyright holders have kindly given permission to quote from the works indicated: Mr. W. H. Auden, "New Year Letter," in *The Collected Poetry of W. H. Auden* (N. Y., Random House, 1945); Harper & Brothers, Gabriel Marcel's *Being and Having* (N. Y., Harper Torchbooks, 1961); Philosophical Library, Gabriel Marcel's *The Philosophy of Existence;* Harvard University Press, Cedric H. Whitman's *Sophocles: A Study of Heroic Humanism;* and University of California Press, E. R. Dodds' *The Greeks and the Irrational.*

Tragedy,

Myth, and

Mystery

$$\underline{\underline{1}}$$

Myth and Mystery

EVERYONE knows that mankind may be facing imminent annihilation, and everyone contemplates the prospect now and then with feelings of dread and satisfaction—satisfaction, that is to say, in the justice of it, that if we are fools enough to trigger the bombs, then nothingness quite properly should be our portion. But not many of us have heard or heeded another threat that lies on the farther side, if somehow our explosives fail to go off. Mankind, the physicians assure us, has physical immortality virtually within his grasp. Disease will some day be eliminated, they tell us; disorders are eventually to be tagged each with its prompt, appropriate remedy; and ways will be worked out by future Frankensteins to replace and replenish our worn organs and tissues with their mechanical and chemical equivalents, or with spare parts from blood-banks, muscle-banks, bone-banks, and ultimately, one must assume, brain-banks. As now our bodies travel through life ingesting and discarding a succession of unnumbered molecules, so that scarcely a single atom remains unexchanged from one year to the next, and so, to quote Hamlet, "a king may go a progress through the guts of a beggar," in the same way the man of the future, of the endless future, may go a progress piecemeal through an infinite sequence of physiques.

This is progress indeed, enough to give us as much pause as the present certitude of death; "for what is man that he should live out the lifetime of his God?" we ask astounded, like Father Mapple in *Moby Dick*. If, barring the exceedingly rare mischance, death becomes a matter of conscious choice, and if each individual must either forever "grunt and sweat under a weary life" or "his quietus make with a bare bodkin," and if we are no longer able to satisfy our curiosity about an eternity of bliss except by entering through the door of suicide, a means of entrance which, according to tradition, leads only to an eternity of hell, then what a dilemma will be ours!—compared to which the "to be or not to be" posed by the world-destroying bomb is merely a child's game of handy-dandy.

When Gulliver came to the kingdom of Luggnagg, having left behind him the flying island of Laputa, that utopia of scientific consummation, he learned of the existence of Struldbrugs—sports of nature produced no one knew how, who could never die. And when he exclaimed over the felicity of such a fate, his Luggnaggian interpreter wanted to "know in a particular manner, what scheme of living I should have formed to my self, if it had fallen to my lot to have been born a struldbrug." Gulliver eagerly replied, painting an idyllic picture of the chances for wealth and ease and liberality that a deathless life would afford, and emphasizing especially the opportunity to acquire unlimited knowledge and wisdom: he would live to see "the discovery of the *longitude*, the *perpetual motion*, and many other great inventions brought to the utmost perfection."

The Luggnaggian laughed at his reaction. Actually, Gulliver discovered, Struldbrugs were despised and hated by all people; their lot was considered appalling. Though most of their misery sprang from the lessening of bodily and mental powers that comes from old age—and the Struldbrugs that our great-grandchildren are to be converted into will presumably take care of that—, yet they were loathed as well because "they had not only all the follies and infirmities of other old men, but many more which arose from the dreadful prospects of never dying. They were not only opinionative, peevish, covetous, morose, vain, talkative, but incapable of friendship, and dead to all natural affection."

But doubtless the learned scientists of the Grand Academy of Lagado, capital of Balnibarbi, which was overshadowed by the flying island of Laputa, could have remedied these vices by sawing into the skull and rearranging the brain-matter, by which means they proposed to reconcile the differences of party-men, or by administering those "lenitives, aperitives, abstersives, corrosives, restringents, palliatives, laxatives, cephalalgics, icterics, apophlegmatics, acoustics" by which they calculated to set erring lawmakers aright. By application of scientific method the Laputians and Balnibarbians could solve every problem, or supposed that they could; and if the tailor who measured Gulliver with quadrant, rule, and compasses came up with a suit of clothes "very ill made and quite out of shape," if the wives of eminent scientists granted their favors to strangers under the very noses of their husbands, who were so rapt in experimentation that they took no notice, such things were little regarded. The creed of Laputianism was Salvation through Science, and those problems that were not amenable to scientific solution were looked upon willy-nilly as solved, or else presumed not to be problems at all.[1]

But Swift went mad, and must always have been mad if
we today are sane. For his fate seems to be taken as proof
that his strictures on science may be discounted. In fact, the
Third Book of the *Travels* still suffers neglect and depre-
ciation, though it functions importantly as the mid-portion
of an exposition which has as its first sections two portrayals
of man's insignificance and as its conclusion the proof that
the life of cold reason may be suitable for horses, but is unavailable to our corrupt humanity. Such messages, sent to
us by every great imaginative thinker from Swift's time on,
are read with undeviating derision. Yet modern man, "Em-
piric Economic Man," as Auden calls him,

> could not silence all the cliques
> And no miraculous techniques
> Could sterilise all discontent
> Or dazzle it into assent,
> But at the very noon and arch
> Of his immense triumphal march
> Stood prophets pelting him with curses
> And sermons and satiric verses. . . .
> The World ignored them; they were few.
> The careless victor never knew
> Their grapevine rumour would grow true,
> Their alphabet of warning sounds
> The common grammar all have grounds
> To study; for their guess is proved:
> It is the Mover that is moved. [2]

If their guess is indeed proved, the news has not yet been
fully communicated to the Twentieth Century. Who can
doubt that Laputianism is flourishing as never before?
Leaving aside as beneath contempt "all the happy endings"
of our mass entertainments, who can survey our popular
magazines without queasiness? Every page either provides

cheap escape from the world that the scientist for the past three centuries has been so rapidly perfecting, or else cele-brates the reign of Mr. Universal Fixit himself, "the expert on human relations," who purveys to us the soporific click-ing of problems outlined, problems analyzed, and problems solved. But perhaps this is to keep one's sights too low; after all, reading periodical literature falls into that class of amusements to which Coleridge assigns "swinging or sway-ing on a chair or gate; spitting over a bridge; smoking; snuff-taking; and tête-à-tête quarrels after dinner between husband and wife." [3] One ascends to the learned journals. Here psychology and sociology, sterile and impotent after their highly publicized divorce from ethics, busy them-selves degrading to the status of problems all the mysteries of individual and cosmic evil. And this they do on the basis of the great discovery that they are exempt from philo-sophical criticism, since every philosophy is conditioned by individual personality and social milieu. But they fail to see that a man armed with such a logical instrument, like *The Mikado*'s Lord High Executioner,

> Cannot cut off another's head
> Until he's cut his own off.

Then if one goes to the schools of philosophy and asks for bread today, one is given, not even a stone, but a calculus. "All thinking is problem-solving," the textbooks on logic be-gin. (Alas for the anciently honored activities of medita-tion, contemplation, and artistic creation, which are airily banished from the realm of thought.) "Philosophy's proper mission," one is told, "is not to talk about anything, but to talk about talking, to prune down all ratiocination to the bareness of mathematics, which is not about anything but itself, and to perfect that scientific method by which we may more quickly reach the goal." What goal? "Why, none, for the end of what used to be the study of ends is now a means to the study of means: philosophy, once the queen of the sciences, is now the handmaid of her handmaids; and the mother of knowledge, by some devilish miracle, has become the daughter of her son. We have reversed the request of Archimedes; we now say, 'Give me no place on which to stand, and I will move the world.'"

And yet, all the same: "It is the Mover that is moved." It is the Solver that is the ultimate Problem. The chief ingredient of every solution is the solver himself, who enters in with all his limitations.[4] For these limitations he can never adequately compensate, limited as he is in his ability to discern them and in his willingness to discount them. He can reasonably use his reason only to the extent that he recognizes that unreason bounds it on every side. As his problems approach more nearly to affecting his self-interest, as, unfortunately, their solution becomes more vital to him, they shade into mysteries.

The term "mystery" need not imply a surrender to mysticism. It can be defined; Gabriel Marcel, in *Being and Having*, makes a distinction between mysteries and problems:[5]

A problem is something which I meet, which I find complete before me, but which I can therefore lay siege to and reduce. But a mystery is something in which I myself am involved, and it can therefore only be thought of as "a sphere where the distinction between what is in me and what is before me loses its meaning and its initial validity." A genuine problem is subject to an appropriate technique by the exercise of which it is defined; whereas a mystery, by definition, transcends every conceivable technique. It is, no doubt, always possible (logically and psychologically) to degrade a mystery so as to turn it into a problem. But this is a fundamentally vicious proceeding, whose springs might perhaps be discovered in a kind of corruption of the intelligence. The problem of evil, as the philosophers have called it, supplies us with a particularly instructive example of its degradation.

In this passage Marcel does not proceed to spell out exactly how a mystery may be "degraded" into a problem, but mention of the "problem of evil" makes clear what is meant. The pertinent question about evil is usually phrased as "Who created evil?" or "Where in the world does evil come from?" Or, if the questioner is more sophisticated, he asks, "How could a God who is all-loving, all-knowing, and all-powerful allow evil to come into the world?" In this very act of formulating the question the individual mind obviously tends to withdraw from the data before it, to *objectify* them in the strict sense, and to exclude itself, the subject, from any possible part in the answer. Only by painfully doubling back on itself may the mind reach the reluctant conclusion, "I created evil." Furthermore, the conclusion is one that we are prone to entertain only abstractly and to classify in the category of truths about atoms, or animals, or other human beings. Marcel enlarges upon this in *The Philosophy of Existence:* [6]

A mystery is a problem which encroaches upon its own data, invading them, as it were, and thereby transcending itself as a simple problem. . . .
It will be seen at once that there is no hope of establishing an exact frontier between problem and mystery. For in reflecting on a mystery we tend inevitably to degrade it to the level of a problem. This is particularly clear in the case of the problem of evil.
In reflecting upon evil, I tend, almost inevitably, to regard it as a disorder which I view from outside and of which I seek to discover the causes or the secret aims. Why is it that the

"mechanism" functions so defectively? Or is the defect merely apparent and due to a real defect of my vision? In this case the defect is in myself, yet it remains objective in relation to my thought, which discovers it and observes it. But evil which is only stated or observed is no longer evil which is suffered: in fact, it ceases to be evil. In reality, I can only grasp it as evil in the measure in which it *touches* me—that is to say, in the measure in which I am *involved*, as one is involved in a lawsuit. Being "involved" is the fundamental fact; I cannot leave it out of account except by an unjustifiable fiction, for in doing so, I proceed as though I were God, and a God who is an onlooker at that.

"He who can live in solitude is either a God or a beast": let us twist Aristotle's well-known saying and apply it to the explication of mystery. Man has no choice but to live in solitude, at least in partial solitude, because of his unique epistemological position: he is the only creature who thinks in time, yet whose thoughts transcend time. He strains under the incessant twin temptations, either of imagining himself a God ("and a God who is an onlooker at that"— certainly not the Christian God, who is very much involved —perhaps a kind of Epicurean god, a quasi-god) or of resigning himself to the status of a beast.[7] Here is the central mystery. Man is both a part of the universe, and apart from the universe; as a subject he may observe himself as an object; he oscillates between subjectivity and objectivity, or rather partakes of both simultaneously; he must come to terms with the temporally-bound percept and the concept which is to some degree freed from time.[8] Ethically and aesthetically he lives constantly in the presence of two worlds which are nevertheless one: the world as it is and the world as it ought to be.[9] Like Captain Ahab, he is a specimen riven from top to toe, who looks out upon a uni-

verse that seems equally split, and who feels that of all
seams and dents this is the one that is alone unsmooth-
able.[10] Yet at the same time he knows that the universe is
one, that he is the microcosm of the macrocosm, that its
essential reality appears again in his essence. But where
and how does the exterior reality leave off and the interior
begin? Is the interior or the exterior prior in logic? Or is
there no leaving-off, but only, against all appearances, a
continuum? In that case one is faced again with the unholy
choice of setting oneself up as a God or of declining toward
the beast.

> Wär' nicht das Auge sonnenhaft,
> Die Sonne könnt' es nie erblicken—
>
> Had not the eye a sunlike nature,
> The eye could never see the sun—

Goethe reminds us, echoing Platonic and pre-Platonic mus-
ings. True, but how much light is reflected in the eye, how
much issues from the eye itself?

"All light is from the Sun," answers one group of modern
thinkers. "All light is from the Eye," says the other.

This is the perennial dilemma of human thought, the
everlasting mystery. But it is the dubious distinction of
modern man, of post-Cartesian man, to have degraded this
mystery to the level of a problem, and then to have "solved"
it by impaling himself on either the subjective or the objective horn. Or worse still, to have pretended that there is
neither mystery nor problem and then, varying the metaphor, to have gone charging at full speed down one road or
the other, without knowing which.[11] We refuse to be awak-
ened from the Dream of Descartes.[12] Our scientists have
laid down as their basic principle, "Have nothing to do with
metaphysics!" Then, on a foundation of metaphysics

which, because it is resolutely not examined, is presumed not to exist, they have raised their "logical constructs" about physical reality.

How, then, do we return to the primeval mystery?

Suppose a group of Western observers watching a primitive ritual, a leopard-dance by some African tribesmen, for instance.[13] If it is a typical group, we may expect three kinds of reactions. A certain number of naive romanticists, deploring the separateness of the Eye and the Sun, and determined to behave as though Eye and Sun were one, will ask themselves, "What are these savages feeling when they enter into this dance? Are they not in some mystical way becoming leopards, leveling the barriers that separate man from the rest of creation?[14] May I not feel the same way? May I not also throw down the bars and enter into the dance?"[15] The savage might welcome these romanticists as fellow performers; there is something to be respected in this sympathetic reaction. Still, the reaction shocks reason, since it leaves reason altogether out of account, and must be felt to be artificial, and even degrading, in the sense of stepping down to a lower level.

Another part of the group would probably be made up of scientist-anthropologists. These assume that the Eye does not exist; they worship the Sun only; they are objective. They say to themselves, "Here we have a problem: why do these tribesmen behave as they do?" And they attack this problem with the most conscientious objectivity. They are resolved to be free from prejudice; no social or cultural biases, no individual likes or dislikes, are to be allowed to distort their perceptions of precisely what is occurring before them. Above all, no philosophical preconception, no twist of ethical interpretation can be admitted into their straightforward accounts; theirs is a descriptive science,

they proudly assert, not a prescriptive code. Their only tool
is reason, a reason cold and impersonal, uninfluenced by
emotionality, the "reason" that they have inherited from
eighteenth-century Rationalism. But they may not have
read that eighteenth-century classic, Dr. Johnson's *Rasselas*,
where Imlac remarks apropos of Egyptian mummies,
"Concerning superstitious ceremonies it is vain to conjec-
ture, for what reason did not dictate reason cannot explain."
For though they strip their thought of all local and regional
dress, they would never go as naked as the savages and
take off that habit which clings to it like the flesh to their
bones, the habit of pragmatic rationalism. When they ask,
"What are these savages doing?" they are betrayed by the
logical prejudices of three hundred years into meaning,
"What are they trying to do? What are they producing?
What is the result? What is the effect of which this is the
cause? What are they getting done?" [16] But these are the
wrong questions, and the wrong questions lead them to an
answer that is at least partially wrong: "The savage is making sure that he will have good hunting. By sympathetic
magic he is identifying himself with the leopard, and
hopes for a share of the leopard's prowess. In his ignorance
he is attempting to do what modern science does much
better. For us the leopard-dance has been outmoded by the
high-powered rifle."

Which is as if an expert in traffic control went into a ball-
room and informed the dancers that they could get
through the room faster by walking. [17]

Still a third set of our modern onlookers would consist of
Freudian or, more likely, Jungian psychologists. Though
vaunting their "objectivity" as loudly as anyone else, they
are, philosophically speaking, subjectivists. Like all who degrade mysteries into problems, they must begin at the be-

ginning, whether there is a real beginning to begin at or not; and the point from which they choose to start their investigations is determined for them by their focus of interest, the individual human soul. So they start out with the epistemological subject.[18] To them "What is the African dancer doing?" means "What need is he satisfying by this activity?" As the old doctors used to explain that opium puts people to sleep because it contains a soporific principle, so the new psychologists account for human behavior by saying that it is the satisfaction of an inner need.[19] Furthermore, they add, this need is a necessary need; it necessitates such-and-such behavior. And if this necessitated behavior is not observable, then there is something grievously wrong—with the patient, of course, not with the theory. In this way the leopard-dance, and all ritual, and all myth, and all religion are not merely explained, but explained away. This kind of scientist prides himself on being more far-seeing and tolerant than the other kind, on the ground that he concedes that man does not live by bread alone; man lives by words as well. But to bring up the question whether these words proceed from the mouth of God is considered irrelevant, even scandalous.

At this point let us suppose that some child, or idiot, or classicist who is not impressed by Greco-Latinisms, asks the childish or idiotic or classical question that all the others have omitted to ask:

"Why is it that men dance leopard-dances, but no leopard has ever been known to dance a man-dance?"

To him the savage might divulge the really interesting reply, which he has been too polite or too suggestible or too bewildered to give to the others:

"Because the leopard feels at home in the world, while a man feels himself more or less a stranger."

In short, he does not dance because he "feels a need to imitate leopards;" this is to indulge in tautology, like the scientist who to the question, "What is there on the inside of things that makes them work as they do?" used to answer, "Energy." Nor does he dance primarily because he wants to get something done by the dance; he does not even want to get the dance done; he wants simply to dance. Nor—though this gets nearer to the mark—does he dance because he wants to break down the barriers that separate men from leopards. We must remember that although a leopard is presumably aware that he is not the same as a man, no leopard has ever been known to dance a man-dance. For while a leopard is presumably aware that he is not identical with a man, he is not aware that he is not totally different. He has never risen by comparison and contrast to the stage of conceptual thought which is the lowest level of reason. Dr. Johnson's Imlac was mistaken in one respect: reason *does* dictate these "superstitious ceremonies;" Dr. Johnson was misled by the eighteenth-century Rationalist's—and the Romanticist's and the objective-scientist's and the subjective-scientist's—error of defining reason solely in opposition to the feelings.

No, the savage's ceremony originates in an awareness that a man both is and is not akin to a leopard. The savage realizes that there is a breach of alienation between himself and the universe, but that this breach can be intermittently closed—not closed in actuality, but mimetically.[20] No matter how intensely, in the ecstasy of the rite, he may feel himself to be one with the beasts, and no matter now nearly he approximates to the beast's behavior, so that to some impressionable observers the savage at the height of his orgy may even seem to be transformed into a real leopard, the fact remains that the rite has been conceived and entered into deliberately by man and that the temporary leopard is bound to resume human form. Reason, will, and emotion are all ingredients in the ceremony.

In art, in myth, and in ritual man symbolizes his position of mystery vis-à-vis the universe.

The philosophers of the Enlightenment dismissed "the puerilities of obsolete mythology" (to use Johnson's phrase) as unworthy of any but satirical notice. Under the influence of romanticism, myths began to be taken seriously, but sentimentally; with his myths the primitive was conceded to have fulfilled a real need and to have discharged a real function in his society.[21] But the need, even if sympathized with and admitted to be permanent in human nature, was looked upon as emotional, and patronized accordingly, whereas the function was regarded as transitional to a more advanced state of civilization.[22] Traces of these two attitudes, the rationalistic and the romantic, are still prominent in modern mythography. In fact, about the only point that contemporary mythographers are agreed on is the rejection of the late-nineteenth-century theory of myth as "mistaken explanations of phenomena."

Aside from this, the contemporary scene is a chaos of warring factions.[23] Euhemerism, the contention that myths are distorted bits of history, has been scotched in every generation and is not yet dead. Often opposed to it is the belief that myth is the offshoot of ritual, but, logically considered, euhemerism and the latter theory are not entirely incompatible: if myths are the verbal equivalent of rites, then in a sense they are records of history, since the rites must have been performed repeatedly in historical circumstances. But myths, of course, are only records of customs, not of isolated events. A similar reconciliation may be brought about in the myth-versus-ritual controversy (and,

in fact, the synthetic view is now pretty generally acceded
to) to the effect that ritual is only the gestural and physical
side of a unified activity of which myth is the verbal side,
and that it is as bootless to argue for the precedence of
either myth or ritual as it would be to debate whether the
dialogue in a play originates in the action or vice versa.[24] A
myth is a scenario for a ritual; a ritual is a dramatic representation that becomes verbalized in a myth. This is not to
deny the possibility, even the virtual certainty, of all degrees of relationship between the two: myth and ritual may
at times have evolved independently of each other; [25]
either may have at times undergone considerable elaboration at the expense of the other; after an initial association
they may have become separated and gone their own ways;
after such a separation they may have been re-associated,
with consequent modifications to either or both. Admittedly the condition of mythology, of any mythology,
whenever it has finally come to be recorded, has been that
of a hopelessly tangled skein. Nevertheless, the connection
of myth with ritual seems necessarily admissible until it is
superseded by a superior single hypothesis; the eclectic
mythographer fights in vain against Occam's Law.

But having explained that myth originates in ritual, and
ritual in myth, what, after all, have we explained? Practically nothing. We have only pushed back to another stage
the answer to the question: What is myth?

There is need of a philosophical, not of a genetic, explanation.

We answer: A myth is a tissue of symbolism clothing a
mystery.[26] Mysteries are not completely inaccessible to the
discursive reason; it is the task of theology to analyze a
mystery as far as possible, to define it and to box it in. But
only symbolically can a mystery be entered, participated

in, coped with.[27] Mysticism is not implied by this definition. Whatever one may think about the credibility of mystics' narratives, they are not here in question, for the alleged direct experience of the mystic has nothing in itself to do with symbolization. Nor, by the same token, is the question one of emotional empathy, reason being shunted aside. Mythical thinking is a valid type of thinking, in spite of the fact that it cannot be classified as problem-solving. That it employs the reason is shown by its selection of the symbols themselves, a selection which is governed by the familiar principle of the appropriateness of the symbol to the matter symbolized, and this principle is simultaneously and inseparably both rational and affective.[28] It is a principle of perceptions and intuitions which yet can be communicated to a certain extent, and to a certain extent argued about and evaluated; if it were not so, all aesthetic discussion would be at an end.

"Exactly," say another school of mythographers; "myth is literature." [29] Before one can agree with this agreement, one must find out what such a statement means, for the members of the school are not really in agreement among themselves, one group convicting myth of triviality, the other granting it a false importance. All depends on whether they are Rationalists or Romanticists—the two classes that comprise all the workers in the "human sciences." Both groups regard literature as "an expression of the feelings," but the Rationalists exalt reason as an absolute, think of literature as entertainment, and belittle myth accordingly, while the Romanticists exalt the feelings as an absolute, consider literature a serious occupation, and assign to myth a jealously guarded but purposely obscure significance. A plague o' both their houses: human faculties ought not to be played off against one another in this fashion. Obviously myth is literature, inasmuch as it is verbal narrative. Just as obviously, all literature is not myth.[30]

We are brought back, then, to the foregoing definition: myth is literature that directly symbolizes man's position of mystery.[31]

Not too much literature does so; some writings, of a reformatory bent, attack the problems of this world almost as squarely as sociological tracts do; most of the rest, if not problem-solving, are on the level of puzzle-working, or perhaps a little below, since the entertainment is derived from the author's solving his puzzle with no effort on the reader's part.

But great tragedy, which is intimately dependent on myth for its material, seems to exist on another level. Aristotle observes in the *Poetics* that the great dramatists of his time had found that they could hardly dispense with subject-matter of a certain kind, namely with myths that had to do with the misfortunes of certain legendary houses.[32] He indicates that such plots had been found particularly suitable because they involved their protagonists in "suffering and perpetrating fearful deeds," because in them the shift from good to bad fortune was due not to wickedness, but to a "great *hamartia*" (whatever Aristotle may mean—of which more later), and because, in the best of them, the protagonist was eventually brought to some sort of recognition of his former ignorance. In all this Aristotle seems to be vaguely aware that there is a connection between the finest kinds of tragedy and myth, and a connection between myth and mystery. But his discussion of these connections does not seem to be very satisfactory.

Parenthetically, it ought to be admitted here that to quote Aristotle on a point of literary criticism is a dangerous

move. Whoever dares to do so is in the position of the
biologist or astronomer of the sixteenth century: if there is
any divergence, or fancied divergence, from the doctrines
of the Master, ninety per cent of all readers assume that
the Aristotelian Scriptures have been interpreted wrongly;
the other ten per cent take one to task for arrant heresy.
But it is impossible to stay away from Aristotelian conceptions and terminology or to remain content with Aristotle's
restricted and timid application of his own discoveries.
Critics commonly complain—though to some it appears to
be a cause for rejoicing—that the *Poetics* has nothing to say
about religion. Cold fish that he is, Aristotle regularly becomes skittish and evasive in the neighborhood of the mysterious.[33] It is enough to point out that if only the stories
of the legendary houses mentioned in the *Poetics* furnished
plots for the finest tragedies, then *The Bacchae*, for one, is
excluded from the first rank. And many other masterpieces
fall foul of one or more of Aristotle's specifications. Therefore we ought to restate the connection between myth and
literature on the basis that what is important is not ad-
herence to Aristotelian canons, but whether the judgment
is valid, or at least suggestive. So restated:

An impressively large amount of what is conceded to be
great literature deals with myths,[34] with stories that symbolize man's mysterious position in the universe. Nevertheless, the greatness of the literature obviously does not de-
pend merely on the mythical nature of its subject-matter.
In the original myth the mystery was doubtless directly
symbolized, as directly, that is, as the process of symbolization will allow. But for later ages, for audiences who were
losing their apprehension of mystery, the authors found it
necessary to rework the mythic material and to shift the
emphasis from bald presentation of the symbolic events to

such a treatment as would promote awareness of the mystery symbolized.[35] (It is of no import whether the authors' approach to this task was fully conscious.) There was need, the authors felt, to bring their auditors back to a clearer understanding of the human condition, to make them perceive through the medium of art what it is almost impossible to bring home to them through discursive logic: that a human being stands as a finitude in the midst of an infinite cosmos and that with this infinity he has simultaneous relations of conjunction and discontinuity.[36] The author therefore had to strike a balance between contemporary verisimilitude and the universal applicability of his mythic plot.[37] So, in the case of a tragic writer, by the manipulation of what Aristotle calls Plot, Character, Diction, Thought—and to a lesser extent by the skillful use of symbolism in visual accessories and in the appropriate musical accompaniment—he had to woo his audience away from the self-satisfaction arising from material progress and pragmatic success and bring them face to face with their insuperable limitations.[38]

Sometimes the audience was to be edified by the unfolding of the drama as a whole; in that case the playwright underscored the mythical features of his Plot and expressed his own insights into mystery through the Thought (*dianoia*) and the Diction. More often he let his audience undergo vicarious education by participating in the enlightenment of a protagonist or some personage near to the protagonist. And of course there could be combinations of these means and various degrees in the use of them. Hence Aristotle is again following a sound intuition when he devotes a long discussion to the delineation of Character. It is at this juncture that he advances his theory of *hamartia*.[39] This concept is too much intellectualized

(after all, he was the heir of Socrates and Plato); *hamartia,*
defined in the *Poetics* as a simple want of information
thanks to which a man might kill a near kinsman by mistake, could easily figure in the most vulgar kind of melodrama. Let us boldly re-define it as a "blind spot" in a
character's make-up, a vast ignorance of some phase of
reality so fundamental that the existence of such ignorance
makes disaster inevitable.[40] And let us, remembering mystery, acknowledge that the existence of such ignorance is
itself inevitable in one form or another.

As mystery presents itself to man in many aspects, any
one of its forms may determine the fate of a human being.
In Aeschylus' *Oresteia,* for example, the *hamartia* is a
blindness to the pattern of universal justice. Looking beneath the details of the myth to its general structure, one
may discern there the Monomyth of the Frazerian school,
the verbal complement of a ritual wherein a king embodying the welfare of a people is sacrificed by his successor.
Into this texture of myth it would seem to have been
Aeschylus himself who interwove some strands of generalized history, the supersession of the blood-feud by a
judiciary and the supersession of a clan-system by the unified life of the Polis. Thus the trilogy can profitably be
interpreted at several levels, but at what seems the
deepest lie the myth and its symbolized mystery. In what
ways are human beings implicated in the mystery of justice,
and in what ways are they, bound as they are, blind to its
workings? In the characters of Agamemnon, of Clytemnestra, and, subordinately, of Aegisthus, the tragedian gives us illustrations of our human proneness to forget
that the observer of the pattern is part of the pattern himself. Here we may see a manifestation of the central mystery: the contemplator of the universe by his very act of

contemplation abstracts, and thus tends to subtract, himself from the universe. Whoever prays for justice is in all likelihood praying for justice to be wrought on all men but himself; whoever regards himself as an instrument of justice is apt to be blind to the fact that, since "it is the Mover that is moved," justice is to be fulfilled *on* him as well as *through* him.

This is the most uncomplicated manifestation of the mystery. But Aeschylus also gives us characters like Cassandra and, most important, Orestes, in whom the sense of mystery itself comes to clearest consciousness. Such characters see themselves as part of the pattern, but only a limited part, and, by themselves alone, an unintelligible part. Through the oracular medium, they have had distinctly revealed to them their roles, passive or active, in the universal play of justice; yet these roles appear to them as doubtfully just. To comply with the revelation seems not so much to carry out a just design as to become embroiled in a confusion of right and wrong such that the just and the unjust cannot be disentangled by mortal discernment: Cassandra's fate seems inequitable because she is only accidentally drawn into the retribution meted out to Agamemnon; Orestes' divinely assigned task is equitable but unnatural. Both must base their own justification on a kind of faith in the existence of a larger design which they may adumbrate to themselves, but may not conceive in all its fullness.

Thus the consummation of justice depends upon the intermeshing of natural and supernatural; Aeschylus quite properly leaves his trilogy at the last on the lap of the gods, so to speak, with the inauguration of that mysterious mixture of personal wrongs and transcendent rights, viz., the political state. Unlike the post-Baconians of modern times, he concedes to suffering its due and awful place in the scheme of things, does not degrade injustice to the status of a problem, and does not, as the Cosmic Tories do,[41] cheapen his vision of the mystery of justice into the solution, "Whatever is, is right." Nor does he, with the Cosmic Whigs, cheapen the past to enhance the present and future.

The *Oresteia* has the additional interest of posing a literary conundrum: May a tragedy have a happy ending?

Something of the same sort of faith in a design overspreading the margins of individual mundane existence is exemplified in Sophocles' *Antigone*. Here the faith is the heroine's, while the blind spot is her adversary's. The myth is again a sacrificial one, but in this case the sacrifice is the offering up of a maiden as a bride to the god of death. Sophocles was penetrative enough to delve deeply into the myth and to discover there two strata of meaning, a pragmatic level where the immolation would appear to be a kind of insurance for the weal of society and an appeasement of the powers of decay and destruction, and, beneath that, a second more primitive level of intuition where, through the slaughtered girl, the tribe might feel itself brought into communion with the powers that have their being beyond the borders of this life. As an artist, Sophocles must have sensed that his own age was in danger of burying under an excessive pragmatism the earlier substratum of religious feeling; for he plays off Creon, the practical man, the overseer of society's welfare, against Antigone, who challenges that welfare in the name of a deeper principle. The whole tenor of treatment, of course, goes in favor of Antigone. Creon, the problem-solver, the practical man, the representative of an ethic of calculation, goes down to as utter pragmatic defeat as he has inflicted on Antigone, who recognizes mystery and commits herself to it and by every token except that of survival vindicates the superiority of an absolute ethic of love.

Antigone may be looked upon as the drama best depicting the mystery of love, that self-contradictory trait of human behavior rising out of man's simultaneous circumscription and transcendence. All the dictates of common sense and the precepts of prudence concur in urging us to evaluate our actions in terms of their consequences; yet this train of consequences leads eventually to death, which is to say it leads to nothing. Meanwhile love, the most powerful of our motivations, ostensibly throws prudential considerations to the winds. But does it really do so? For, by valuing things for themselves alone, it to some degree establishes reality in its eternal aspect, and so sets death at defiance. These are some of the facets of mystery that the myth of Antigone disclosed to Sophocles' insight.

For literary criticism, the play is a pagan test case: It is certainly a tale of martyrdom, yet many critics agree in affirming that Christian martyrdoms do not afford properly tragic material. Is *Antigone* then not a tragedy?

Whatever may be said to that, opinion is unanimous about *Oedipus the King*. Almost everyone has echoed Aristotle's judgment that here if anywhere we have tragedy, tragedy *par excellence*. And here, if anywhere, we have what has been defined in the foregoing pages as mystery. The greatness of *Oedipus* depends to a large degree on its fit symbolization of man's mysterious status. Here we are confronted by a protagonist who is virtually the incarnation of the human problem-solving faculty. An uninvolved stranger, he has come to Thebes from afar, disinterestedly answering the Sphinx's riddle, and freeing the people from affliction. The same man, on the outbreak of another plague, tries to cure the pestilence with the same abstractive, analytic, impersonal intellection. But as the process of solution develops, the situation becomes more and more concrete, implicative, individual, until he encounters himself at the center of the problem that he has attacked, as it were, from the outside. His initial triumph in riddle-guessing is the veritable cause of his defeat in the second attempt; for he has supposed that he found an answer when he formulated the generalization "Man" in response to the Sphinx's dark question, only to be forced to learn that there is no generality of Man, that there are only particular men, and that of all these the one most in question is he himself, Oedipus. Evil begins at home. Thus Sophocles, from mythic matter very similar to that which Aeschylus elaborated in the *Oresteia*, namely the myth attendant on a succession of scapegoat-kings—Laios to Oedipus to Creon—extracts understandings different from those of his predecessor, while dramatically showing us the way to the same "still point of the turning world."

Euripides is more psychological than the other two Greek tragedians, it is usually said, and by this it is usually meant that he is more concerned with offering character portraits than with working out probable plots. Be that as it may, for our purposes Euripides is more psychological in a profounder sense. Whereas the other two had been interested in symbolizing the concurrent continuity and discontinuity of the single man in relation to his world, Euripides attempts to trace this not completely divisive fissure in the individual psyche itself. Do we fondly dream that psychology and ethics can be separated? In his *Hippolytus* Euripides shows that such separation is unthinkable. Do we imagine that the intellect is ethically neutral, that ignorance is *ipso facto* innocence and that guilt can

be found only in company with full knowledge? In the
same play the author makes clear that the truth is far more
complex, that one may sit in judgment on man's intellective
activities as well as on his overt actions. Do we assume
that we may begin our analysis of the human psyche by
postulating as basis either man's cognition or his needs,
drives, urges, desires? But the play shows that such a
postulate is wholly artificial, every part of man's soul—
will, intellect, and desire—being both cause and effect of
every other part. So the drama of *Hippolytus* plays the
changes on the mystery of the ultimately unanalyzable soul.
To present this mystery the playwright contemplates
phases of guilty ignorance, types of blind spot: in the narrowly blind Hippolytus, who does not desire to know the
scheme of nature; in the rashly blind Theseus, who fails to
bring his will into play and to investigate with due delibera-
tion the circumstances of his wife's death; and in the consciously blind Phaedra, who chooses to behave as though
she does not know what she knows that she knows.

Thus *Hippolytus* deals with man's internal complexity in
its quality; the same author's *Bacchae* treats the same
psyche quantitatively, that is, it raises speculation about the
extent and boundaries of the soul. As a study of the inter-
penetrating relationship between human and divine, *The
Bacchae* is unique in introducing a god, Dionysus, who
functions throughout as one of the main characters; and as
a study of the overlapping of mental and extra-mental, it
represents that god as entering into and taking over the
soul of the human protagonist, King Pentheus. Pentheus'
blind spot is his presumption of imperviousness to emotion. But emotion is man's most ineluctable and powerful
bond to his universe; the more passionately one desires to
snap the link, the more assiduously one forges it.

Pentheus is perhaps the most striking example of that type of tragic hero who is enveloped in catastrophe without ever coming to recognize his defect of understanding; like Agamemnon and Hippolytus, he is never vouchsafed an inkling of what in himself has led him to his fate; he stands at the extreme of unenlightenment, on a scale in which such characters as Hamlet, Orestes, and Lear are nearer the middle position, while Oedipus and Creon represent a progression toward that full realization of mystery which is from the very start the endowment of Antigone and St. Thomas à Becket (of *Murder in the Cathedral*).

Hamlet's place in this series may seem odd at first glance. But discarding our Romantic preconceptions and viewing the Prince as something both more and less than a matinee idol, we can see that, reflective as he is, he never learns to reflect rationally and connectedly upon his own shortcomings. He is blind to the ideal self that he was created to become, and by a defect of charity he fosters within himself the deadly sin of despair. Between the Greek tragedians and Shakespeare we see the unmistakable marks of Christianity's intervention; the theory of an ideally perfect self implicit in the natural man was one that Christian thought constructed on Greek foundations. Shakespeare, in *Hamlet* and *Lear*, had to do with mythic material of ancient and pagan provenience, which almost certainly was explanation connected with primitive *rites de passage*. He may not have been aware of all the mythic vestiges, attenuated as they were, but they provided him with fitting symbols for mystery. The self-consciousness with which he could have his heroes probe the depths of their being was a Christian legacy; the simultaneous disparity and coherence of that which is and that which ought to be was ready to his hand in the transmitted myth. This mysterious con-

junction-disjunction is handled in *Hamlet* mostly in relation to the individual self; in *Lear* it becomes the theme of
Nature-actual versus Nature-ideal. Hamlet is blind to his
own perfecting; Lear fails to see that the natural world
implies its fulfillment in super-Nature. Lear's tragedy is
therefore more cosmic than Hamlet's, and because Lear is
carried further along the road to self-knowledge, almost in
fact to the goal itself, his drama is more enlightening to the
audience.

One modern play, Eliot's *Murder in the Cathedral*,
though it might seem on several counts not to belong in the
class of works referred to above, reveals itself as akin to
them in a very important respect. True, it is based, not
on a myth, but on a series of historical occurrences, and it
shows, not a good man with a blind spot, but a saint who
foresees his catastrophe and rushes to encompass it. Yet the
play, treating as it does the human being as at once both
actor and sufferer, and having for its central concern the
double aspect, both temporal and eternal, of human events,
obviously is to be ranged with those works of literature
which portray what we have called mystery. For this reason Eliot could mythicize his material, and was able to do
so precisely because the historical character in the center
of his plot willed to mythicize his own fate. In *Murder in
the Cathedral* myth and history become one.

The foregoing remarks will be amplified in the essays
that follow.

Aeschylus' ORESTEIA

The Marriage of Heaven and Earth

THE ONLY version of the Agamemnon-Clytemnestra-
Orestes myth that we can be sure of as antedating Aeschylus' treatment is the story given out piecemeal in the
Odyssey. When the epic has scarcely begun we are told
how Orestes slew the "blameless" Aegisthus in retaliation
for seducing his mother and killing his father—crimes of
which Zeus himself had sent Hermes to give Aegisthus fore-
warning of the consequences (*Od.* I, 28–43); and later it
is added that Orestes gained great glory from his deed
(298–300). The details of the murders of Agamemnon and
Cassandra are revealed only gradually, further on in the
poem, in the responses of Nestor to Telemachus
(III, 246 ff.), of Proteus to Menelaus (IV, 512 ff.), and of
the ghost of Agamemnon himself to Odysseus at their meeting in the Kingdom of the Dead (XI, 387 ff.). Pieced out
from these sources, the Homeric version runs as follows:

When King Agamemnon set out for Troy, he left a
minstrel with his wife Clytemnestra, and gave him de-

tailed instructions to watch over the queen. And while the Achaeans were enduring the pains of war, Aegisthus took his ease in the country of Argos, where his father Thyestes had once been king, and tempted "goddess-like" Clytemnestra with many a wheedling word. But for a time she kept her mind pure and turned him a deaf ear. Aegisthus at last seized the minstrel, took him to a desert island, and left him there to be a prey to the birds, after which "he willing led her willing to his house" (III, 272). To signalize his unexpected success, on the altars of the gods he burned meats and made votive offerings of gold and precious fabrics.

Then he and the queen plotted to kill the rightful king on his return (but not until Odysseus hears the narrative from Agamemnon's ghost is the queen's part in the plot at all emphasized). Aegisthus stationed a watchman on some vantage-point, promising pay of two gold talents, and after a year of watching, the announcement came that Agamemnon was approaching. Meanwhile, Menelaus, who would never have allowed the dastardly crime to happen, or at least to go unavenged for any length of time, had been struck by a storm off Cape Malea and blown with half his fleet to Egypt, where he spent several years amassing wealth. Agamemnon, also, had encountered bad weather at Malea, but had managed eventually to land. And there Aegisthus met him, with horses and chariot, inviting him to a feast in his palace, where the tribe's twenty best men were already waiting in ambush. Agamemnon, kissing his native soil and greeting the old familiar sights with tears, accepted Aegisthus' invitation without suspicion. Thus he was butchered at the feast like an ox at the manger, all of his retinue were slaughtered like pigs, and all of Aegisthus' twenty died in the melee, too. And as Agamemnon lay helpless and wounded to the death, Clytemnestra slew the screaming Cassandra over his body, and turned away from her husband without having the decency to close his mouth or eyes.

For seven years thereafter Aegisthus ruled tyrannically in Mycenae, until in the eighth year Orestes came back from Athens and killed him; and during the banquet which Orestes gave for the Argives, to celebrate his triumph over his baleful mother and her cowardly lover, Menelaus finally returned from Egypt and shared in the rejoicing, thus fulfilling the prophecy made to him by Proteus on the Egyptian strand.

So Homer. It looks as though his version were a much-changed elaboration of an old myth describing the transmission of the kingship of Mycenae to a series of successful challenger-husbands of the goddess-queen Clytemnestra. Hence the succession, more or less regular: Agamemnon—the minstrel—Aegisthus—Orestes; somewhere along the line of pre-Homeric tradition it must have been no longer understood that each consort of the Mother Goddess was looked upon as her son as well as her lover, and this distinction was conferred exclusively on Orestes, who then was made into an avenger rather than merely another in a sequence of challengers.

But Homer himself seems uncertain of just what happened to Clytemnestra, for he never says specifically that Orestes killed her; the verses in the *Odyssey*, after telling of the death of Aegisthus, simply add a vague mention of the funeral feast "of his baleful mother and her cowardly lover" (III, 310). Aeschylus was not the one to have changed Orestes' role in this way; surely the commentators are right to see here marks of the long-previous passage from matriarchy to patriarchy; yet with some confidence other changes can be attributed to Aeschylus. If his tragedies were, as he called them, "slices from Homer's banquet," it is obvious that he carved up his ox somewhat differently from Homer. As indicated above, between the *Odyssey* and the *Oresteia* the role of Aegisthus had been considerably toned down, while the role of Clytemnestra had been considerably intensified. Granted that this heightening of the woman's part may have been suggested by Agamemnon's fierce denunciation of his faithless wife in the *Nekyia* episode of the *Odyssey*, still the lessening of her lover's stature calls for some explanation.

Another change of detail is to be noted: instead of having Orestes arrive from Athens for his revenge, Aeschylus follows a different version, which could hardly have been original with him, since it appears in the majority of our widely divergent stories, having the heir to the throne spend his years of exile in Phocis, at the court of King Strophius, where his model friendship with Pylades was contracted. Still the Homeric mention of Athens must have lingered in Aeschylus' mind, and have suggested to him the splendid finale of his whole trilogy, so gratifying to the local patriotism of his audience: if he could not have Orestes set out from Athens on his mission of revenge, he could assuredly have him end it there. And can we hazard the guess that the use of Athens as the final setting suggested the introduction of Athena, goddess of wisdom, as the final arbiter of the questions about the mystery of justice? There is general agreement that it must have been Aeschylus, and not antecedent tradition, who introduced the elaborate divine machinery that motivates the trilogy from the beginning and completely takes over its workings at the end. Why did he do so? What did he see in the myth as he found it, and for what purpose did he so transform it? [1]

He had at hand a myth describing a series of slayings, each one of which had been made to appear a retribution for the one preceding. And his material also contained a family curse, in which the sins of the fathers are visited on the children. The recurrent theme was one of guilt expiated by the guilty and of guilt expiated by the innocent. He had therefore ready for use a story symbolizing the mystery, or rather the mysteries, of justice.[2]

The curse on the House of Atreus is the feature most likely to strike the modern reader as primitive, alien, and incomprehensible, a throwback to a darker age than even Homer's. The emphasis on it, combined with the prominence accorded to the sacrifice of Iphigenia, which Homer also knows nothing of, lends some color to the adjectives that have been used to describe Aeschylus' thought: "stern, unbending, archaic, pietistic." [3] But was the tragedian in fact merely an inconsistent and unquestioning transmitter of orthodoxy? Such a description in modern times amounts to little less than a charge of obtuseness. One may well doubt whether there was in that age any considerable body of religious doctrine to accept and transmit; Aeschylus, like Homer, may have been as much a shaper of orthodoxy as a trafficker in it. Surely the changes he made in the tradition, whether they appear to our eyes progressive or retrogressive, were made deliberately for the purposes of his theological symbolism; and a little contemplation of the mysterious nature of the ethical questions dealt with in the *Oresteia* should show that in the light of the justification of justice this symbolism itself is justifiable.

To one who faces the facts without flinching, there can

be no doubt that the sins of the fathers are indeed visited on the children; that the sins of ancestors descend to their descendants; that the sins of past societies are the agonies of our own.[4] (And we, too, busy ourselves manufacturing disasters for our posterity.) There is no doubt, in short, that the sins of the guilty are visited on the innocent.[5] This is precisely what we mean by injustice, and it arouses our indignation. If a man takes up an axe with hostile intent, we are indignant; if he proceeds by accident to chop off his own toe, we are pleased. We would have injustice transmuted into justice swiftly, simply, measuredly, and with an immediately apparent identity of doer and sufferer. And we are indignant that this seldom comes about.[6] We see doers suffer apparently too little or apparently too much; we see sufferers suffer without doing; we see doers suffer long after the deed has apparently lost effect; and we feel therefore that we live in a world in which justice is not ultimately guaranteed. We forget that to feel so is to lose the concept of justice itself. And if justice does not exist, how is our indignation at injustice to be justified?

Continuing these elementary observations, we ask ourselves: What is justice? "That principle of order in the universe by which every man suffers his own self," Plato once replied.[7] Long before Plato's day Aeschylus had given a definition at once narrower and more inclusive, more natural and less subtle: "That principle of order in the universe by which every man's internal evil, his evil purposes and deeds, is balanced by the evil that comes from without, the evil of suffering."[8] As no man can survey the whole universe, the concept of justice must be compounded nine-tenths of faith.[9] Consciously or not, willingly or not, such faith is always tendered, for so deeply implanted in man's soul is the desire for justice that the criminal either craves

punishment for his crime or labors to convince himself
and others that no crime has been committed. No man
can say, "I have done evil; *therefore* I must not suffer." He
knows obscurely that to say so would be to abandon the
knowledge of good and evil and with it the distinction between truth and falsehood, thus to land in the intolerable
chaos of unreason. And yet, to be sure, we all try to say
this; to do evil and abide by evil is to attempt proof of this
impossible proposition.

Justice is, then, a mystery.[10] Its unexceptionable validity
must be presupposed if we are to begin to think at all. To
its mysteriousness two factors contribute, one being the
circumstance mentioned above, that, to our frequent exasperation and even incredulity, the vaster part of the justice-
pattern is inevitably shrouded in darkness, out of which
there come fitful gleams to give us intermittent reassurance.
And even more important is the second consideration,
that the individual, as he contemplates the world in search
of this pattern, falls into the almost inescapable *hamartia*,
moral blindness, of forgetting that he himself is not merely
spectator, but actor as well. He excepts himself, who
should be the pivot on which this all-encompassing order
rotates, and this in turn causes in him a double delusion.
First, he defines justice in non-personal terms, praying with
Aegisthus and Clytemnestra in *Agamemnon*: "Let justice
be done—on others." [11] And, secondly, he unconsciously
exempts himself from participation in elaborating this universal pattern, hesitating to take upon himself the apparent
guilt and pollution that the punishment of injustice sometimes requires.[12] This twofold existential withdrawal entails
the untenable assumption that innocence consists of inac-
tion and that sins of omission do not exist. For which of us
is innocent? The gods must use the guilty to check the

guilty and must employ the polluted to expunge pollution: after all, they have agents of no other kind.[13] To their eyes, and to their eyes alone, out of the tangle of earthly injustices emerges the divine design of justice itself.[14]

Hence the finale of the *Oresteia*, the transformation of the Erinyes into the Eumenides by the goddess Athena's use of divine persuasion, the domiciling of the dread deities in Athens, and the reconciliation of the old gods with the new, the powers below with the powers above, signifies far more than a mere gratification of the Athenian audience's and author's local pride, or a consolation to the diminished court of the Areopagus—most readers have sensed this, at least—, but even far more than the civilizing of the primeval lust for revenge and the transferral of judicial execution from the personal clan or individual to the impersonal polity. So much could have been made clear, and it should have been and was made clear, without the elimination of the human actors from the scene. Critics have not failed to object to the disappearance of Orestes halfway through the *Eumenides* and to the complete usurpation of the action by Athena and the Furies, who are after all, they say, abstractions, of no appeal to the modern mind.[15] But this may well be a judgment on the modern mind rather than on Aeschylus or his play. For it will be seen from the very definition of justice that any exhaustive treatment of the subject must necessarily ascend from the plane of the human to that of the divine.[16] If justice is taken to mean anything more than the sum total of physical "laws," and it must be taken to mean more, or else it is a superfluous concept, then it must presuppose a supernatural realm which comprises those relationships in its pattern that are invisible, intangible, imperceptible, and even supra-rational, and it must find the larger part of its sig-

nificance in that complementary realm.[17] Justice is the sense
of cosmic order,[18] and the cosmos is only minutely palpable to us either in actuality or in potentiality. The longing
for justice brings us to religious faith, or it brings us to
nothing.[19] "All our efforts," said Dr. Johnson, "end in belief,
that for the Evils of life there is some good reason, and
in confession, that the reason cannot be found." [20] So
Aeschylus appears to have felt. The finale of the *Oresteia* is
truly final, the human story being prelude and accompaniment to the interplay of the gods' activities.

What are the characteristics of these Aeschylean gods? [21]
It must be answered that in the first place they seem to
have been conceived of as aspects of a single deity, who
more or less for convenience' sake is identified with the
traditional figure of Zeus. The author seems to have been
anxious to make this point as early as possible in his work,
since it is introduced rather abruptly in the first Chorus of
Agamemnon (160 ff.). Yet his manner of phrasing this
monotheistic doctrine seems curiously offhand:

> Zeus—whoever he is,
> If this name is acceptable to him
>   as a mode of address,
> I call him by it.
> Weighing everything in the balance
> I have nothing to liken him to
> Except Zeus—

This manner is not the hesitancy of a man advancing revo-
lutionary opinions, but resembles rather the practice of
those more enlightened among the later Greeks who spoke
of a singular *theos* or of plural *theoi* almost with indifference.[22] The point was that the multiplicity of the divine
should be recognized as it revealed itself in multiple

phenomena to human experience, while the essential one-ness of divinity should be constantly and simultaneously kept in mind.[23] Hence no educated Greek, or Roman either for that matter, had difficulty being monotheist and poly-theist at once.[24]

In contrast to this offhandedness is Aeschylus' tone of in-sistence in the next stanzas, the substance of which has either been misconstrued or ignored:

> And he who was formerly great,
> Brimming with wanton pugnacity,
> Shall be said never to have been.
> And he who existed after
> Thrice chanced to be thrown
> And vanished before his champion.

The reference is to Uranus and Cronus, the grandfather and father of Zeus according to the old theogony, and the usual explanation is that we have here Aeschylus' concep-tion of an "evolving deity." [25] The arguments for positing the existence of such a conception seem to be these: The Zeus of the *Prometheus* trilogy is just such a developing god; in *Prometheus Bound* he is shown as cruel, vindic-tive, and drunk with new-won power, but in the two suc-ceeding plays, now lost, he must have been intended to mellow and mature. Also, in the *Prometheus* plays, this crudity on Zeus's part is closely connected with the over-throw of the older gods by the newer generation, an up-heaval referred to in the very passage translated above and made much of in the concluding section of the *Eumenides*.[26] Lastly, the progressive humanization of hu-manity that is the theme of the *Oresteia* trilogy on its mun-dane side suggests a parallel on the divine plane: the progressive "deization" of the deity.[27]

Such appears to be the reasoning; there are fatal objections to it. In the first place, there is no proof that the *Prometheus* trilogy embodied the figure of a developing god. In the one play extant we have only Prometheus' side of the story; in the two companion plays that are lost Zeus may, as most of the restorers say, have been portrayed as undergoing a maturing process, or he may have been represented as misunderstood all along; we do not know; at all events it is the height of scholastic folly to impose a conjectural interpretation of a fragmentary work on another and later work that is whole and entire.

Furthermore, it is assuredly never stated in the *Oresteia* that the transition from an older to a newer generation of gods stands for any development in Zeus himself. On the contrary, Aeschylus seems desirous of disparaging the myth of divine succession; Uranus, the oldest of the gods, "shall be said never to have existed," and Cronus, Zeus's father "vanishes" or "retires" after his overthrow by his son. It sounds as though the dethronement of the older gods were intended to represent a supersession of more primitive by more humane ideas, culminating in that conception of perfect justice which is Zeus, rather than any growth in the godhead itself. A similar deprecation is to be sensed in Apollo's answer to the Furies' charge in the *Eumenides;* when he has just maintained that the murder of a mother is in no way comparable in seriousness with the murder of a father, the Furies take issue (640 ff.): "By your reasoning Zeus puts more stress on a father's fate. But he himself bound his aged father Cronus. Does this not contradict your contention?" Apollo replies indignantly:

All-detested monsters, O loathesome to the gods! Fetters may be loosened; they have their remedy, and many are the devices that can do the trick. But where a man is concerned, when once he is killed and his blood spilled in the dust, there is no raising him up again. My father has not decreed any magic spells to reverse this state of things, but, as for all else, he throws all down and sets all up, and without exertion or loss of breath he abides.

It would appear that, in this answer, the old doctrine of "All things flow; nothing remains" was being deliberately restated as "All things flow by the will of God, and God remains." Apollo is not indulging in embarrassed subterfuge here, as he has sometimes been said to be doing; rather he is emphasizing the argument that the condition of mortal men is in no way to be compared to the unconditionality of the immortal gods. And we perceive then that the point throughout is this: that however the aspects of the god-head, as revealed to human sight and mind, may seem multitudinous and contradictory, the godhead itself is one and unvarying, and we remember the import of the Chorus: Uranus—Cronus—Zeus—the name does not matter; but probably, all in all, Zeus is the most fitting term. This is summed up in the famous stanza that follows in *Agamemnon* (176 ff.):

God fixed this road to wisdom, and established this as his prevailing rule: "Suffer and learn!" [28] Pain-recalling toil drips down the heart in sleep; to men unwilling comes wisdom. This bounty of the powers divine, who sit on their awful thrones, is mighty, violent.

The contrast between toilsomely developing man and serenely perfect deity could hardly be more forcefully put.
And this contrast reminds us that, after all, the concept of a perfectible god is in the highest degree illogical. The whole notion seems to have been invented by the post-

Darwinian nineteenth century, which wished to salvage some sort of faith out of what was taken to be the utter shipwreck of religion. Thus it came about that Life Forces, Creative Evolutions, and Infinite Perfectibilities were strung up behind the altars.[29] To foist off such a belief on Aeschylus is to perpetrate a dreadful anachronism. Having been told that God is perfectible, Aeschylus would certainly have asked the common-sense question, "In accordance with what higher standard is he being perfected, or perfecting himself?" If there is such a standard, by definition it is the divine; it should be worshiped instead of Zeus. If, on the other hand, there is no fixed standard, to say nothing of the inescapable inference that the whole idea of perfection becomes nonsense, where is our guarantee of universal justice? How can God, who is not yet himself just, be the guarantor? But if God is not the guarantor of justice's eternal triumph, then he belongs to that category of entities that ought not to be multiplied beyond necessity, and we need not posit his existence at all.

"Still, and for all that," it may be objected, "Aeschylus may not have thought so far into these implications, and there does seem to be a kind of metatheosis in the compromise between the Olympian gods and the chthonic gods that is effected by Athena at the end of the trilogy." [30]

The important question, according to this, would be: Does Athena bring about an essential change in the character of the Erinyes in this climactic scene? And the answer in turn depends on the answer to this prior question: What is the nature of the Erinyes to begin with? It may be shortly stated: they are spirits of retributive justice, especially in its emotional and intuitive aspects. They are female themselves, and intimately associated with the female half of mankind, which the Greeks habitually regarded as predominantly emotional and intuitive; because of their disconnection with the light of reason, they are looked upon as Daughters of Night, spirits of Earth and chthonian genii. Presented initially as a kind of matriarchal embodiment of the blood-feud, they preside over the avenging of only those crimes that violate relationships of descent. Therefore they activate Clytemnestra, who is the incarnation of an Erinys herself,[31] to seek retribution for the sacrifice of Iphigenia, and, in the absence of any available human agent, they must appear in their own persons to punish Orestes for the killing of Clytemnestra. All this is unnecessary restriction of their roles, as their most determined opponent, Apollo, points out, for they should in reason take upon themselves the punishment of transgressions against those related by marriage also. Furthermore, as he demonstrates, they are liable to be dispossessed entirely if a new biological theory of genetic relationships should gain acceptance.

So the climatic scene actually represents, not a narrowing, but an enlarging of the Furies' sphere of activity. Heretofore, they had been mere personifications of vendetta and revenge, and of a strangely delimited form of vendetta at that. Revenge is an unsatisfactory and unreasonable form of retribution at best, for in it retribution depends for fulfillment on the availability of some individual who can be screwed up by personal emotion or social pressure to the pitch requisite to ensure performance; equally unsatisfactory is the fact that it makes no fine distinctions, and, being personal, may find expression out of all proportion to the offense. There is something almost pathetic in the circumstance that Clytemnestra has no living relative to avenge her, and must conjure up into the sight of men the spirits of retribution themselves. If the vendetta, and the vendetta only, had held sway, the death of Clytemnestra would have gone unavenged, and it actually does go unavenged in the Homeric version, which ends with Orestes triumphant.

Whether Aeschylus or a predecessor added the expiatory sequel, Aeschylus at any rate did not furnish such a continuation of the story for the purpose of discrediting retribution. The Erinyes are in no way to be dishonored. As they say, collectively (*Eum.* 393 ff.):

> My privilege of old abides;
> And though consigned beneath the earth
> In gloom ill-lighted by the sun,
> Dishonor never is my lot.

Far from being shamed, they are domiciled in Athens and given free run of the city and its population. They are to be accorded the first fruits of the land, are to hold sway over childbirth and marriage, and are to be the guardians of civic affairs. Athena assures them that not one jot of the law of retribution shall pass away, that she comes not to destroy but to fulfill. However overmastering to the modern interpreter the temptation may be to suppose that somehow the old law is being mitigated or modified, the fact remains that the whole *Oresteia* closes with the populace of Athens singing a hymn of praise and welcome to the goddesses of retributive justice, those same snake-haired, bloody-mouthed, fiery-eyed deities who, we are told, caused several of the spectators to faint when they made their first appearance in the orchestra and who have not changed their costumes or their characters in the interlude.

This emphasis on retribution is unpleasant, needless to say, to modern sensibilities. Modern man, having abjured all sense of mystery, has forfeited all comprehension of how

eternity might interpenetrate with time; the necessity of
punishment embarrasses us at its best, and we prefer to
speak not of punishment, but of reformation; all our
penological theorizing points firmly to the future and away
from the past. But in older thought, in attitudes that seem
still ineradicable, retribution is looked upon as somehow
redeeming the past, since it completes the pattern which
unfolds in time but exists in eternity. This is the pattern
which Aeschylus presents the gods, in their immutability,
as perceiving. But modern commentators would like to
suppose that Aeschylus means something other than he
says. They would like to suppose that he means that the law
of retribution is ultimately converted into deterrent, or better still, rehabilitative justice. But, on the contrary, he
seems to be asserting stubbornly that the *lex talionis* is at
base the only kind of justice that exists.

Is this merely another measure of his limited archaic
mentality? Or is he mysteriously more right than we are,
perhaps? For though we repudiate punitive justice in theory, we cannot eliminate it in practice. Why is this? The
answer seems to be that retribution is the irreducible content of any definition of justice; beyond this mystery our
thought can go no further.[32] If on the one hand deterrence
were the principal aim of our judicial systems, it has been
well pointed out that the guilt or innocence of the con-
victed would then be quite irrelevant; the authorities might
just as well arrest a man at random on the streets and
string him up, with the notice that this is an illustration of
what happens to murderers; the deterrent effect would be
the same as though the victim were really guilty. A somewhat similar objection might be made to rehabilitative justice, which would take as the whole purpose of our penal
systems the production of "useful members of society" (re-

pulsive phrase! Who is going to use them?). This seems on all accounts to be the favorite definition of justice in the eyes of modern theorists. Yet murder, as all criminologists assure us, not being a crime that is likely to become habitual, it is hard to see why, according to this theory, murderers should even be molested at all, nor is it easy to understand why burglars and thieves, who commit crimes for gain, should be shut up in prison: why not give them pensions? By this means society would acquire any number of useful members.

That these suggestions sound outrageous is simply due to the fact that all of us are at bottom believers in "an eye for an eye," and cannot be shaken from this belief without abandoning reason itself. The evilly intended deed must be compensated for by proportionate suffering: this is the Law, and we cannot escape it. Nor can we explain it in other than these very terms; justice is just simply because it is justice, which is to say that the Law has been established by powers which are superior to the powers of the human mind.[33] Such powers are, Aeschylus says, divine.

Hence it is something of a mistake to assert, as is often asserted, that the *Oresteia* is one vast theodicy; in the strictest sense of the word it is nothing of the kind.[34] No attempt is made by the poet to "justify the ways of God to men." True, we are told that the gods send suffering to men in order that the latter may attain wisdom, but as wisdom is mainly a matter of reconciling oneself to the inscrutable ways of the gods, not much justification is to be found here.[35] Orestes' chief defense at his trial is the plea that he was commanded to his murderous deed by Apollo, with the threat of dire penalties if he failed to act, and Apollo does not deny this responsibility when he takes over as Orestes' advocate.[36] Furthermore, Athena at the trial's end grants Orestes acquittal for reasons that seem capricious at best. And at the very beginning of the trilogy, we are reminded that Artemis virtually ordered the sacrifice of Iphigenia, apparently in compensation for crimes that had not yet even been committed, namely the slaughter of the innocents at Troy.[37] Yet all these things must be accepted as just in a way that passes human understanding, for the Establishers of the Law are by definition just. For if God be not just, where is justice to be found, whereby we may even justify our disapproval of its absence?

So, too, then, are the Erinyes just, being divinities.[38] And though it may seem to the casual reader, as it seems to the goddesses themselves at first, that their divinity is impaired by the release of Orestes, such is not really the case, as Athena convinces them.[39] For retribution has actually been exacted after all. One must recall the definition of basic justice, punitive justice: the evilly intended deed must be compensated for by proportionate suffering. One may easily see that if the intent is examined minutely and if the proportion between this internal, intentional evil and the external evil of the imposed suffering is carefully weighed—"let the punishment fit the crime," in short—, there is no abrogation of the retributory principle itself, but rather a corroboration of it. Apollo, then, as god of light, and Athena, as goddess of wisdom, come not to destroy the Law, but to fulfill it.[40]

Thus there is no diminution of punitive justice when reason intervenes in order to do all that reason can do, which is to put under close scrutiny the two sides of the balance, the evil intention and its compensatory suffering.[41] If the punishment is to fit the crime, the extent of the crime must be ascertained with care. This is the purpose of introducing the judicial process, which is instituted precisely because personal revenge may strike blindly and, in the name of justice, unwittingly leave a residue of evil which must in its turn be expiated.[42] The court called into existence by Athena proceeds at once and without question to a precise determination of the gravity of the crime. And immediately it is made clear that Orestes' deed of blood has been performed with quite different intent and in quite different spirit from Clytemnestra's.[43] Orestes stresses the fact that his action was the result not of a plot contrived in the secrecy of an adulterous bedchamber, but of a divine design promulgated in the sanctuary of the god of light.[44] To acquiesce as a diffident and hesitant agent of the gods is a far different thing from conceiving oneself a veritable incarnation of justice, as Clytemnestra has done.[45]

And this is the second point in Orestes' favor, the fact that he does hesitate, that he is fully self-conscious and therefore self-distrustful, and that he is subject to qualms of aversion in the face of his dreadful duty and of self-reproach at his failure to discharge the office directly. A scene of prolonged self-exhortation is necessary before he can lash himself to the requisite pitch of murderous passion, to which he is aided by the instigation of his sister Electra and the Chorus; [46] even then, at the critical moment of the slaying, he wavers and appeals to his friend Pylades to confirm his resolution. All these marks of self-doubt have been many times discussed,[47] and they are in marked contrast to the sinister aura of excited anticipation that emanates from Clytemnestra in the early scenes of *Agamemnon*.[48]

Even more distinctive, of course, is Orestes' emotional revulsion after the murder. This is the third and most important of those psychological differences that so materially qualify and diminish the evil of his intention. After his crime, the son surrenders himself to the Furies of guilt, whereas the mother and her paramour have tried, by barbarously cutting off the corpse's extremities and tying them beneath the armpits, to forestall the vengeance of the murdered man's spirit. Furthermore, with a kind of hideous joy Clytemnestra gloats over the bodies of Cassandra and her own husband and puts Agamemnon away hastily into the earth unmourned. There is a striking and instructive diversity of mood in the tableaux that ensue upon the two murders. Clytemnestra is bursting with fierce exultation as she smiles down at the dead Agamemnon and his dead lover (*Ag.*, 1444 ff.):

> So he lies, and there lies she,
> Who chanted forth a dying groan like a swan's,
> And *that* was the lover of *this*.
> Not to his bed, but to mine
> And my lover's, shall she add
> The final relish of enjoyment.

But Orestes, above the bodies of Clytemnestra and Aegisthus, is defensive and regretful.[49] After displaying the rent robe in which the slain Agamemnon was entangled, he concludes:

> But I am in pain for these deeds
> And for this suffering and the whole race,
> Bearing the unenviable blots of this triumph.

This mention of "unenviable blots of triumph" is proof of his realization that the human executor of justice inevitably besmirches himself with the very injustice that he is seeking to expunge.[50] Precisely here lies the clear superiority of his consciousness to that of his mother; to her, injustice is

a problem to be solved, a knot to be cut; to him it is a
mystery to be entered into.[51] He obscurely suspects that
what he, being only a part of the design of justice, looks
upon as a chaotic tangle of guilt and innocence is from the
perspective of the gods an orderly pattern; but Clytemnestra imagines that she herself is standing apart from
the pattern and weaving it. She supposes that by dispatching her husband she has dispatched the problem of
injustice; Orestes knows that the chain of guilt stretches
to infinity.[52]

Not only, then, does the courtroom process bring to
light the fact that the intentional nature of Orestes' act
differs widely from his mother's, but also it helps to fulfill retributive justice more exactly in establishing that he
has paid for his crime in suffering, and in suffering suffi-
ciently. Unlike Clytemnestra, who reigns for years in Argos,
living at her ease up until the short period of apprehension
that precedes her sudden death, Orestes is not permitted
to succeed to his ancestral throne, as he prays to be able to
do, until he has undergone a course of torment over a wide
expanse of space and time. Because of these sufferings consequent upon his crime, he can be adjudged to have already given satisfaction, and the Eumenides are bound to
concede that his acquittal does not really frustrate retribution, but signalizes its exaction.[53]

So the dread spirits of justice are bound by logic
(Athena) and by the majesty of Persuasion (Peitho) to
acknowledge the conditions of their own perfection.[54]
When they chafe at the alleged insult implicit in Orestes'
release and refuse the proffered domicile as part of the
state, Athena wins them over by showing them that
their refusal is a contradiction in terms. They threaten to
punish the Athenians for the wrong they have suffered; yet

how, Athena asks them, can they bring justice to bear on the Athenian Polis, while they themselves, the Spirits of Justice, are simultaneously rejecting any part in it? This would be both to participate and not to participate in the life of the city. So Athena puts it (*Eum.*, 887 ff.):

> But if you are unwilling to remain here, then it cannot be justice that you should vent your wrath or spite on this city here nor do harm to its populace; for it is available to you to hold your place in this land, justly honored in every respect.

It is by this argument that the ancient goddesses are won over,[55] and the Erinyes begin to be transformed into the Eumenides, in essence the same as before, but enormously richer in function.

Nor are they the only gainers by the change. Athena, too, cannot afford to weary in her efforts to reconcile them, for she knows well that without them no city can endure.[56] By this reconciliation of the chthonian with the celestial deities a sort of sacred marriage of Heaven and Earth is effected;[57] Athena as representative of Zeus, the Lord of Heaven, gives orders for the torchlight procession to escort these Earth Goddesses, as in a bridal, to their new home beneath the earth, whence they promise increase of crops and children to the land. By this wedding of wisdom to the emotional impulse of retribution a just social life for mankind is made possible.[58]

We are reminded of the primitive ritual of the sacred marriage which underlay the Agamemnon-Clytemnestra-Orestes myth from its inception; we recall the ancient Near Eastern ceremony in which the king as surrogate for the Lord of Heaven was reunited to the queen, the representative of the Earth Mother, and by which was thus re-enacted the creation of the world, and at each New Year the foundations of society were thus relaid.[59] And even more vividly we remember the yet more savage and primitive rite in which the god-substitute shed his blood as postlude to his matrimonial duties, and thus fertilized the earth anew. This sacred marriage which passes so quickly into the sacred death and resurrection has already been forecast by Clytemnestra toward the beginning of the trilogy, after she has described the threefold ritual blow with which she dispatched her spouse (*Ag.*, 1389 ff.):

> And breathing out a sharp spurt of sacrificial blood,
> He struck me with a dark-red drizzle of dew,[60]
> Struck me, rejoicing as the seeded earth rejoices
> At its god-given delight in the birth-pang of the bud.[61]

A strange saying this, and a gratuitous bit of bloodthirstiness, unless appreciated in all the richness of its mythic significance.

In the original storehouse of myth from which this passage is ultimately drawn, Clytemnestra may have symbolized merely the earth, her slain and mutilated husband merely the sky, and his blood-drops merely the rain.[62] But these things became in turn for Aeschylus symbols of much profounder mysteries. Clytemnestra for him does not merely embody the Eternal Woman [63]—a mannish woman, to be sure, mated with Aegisthus, a womanish man [64]— whose submergence beneath her husband's blood forebodes her eventual defeat by her husband's male offspring, just as her reincarnations, the Furies, are eventually to be dominated by the representative of Zeus,[65] the Eternal Father.[66] Nor is she only the everlasting Night of intuition and emotion,[67] whose darkness is to be penetrated and defined by the higher powers of light and reason; for the triumph of reason over against emotion is not destined to be complete, but is to resemble more of a reconciliation than a triumph, so that the trilogy ends with the same interplay of light and darkness as it began. Clytemnestra is of course all this, but, being the earth, she is unenlightened humanity as well, and the drizzle of blood that falls on her from her lord, Agamemnon, Zeus's surrogate, is that rain and dew of suffering which falls upon all the characters of the drama from beginning to end, the "pain-recalling toil that drips down the heart in sleep," from the Watchman's vexing dew and the Herald's troublesome rain to the terrible visions that come out of the sky, Clytemnestra's nightmare, Orestes' divine ordinance of retaliation, and the final vision of cosmic order that is at once the source of mankind's illness and of his redemption. For the rain is creative divinity, the earth is fecund humanity, and the fruit is justice.

Sophocles' ANTIGONE

Eros in Politics

THE GREEKS and Romans, even as we do, had book digests
and plot summaries for those literature-lovers who love to
read anything about literature rather than literature itself.
One of the summaries attached to the manuscripts of
Antigone goes as follows:

> After Polynices has been killed in single combat with his
> brother, Creon has his body dragged off and left exposed,
> announcing that anyone who buries it will suffer the penalty of
> death. Antigone, Polynices' sister, attempts the burial and suc-
> ceeds in throwing some dirt over the body without being de-
> tected by the guards. Creon threatens the latter with death if
> they fail to catch the culprit; they clear the dust from the body
> and watch it as before. Antigone, finding the corpse bare again,
> betrays herself with her anguished cries. She is taken to Creon,
> put to the examination, and enclosed alive in a tomb. Teiresias
> predicts the dire results of it all: Antigone hangs herself;
> Creon's son Haemon, who wanted to marry her, despairingly
> commits suicide over the body of his beloved; and Eurydice,

Creon's wife, kills herself in grief over her son's death. The end
of the play finds Creon bewailing the deaths of his wife and son.

There are few references to the myth of Antigone aside
from this play, and it is sometimes thought that the story
must have been of Sophocles' own manufacture.[1] This can
hardly be true, for a number of reasons. Greek playwrights
did not invent their plots, in our understanding of the
word; they applied their powers of invention to elaborating
and vivifying such myths as were traditional. Quite different versions of the myth were used by Euripides: in a
lost *Antigone* he had his heroine bear a son to Haemon,[2]
but in the *Phoenissae* Creon has to leave off pressing
Antigone to marry Haemon—in accordance with her
brother Eteocles' dying wish—when she threatens to kill
her unwanted bridegroom on their wedding night.[3] By
the accounts of another author, she was burned to death
(along with her sister Ismene) in the sanctuary of Hera by
her nephew, Eteocles' son,[4] and Hyginus[5] shows us the
myth in the process of becoming a fairy tale: Antigone,
apprehended while trying to bury her brother Polynices, is
turned over to Haemon for execution; he falls in love with
her, and—like Snow White and countless others—she is
not killed but committed to the care of shepherds, who rear
her son; the son, of course, when grown to manhood, takes
part in games at Thebes and is recognized by his wicked
great-uncle because of the mark of the dragon's brood on
his body; the outcome of it all is that Haemon has to kill
Antigone and himself.

The fact that in Sophocles' play the girl is first shut up in
a cave to starve and afterward hangs herself is enough to
arouse suspicion; a double means of death seems to be a
sign that varying traditions were somehow synthesized.

Was she a cult figure, like the similarly named Erigone,[6] the daughter of Aegisthus and Clytemnestra, who hanged herself in disgust at the acquittal of Orestes and whose suicide was commemorated in Attica by swinging from trees and hanging dolls from tree-limbs at the Festival of Aiora?[7] Erigone must have been a Hanged Goddess, like certain forms of Helen and Artemis, embodying the fertility of trees. Another Hanged Goddess was Ariadne, who brings us back to the Labyrinth or Cave, in which Antigone was entombed, and the symbol of the Cave carries us, perhaps, far back into the Stone Ages. The Cave was the Tomb and the Womb, the first and last home of mankind; it was the passage to the other world.[8] In a cave or its equivalent, the initiate awaited his rebirth; and in earlier times, the maiden victim must have waited in a cave for her union with the God of the Underworld.

Sophocles' Antigone is likewise the Bride of Death, there can be no doubt of that; she is the virgin who gives up all hope of earthly nuptials in order to embrace Hades as her husband. "Look at me, citizens of my native land," she says (806 ff.) as she is being led to her living entombment, "taking my last steps, gazing my last at the light of the sun. And never again! But Hades, with whom all sleep at last, is leading me alive to the shores of Acheron. No wedding-march is my portion; no marriage-song is my hymnal, but to Acheron I shall be bride."[9]

At this point in the play there is an odd change in the attitude of the Chorus; sympathetic before, they become slightly abusive, and Antigone reacts to their words out of all proportion to their stringency, claiming that she goes to her death derided (839 ff.), unpitied, and utterly friendless. It would seem that we have here the typical scapegoat procession to the sacrifice, during which the victim was ceremonially cursed, on her way to what she addresses as "O tomb, O bride-chamber!" (891). If Antigone is "in love with death," to the amazement of the Chorus, who have thought that "no one can be such a fool as to be enamored of dying" (*thaneîn erâi*—220), it is not because she is obsessed by some Freudian death wish, but because her story, like those of Danae, Lycurgus, and Cleopatra in Stasimon Four,[10] was a transmission to Sophocles' time from the dim days of human sacrifice.

Many primitive peoples, as is well known, were in the habit of offering up a victim annually, or more or less frequently on extraordinary occasions; such ceremonies often took the form of wedding a virgin to a god. Pragmatic mythologists say that this was done in the hope of immediate tangible benefits: abundant crops, good hunting, fertile wives, at the very least a let-up in untoward circumstances. But if we reflect that the primitives in question were never post-Renaissance Westerners, we may beg leave to doubt. In the same way we are told that the ancient Egyptians and other early peoples harbored a real anxiety about the disappearance of the sun every evening, and felt it incumbent on them to practice incantations before dawn to induce the sun to come up again.[11] Perhaps so, perhaps not. It seems more likely that the ancient Egyptians knew very well that the sun would come up, chanted to or not chanted to: they simply wanted to "get in on the act." Man wants to participate in the rhythms of nature and to penetrate into nature's mysteries. And what more mysterious than death? Could not the human sacrifice represent an effort vicariously to cross the border of the living and visible world? Could not the human victim, into whom the dread of the tribe was projected, represent a pitiful effort, in her marriage with death, to come to loving terms with those eternal powers which encompass the whole life of man? The custom was abominable, doubtless; but the motives that prompted it are not wholly incomprehensible.

If we assume that the heroine's Wedding with the Death-God is the climax of the play, what can Sophocles be supposed to have meant by his treatment of the actions leading up to this? What phase of the mystery did he wish to underscore? The answer is that he apparently wanted to focus his audience's attention on the conflict between two codes of ethics, both of them perfectly familiar to the Greeks, and both of them perennially available to the human mind.

In a well-known passage from Book Two of Plato's *Republic* (357b-d), Glaucon points out that there are three commonly accepted meanings of the word "good," the second being actually a combination of the first and third: that there are, first, a class of things which are good in themselves, absolutely good; second, a class of things which are good in themselves and also productive of good results; and third, a class of things which are called good only because they lead, presumably, to consequences which would fall within the first class.[12] It becomes the endeavor of Socrates throughout the remainder of the *Republic* to demonstrate that justice, the topic under discussion, is to be classified with those things which are absolutely good as well as good in their consequences. Nor does he consider his task discharged until—to the disgruntlement of every pragmatic-minded reader—he has torn away the veil that separates this transient world from the world of eternal verities and shown that the justification of justice depends ultimately upon its substantiation in that order of true being which is certainly the only final source of power simply because it is the only final realm of reality.

(Hence the irrelevance of that criticism of Plato which accuses him of "taking refuge" in the Vision of Er because he cannot otherwise solve the problem of the definition and vindication of justice. Of course that is Plato's conviction all along: it cannot be solved otherwise.)

Again in Plato's *Crito* pretty much the same issue is broached, there appearing in the form of a clash between the practical course and the ideal, between the choice of a good that leads to other goods and the direct preference of the good in itself. The similarity of dilemmas is not fortuitous, of course, for surely Plato had the career of Socrates in mind when sketching the contrasting portraits of the "happy undeserving" Unjust Man and the "wretched meritorious" Just Man that follow Glaucon's analysis of goods in *Republic*, Book Two (360e ff.). In the shorter dialogue, Crito, in so many words, presents the question as it would occur to the mind of the natural man: "In a conflict between practical good and ideal good, is it not better to choose the practical? Especially when the ideal choice means nothing less than death, which for the individual is the elimination of all consequences whatever? Is it not better on the face of it to cling to life at any cost?"

Aristotle, that paragon of the natural reasoner, would have approved of Crito's formulation of the question; in Book One of his *Ethics* he rather airily asserts that the *summum bonum* must be attainable by man (*kte·tòn anthró·po·i*), thereby implicitly refusing to let his inquiry stray into the pursuit of any good that may lie beyond the confines of this life.[13]

There is a story told of Gertrude Stein that in the last hours of her life she roused herself from coma to address her lifelong companion with the query, "Alice, what is the answer?," and that having fallen back to remain insensible for some time she again roused herself to speak her last words, which were, "Alice, what is the question?" Socrates, it will be remembered, attempts by and large to show that Crito's question is not well formulated, that to the question as Crito puts it there is no answer. Truly a man should not ask, "In a conflict between practical good and ideal good, is it not better to choose the practical?" The putting of the question in these terms is responsible for the vulgar notion of the idealistic fool. There is a question rather that runs before, that is logically precedent: "In the long run is it possible for the practical and the ideal to clash? Is not any ultimate conflict between practicality and ideality delusive?"

Socrates' answer is that it is delusion indeed, the philosopher's real task being rather to distinguish between true and false ideals. Here we have the basis of the whole Platonic enterprise, the attempt to lay a foundation of ontology on which an ethic might be constructed. Cicero, as a good Academic, follows his master; in the *De Officiis* he develops the implications of these views (3.3.11):

. . . dubitandum non est quin numquam possit utilitas cum honestate contendere. Itaque accepimus Socratem exsecrari solitum eos, qui primum haec natura cohaerentia opinione distraxissent.

It is not to be doubted that a clash between practical conduct and ideal conduct is impossible under any circumstances. And therefore tradition has it that Socrates used to call down anthema on the heads of whoever it was that first instituted a specious theoretical distinction between two things which are ontologically inseparable.[14]

Who was it, then, who initiated this sophistical categorization? Probably some members of that motley group

known as the Sophists. The malodorousness of their reputation—and they surely deserved some of it—must have
arisen from a general tendency of theirs to let *utilitas* prevail over *honestas,* in political matters at any rate.[15] The
concern of many of their contemporaries, Parmenides for
example,[16] with the problem of the One and the Many, a
problem that is likely to strike us as somewhat academic
today, must have sprung from the realization that a philosophical pluralism, by positing more than one ultimately
discrete reality, inevitably leads to an ethical relativism
that may degenerate into no ethics at all.

In writing his *Antigone* Sophocles seems to have been
swayed by something like the foregoing considerations, for
the play brings into sharpest focus the truth that human
beings waver between an ethic of calculation and an ethic
of faith and love. Yet any ethical calculus, from the lowest
to the highest, from the most selfish hedonism to the noblest
utilitarianism, is in time and of time, in causality and of
causality, converting value into an endless process of becoming.[17] (It is not surprising, then, that modern positivism,
bound as it is to the cause-and-effect relationships of scientific method, is so helpless to construct ethical codes or to
erect aesthetic standards, having rather to issue its ad-
herents an empty promissory note on a future habitation
that science is somehow impossibly to build.) The ethic of
love and faith is different. By valuing the object or action
for itself alone it dispenses with all results. Nor is anything
sentimental or romantic implied here; no occurrence is com-
moner than to fix our evaluative faculties on an object without calculation of temporal consequence. Did anyone ever
really love a baby for the adult that he might become?
"What youthful mother," asks Yeats ("Among School Children"), ". . . Would think her son, did she but see that

shape / With sixty or more winters on its head / A compensation for the pang of his birth, / Or the uncertainty of his setting forth?" Did anyone ever love a great symphony because it eventuated in dead silence? Works of art are autotelic: "Thou, silent form, dost tease us out of thought, As doth eternity," says Keats to his Grecian Urn. Love, by abstracting its object from time and from causation, eternizes it, and at this point passes into faith, into the belief that such eternizing has some basis in ultimate being and is thus the most practical kind of practicality.

"There are many clever and fearsome things, but none is a cleverer or more fearsome thing than man," sing the Chorus in *Antigone* (332 ff.). "Man subdues the sea and the earth," they continue, in effect, "outwits work animals, wild animals, and fishes, fashions language and founds cities; through all the future he finds his way (*pantopóros áporos ep' oudèn érchetai / tò méllon*). But he shall find no way through death (*Háida mónon / pheúxin ouk epáxetai*), for death is the no-future."

This Chorus has often been interpreted as a kind of humanistic hymn; the first lines only are quoted, or the interpreter lets his analytic powers or his attention flag before coming to the climax of the song. But it is anything but a celebration of humanism. The humanist is all too prone to take man as the measure of all things, or at least to look on man as the repository of the ultimate values. But the point of the Chorus, and of every line of *Antigone*, is to show precisely that man cannot be the measure of anything, being himself strictly measured and delimited by death.[18] The measure of all things is, of course, God, that which is Above-Man, which is Not-Man. No human being who looks on himself as the center to which all else should be referred—and humanistic "love of mankind" is always

specifically love of oneself—can possibly reach the stage
of self-surrender that is predicated of the heroine of this
play.[19] Even "to know" and "to appreciate" are lesser degrees of the verb "to love," all of these activities implying
the submission of the self to its object.[20] The best musician,
to speak in Socratic language, is he who is most subservient
to music; the least obtrusion of personal interest produces
a dissonance fatal to the harmony of the whole. In much
the same way this Chorus reminds us by implication that
he who would save his life must lose it.

It follows that the noblest ethic of calculation cannot
encompass death, the end of the whole chain of consequences. When faced with death, or rather when faced
with a choice between death with honor and survival with
ignominy, it is impossible to ascertain an Aristotelian
mean. The situation itself admits of nothing but extremes.
The truly tragic situation is always of this nature; it is almost by definition a case in which the ethic of calculation
reveals its insufficiency. Hector, as he faces Achilles by the
walls of Troy in that prototype of all tragic crises, has
found that the time for parleying, for bargaining, and for
evading is past. Nor can he flatter himself that a noble
death will produce any desirable results. Will his dying
well help to save Troy? No. Will it palliate the suffering of
his fellow Trojans by one jot? No. Will it mitigate the lot
of his father or mother or wife or child? No. Will it ensure
his body considerate treatment afterward? Certainly not.
It makes no difference in the scales of fate; it has no good
effects in the course of time. Yet it is good.

That Antigone is in a similarly tragic situation is obvious;
she mentions that her reward is not only death, but the ob-
loquy of being thought to have acted impiously toward the
state (919–24). Thus she is not even to have the consolation

of thinking that she has won some posthumous glory by her deed. Nor is the comfort or rest that she may have given to her dead brother's spirit at all emphasized in the play.[21] It was good that the ceremony should be performed; it had to be done; and she did it. It is perhaps to point up the inapplicability of the ethic of calculation to her case that Sophocles puts into her mouth the speech (905 ff.)—so shocking to romantic readers—to the effect that she would not have risked this certain death for a child or a husband, since either might have been replaced in the course of nature, whereas, with both her parents dead, she could never have another brother. Some editors have wished to athetize the lines; others have called them an inept borrowing from Herodotus; still others have considered them an indication of Antigone's unamiable personality.[22] But surely she is merely putting as strongly as possible the inescapability of her moral dilemma: in the situation that confronts her there can be no shuffling; she cannot beguile herself with the thought of a future reparation of any sort; she must choose between utmost nobility and utter cowardice.

Admittedly her ethic also may be called calculating in a certain sense.[23] But her calculations are based upon that which transcends life, and hence upon the absolutely unknown.[24] Unlike Creon she does not reckon on probabilities, those extrapolations of our past experience, but she rests upon hopes, and these hopes embrace a minimum of content.[25] All of her detailed descriptions concern the world which she is leaving rather than the underworld to which she goes; of the latter she knows only that, compared to the duration of our death, the duration of our life is brief indeed. That all will be well in death, she herself questions (521): "Who knows whether these things are holy in the world below?" (To be sure, the query is raised to throw doubt on the rightness of Creon's procedure, but it equally throws doubt on her own.) Antigone merely nurses the hope (*en elpísin trépho* ·) that she will meet father, mother, and brother in the afterlife, and that her conduct will have been approved by them (897 ff.). Since Creon thinks that "profit resting merely on hope has often destroyed men" (221–22), in his eyes she is a fool, as he is in hers (469–70).[26]

Between these opposed ultimates of Holy Fool and Natural Fool of Fortune (to use Shakespeare's phrase), two fools of lesser degree are personated. Ismene is the obeyer of impulse, pursuing no consistent line of action; she does not share the noble inflexibility of Antigone, but in her two chief appearances in the drama presents first a picture of simple fear and then one of simple affection.[27] She is acquainted with love, but not with her sister's transcendent love confirmed by faith.[28] More significant is the figure of the Guard, who is far more than the mere comic relief he is usually taken to be. He is rather a sardonic caricature of the calculator, a representative of Creon's ethical position reduced to its narrowest bounds.[29] A sly pettifogger, who "fences off the action on all sides" that his aim may be good (241–42), the Guard has no thought for anyone but himself. He is comical precisely because he is portrayed as the Natural Man on the lowest level; as such he can furnish the audience that feeling of superiority noted by Aristotle as essential to comedy. As a Natural Man, he anticipates a certain amount of suffering, but hopes that it will not be beyond the common measure (235–36), and he sums up the code of his tribe admirably (439–40): "Nothing is so important to me as saving my own skin."

Such is the logical conclusion of Creon's system of this-
worldly calculation, for it must be remembered that he, too,
considers all concern with the afterlife merely "wasted effort" (*pónos perissós*—780). As events move on toward the
play's end, he is allowed to save his own skin, but to do
nothing more. It is fitting that his threat to the Guard
should come to apply to himself (308 ff.): "Death (Hades)
alone will not be sufficient punishment for you; first you
must be strung up alive and exhibit an object-lesson in impiety (*húbris*)." [30] After Creon learns that Eros, the god of
Love,[31] can be more destructive than money, which was the
only power his calculating mind had recognized before,[32]
he becomes, when Love has robbed him of his wife and
son,[33] only a "breathing corpse" (*émpsuchos nekrós*—
1167), a living object empty of profit or pleasure.[34]

Both Antigone and Creon are destroyed by love, for it
is Creon's own love for his wife and son that makes his
tragedy possible. Eros is thus the leading personage of the
play.[35] And this fact seems to make nonsense of the old
question whether the drama is a "diptych," [36] half Antigone's play and half Creon's play. Such a discussion could
arise only in the persistent attempt to read Greek tragedy,
and indeed all Greco-Roman, medieval, and Renaissance
literature, in terms of the post-Renaissance interest in "personality." [37] Many a book on Sophocles has consisted of
little more than "character studies" (which more properly
should have been labeled "personality studies"), but the
harvest in this field is a lean one.[38] And many a reader of
ancient plays has been betrayed into looking for what is not
to be found there in any abundance, with the result that he
has closed the book, muttering, "This is poor stuff, compared to the latest novel." In our hunger for idiosyncrasies
we fall with delight on the Guard in *Antigone* or the Nurse

in the *Choephori,* not realizing that these are "personalities" precisely because they are shallow and ethically of little significance.[39]

You will search in vain through Greek literature for personalities; the Greeks had neither the word nor the idea. "Personality" is a modern notion, a parasitic growth on the generally discarded concept of "the soul." The older belief in the soul implied that there is within each human being a unique and precious pattern of individual perfection and that each man's life has meaning and value only insofar as this pattern is realized in habit and action; the weakening of this belief in modern times has caused a shift of emphasis to "personality," a superficial concept which, under the guise of providing a basis for respecting each individual's worth, merely bolsters human vanity by putting a premium on any trait whatever which may serve to distinguish one mob-man from his fellow mob-men.[40]

Romanticism seized on the notion of personality with eagerness, and Romantic critics, Sainte-Beuve chief among them, made it the cardinal principle of their criticism. Modern psychology, also, has found the category an attractive one; the word is conveniently free from the religious connotations of "soul" and the ethical associations of "character." But modern psychologists can agree only on what personality is not: it is not other-worldly; it is not to be explained by thoughts that overleap this life and this little world of man. Accordingly the modern critic must look askance on such a "personality" as Antigone would appear to possess, and must convict her of harboring complexes and urges repellent to the norm.

Equally anachronistic is all commentary to the effect that Antigone has a martyr complex, that she is possessed by a stubborn death wish, that she lacks tragic stature because she knows that after her death she will be rewarded for her virtue a hundredfold. All this is commentary couched in terms of that very ethic of calculation which Creon approves and she herself rejects. As a martyr, she is a tragic figure precisely because she acts in terms of that other ethic; she does not know, she believes; in fact, the one thing that she does know is that her reward will not be in the nature of the rewards of this life. Is she a religious martyr, then? [41] If with this word we indicate one who by his suffering is willing to witness to the validity of what he cannot know, it is hard to see that she can be called anything else. Her martyrdom rests squarely on the fact that she has love and faith, but not knowledge.[42] She calculates, or rather speculates, that the ethic of temporal and causal calculation is illusory and inadequate, and that true gain lies somehow on the other side of death.[43] Antigone, the Bride of Death, speaks of *kérdos*, "gain and reward," but her wager is that he who acts only in the light of natural reason is aligning himself with a power that is certain, even in the light of that reason, to be no power at all.[44]

We recall that this heroine is, mythically speaking, a human sacrifice such as was offered up by the tribe in order that, through her assumption into the state of death, the whole people might participate in the mystery that encompasses life at its beginning and at its end. If one subscribes to the ethic of faith rather than to the ethic of calculation, one must, however much deploring the savagery of its expression, concede that the intuition that prompted this primitive behavior was perfectly sound: the mystery at the root of *Antigone* is the belief that the powers beyond human power, beyond this world and beyond this life, are somehow pleased and appeased by actions that show contempt for life and world.[45] This may be the explanation of why regularly the victim was honored by the population—before being ultimately dishonored and disposed of—and of why he or she felt it an honor to be so singled out. To this affinity of the superhuman with the supernatural Antigone attests; time, cultural attrition, or Sophocles himself had stripped away the more sanguinary reminiscences of the primitive ritual and had left her a martyr to the basic mystery of mankind face to face with death.

Politics, we are told, is the art of the possible. The politician Creon's bafflement when confronted by the martyr Antigone is the bafflement of the practical man when crossed by the advocate of impossible ideals.[46] The former supposes that the latter is pursuing some good which is different from his own good; let Antigone pursue it then, Creon says, and let her take the consequences. He fails to perceive that her belief is: *dubitandum non est quin numquam possit utilitas cum honestate contendere.* The conflict is between a person who thinks that there can be such a fundamental ontological conflict and a person who has faith that there can be none. For Antigone believes that Eros is the greatest of all powers, and that even in politics he shall ultimately prevail.[47]

Something of Antigone's conception of the good was in the older Greek ideal of *arete,* the ideal of the Homeric hero and of the aristocracy during the "Greek Middle Ages." The aristocrat, as one of *hoi áristoi,* "the best," had the advantage of being able to act in accordance with an absolute code, as opposed to the codelessness of base and self-seeking calculation subscribed to by *hoi kakoí,* "the low, the cowardly, and the worthless." [48] This was no simple question of aristocracy versus democracy; for many Athenian statesmen, such as Cimon and Pericles, as well as statesmen in later ages such as Cicero and Jefferson, were

able to pursue the aristocratic ideal in a more or less demo-
cratic context. Sophocles also was an aristocrat. Living in
an age of selfish demagogues who were discarding the
older ethic as politically impracticable [49] and of sophistical
moralists who were likewise rejecting it as indefensible in
terms of natural reason,[50] he wrote *Antigone,* we may suppose, as an affirmation of the ancient ideal.[51] In it the ethic
of love and faith incalculably triumphs over the ethic of
calculation. Eros, that terrible and tender god of love, turns
out to be the most powerful force in the universe after all
(781 ff.):

Eros unconquerable in battle, Eros, you who fall upon the
    treasures of men,
And rest all night on the delicate cheeks of a girl,
You who stride the seas and frequent the flock in its fold:
Among the deathless you are inescapable,
And men, creatures of a day, you rob of all reason.

So the victory of Love, which grows more certain from the
moment when the Chorus sing this song to the end of the
play, counterbalances and grows out of the victory of Force
with which the play began.[52]

As a result of this presentation, we learn, Sophocles so
pleased the electorate that he was chosen by the *demos* of
Athens to the office of *strategos.* We may assume that he
did his duty, but history does not record whether in this
office he met with any great measure of practical success.

4

The Existential Oedipus

EXISTENTIALISM has suffered the fate, certainly rare among philosophies, of becoming a fashionable byword. The results of this are such as might have been expected: satire, contempt, and misunderstanding on the part of the general reader; hostile criticism and supercilious interpretation on the part of the professional thinker. Generally speaking, philosophers outside of Germany and France find it hard to take existentialism seriously, being committed to an orthodoxy of a very different kind. Nor has the school's reputation been helped by the political vagaries of some of its leading exponents. In spite of all this, existentialism deserves to be taken seriously, if for no other reason than that it addresses itself to a serious task.[1]

The task of the existentialist thinker is similar to that of Socrates in the late fifth century B.C.: to bring philosophy back from a preoccupation with merely linguistic and narrowly pragmatic considerations—such a concern with ancillary studies being certain to lead to moral indifferentism —and to focus on philosophy's only proper point of concentration, a concern with ethics, thereby setting again for the activity of human thought the only goal that can evoke in a human being a sense of personal urgency. From Socrates onward the ancient world never forgot that the Groves of Academe are indeed barren ground unless they bear fruit in ethics.[2] Yet in most schools of philosophy today, if the layman dares to enter in search of an ethic, he will meet with as little welcome as Oedipus says he found in the shrine of Apollo: "Phoebus contemptuously dismissed the question I had come to put, and spoke instead of wretched, fearful matters, hard to bear" (*Oedipus Rex*, vv. 788–90). The questioner will be told that the terms of his query are meaningless, that the ground of his inquiry is, being metaphysical, nonexistent, and that he must wait a few centuries anyway, till science finds the answer.[3]

So completely has the modern age forgotten Socrates' lesson! The abstractness of absolute idealism, the impersonality of scientism, the absence of moral challenge in bourgeois optimism—in the nineteenth century all these stirred the bile of Kierkegaard and Nietzsche, just as the continuing ethical indifference of twentieth-century positivism provokes the reactions of Heidegger, Jaspers, Marcel, Sartre, and others. Existentialism has thus mainly arisen in protest against the excessively abstract and excessively impersonal direction of modern rationalistic thought. It may be defined, then, as including all thinking that by a method of introspective empiricism throws particular emphases on the ethical issues involving the individual self.[4] These emphases are placed on the following: on a rigorous inspection of concrete, primary experience— experience, that is, as it presents itself to the individual, as opposed to the interpreted, secondary data of science and abstractive reflection;[5] on the actual situation in which the individual finds himself, *la condition humaine;* on the individual's personal commitment or lack of commitment of himself to that situation, his willingness or lack thereof to become *engagé,* "involved, committed"; on the peculiarly human character of pledges, promises, and loyalties, which constitute the ethical life of human beings in contrast to the life of the lower animals; on the individual's relationship to fate and freedom; on the emergence or nonemergence of what may be called a Self.[6]

Existentialism is far more of a methodology than a coherent body of philosophic doctrine; its exponents differ widely among themselves; some are to be found in every major division of religion, and others center all their thinking around the denial of, or opposition to, a God. But a persistent and honest attempt to examine the primary data of experience is enough to mark a thinker as existentialist, and such an attempt necessarily involves him in a process of constant self-probing. He thus finds himself in the position of being both prescientific, in that the data of science must appear to him secondary, conventionalized, and overschematized, and at the same time empirical beyond the claims of the traditional empiricists, who long ago traded their so-called "experience" for a mess of mathematical abstractions. With his eye so uninterruptedly fixed on the inner workings of himself, the existentialist is naturally brought face to face with the question that Oedipus wished to put to the Delphic Oracle, "Who am I?," with the question implied in the riddle that the Sphinx put to Oedipus, "What is man?," and with the question that the people of Thebes brought for solution to their King, "Who is the guilty one?" And acting as he does in the double role of investigator and investigated, he becomes acutely aware that these questions are not problems, but mysteries, which the solver cannot solve without solving himself.

The reader will recall that "a mystery" was defined, in Gabriel Marcel's words, as "a problem which encroaches upon its own data," and that problems turn into mysteries in proportion as they draw nearer to the central concerns of the individual self. A human being is so inextricably entangled in his environment, temporal, material, and interpersonal, that he cannot logically make a clear distinction between himself and that which is without him; yet this distinction is precisely what logic, in order to function at all, assumes to be made. He indulges in the worst form of self-forgetfulness, forgetting namely that it is a self that is thinking and a conditioned self that is conditioning the results of thought. These are the human limitations to which existentialists wish to resummon our attention.

Sophocles, of course, was not an existentialist philosopher.[7] But it would perhaps not be too anachronistic to maintain that he wrote at a time when the intellectual situation was somewhat analogous to our own, that his reaction to it was somewhat similar to that of our existentialists, and that consequently his works deal with issues that are substantially the same as those treated in modern existentialist literature. Oedipus, in *Oedipus Rex*, confronts the dilemmas of personal commitment as opposed to intellectual abstraction, of his own relationship to fate and freedom, of apparent existence and true being, of the acceptance or rejection of emergent selfhood; he is, in short, faced with the prime mysteries of human existence: his story, as handled by Sophocles, if not strictly existentialist, may at least be called existential.

The verse summary of the play, ascribed to Aristophanes the Grammarian, runs as follows:

Taunted on all sides with the charge that he is a foundling and not his father's real son, Oedipus leaves Corinth to inquire of the Delphic Oracle who he is and who is his father. And coming upon Laius on a narrow wagon-road, poor Oedipus kills his father unwittingly. Afterwards, having answered the fateful chant of the terrible Sphinx, he shamefully shares the bed of his unknowing mother. Plague and widespread disease there-upon fall on Thebes; Creon is sent to the Delphic hearth to find a remedy, and from the mouth of the mantic god he hears the pronouncement that Laius's murderer should be brought to justice. So wretched Oedipus, learning that he is the man, puts out both of his eyes with his own hands, and his mother de-stroys herself by hanging.

It is interesting to note that in some versions of the myth Oedipus continued to rule Thebes for many years after the disclosure of his transgressions, apparently not much af-fected by Jocasta's suicide.[8] But in the classic version treated by Sophocles we have a double story, not only a fictionalization of some sort of murderous contest in which a new aspirant to the hand of the incarnate Great Mother,[9] the Lady of the Crossways where the three roads met, had to kill his predecessor and later undergo death or expulsion as a community scapegoat, a *pharmakos,* in his turn. The hanged Jocasta, also, seems to have originally been a *pharmakos*-figure, exactly similar to the hanged Antigone.[10] Such sacrifices were made, we are told, in order to appease the powers of nature and thus ensure that the society might enjoy a year of fat crops and fertile wives. We can object only when assured that this explanation explains all.[11] If this is all that the story of Oedipus originally meant, then what was its attraction for Sophocles? Granted that the primeval import of the myth had been considerably modi-fied, even softened, yet the main elements were ineradi-cably brutal and grotesque. How did he manage to see in it such striking symbolism of man's ineluctable fate and cir-cumscribed existence? [12] If the myth was merely a bumbling aetiology, only an attempt to account for ceremonies that had long since lost their practical significance, why did it, and why does it, along with its sister myths, prove so hospitable to profundities of philosophical and theological interpretation? Could such ideas have been already present in primitive religion?

The answer may well be that they were, in germ at least. The full mystery was in the Oedipus rite and the Oedipus myth from the beginning; all honor to Sophocles that he had the genius to see it and to bring it out. Not practicality, but *participation* is the motivating principle of religious ceremony. A scapegoat must be found at the turn of the year not primarily because the tribe hopes that a good season is made certain by that means—surely the tribesmen could remember many a year when the ceremony had no such effect—but mainly because man cannot bear for the year to turn without his having joined in the turning. He feels himself a part of nature, yet somehow strangely expelled from nature. His rites are his pathetic attempt to make a home for himself in an alien universe. The dominant philosophy of today says that in our age for the first time we can honestly come to terms with our expulsion, face it bravely, master both ourselves and this indifferent world. If it were so, it would be well. But the existentialist counters with the reminder that our alienation is not complete, that man against nature is but one part of nature against another, and that the notion of man's divorcing himself from the cosmos is a separation from order and a delusion more dangerous than any that led to primitive sacrifice.

That Sophocles was similarly in opposition to certain intellectual tendencies of his time, that he set himself against the trend toward a facile and narrow rationalism: these

have become critical commonplaces.[13] He is usually contrasted with Euripides in this,[14] frequently to the advantage
of the latter, who is admired for his liberal-progressive
spirit; whereas Sophocles is likely to be depicted as a somewhat dim-witted conservative, pietistic, obscurantist, devoted to the intuitive and the irrational. Such epithets are
the usual weapons of rationalists in their quarrel with anyone who—as Sophocles undoubtedly does in *Oedipus Rex*
—attempts to point out the limitations of human reason.
This quarrel is almost always conducted in false either-or
terms: after all, there is no such person as an "irrationalist." No one has ever consistently argued for deliberately
hampering the activity of reason, if only because he could
not allow his own reason to be hampered in defense of his
position; no thinker has ever thought that human reason
should not be permitted to go as far as it can: there have
simply been many to add that, having gone so far, it must
not rest in the unreasonable conclusion that it has gone all
the way, or that, having gone farther than it can, it must not
conclude that it is any longer reasonable. Sophocles in
Oedipus Rex surely attacks intellectual pride; he does not
attack the intellect as such.[15]

Intellectual pride arises from the exaltation of the intellect to the neglect of other parts of the soul, and seems
most likely to be a common vice of ages when there pre-
vails a system of psychology that treats human behavior in
simple terms of appetite and of schemes for its satisfaction.
The Sophistic psychology of Sophocles' day was like this, if
we are to believe Aristophanes and Thucydides, and in a
somewhat similar way modern psychological thinking virtually ignores the human will. And precisely here is the
source of the difficulties encountered by modern commentators in applying Aristotle's *hamartia* theory to *Oedipus.*

Hamartia to them must mean either a "moral flaw" (an isolated misdeed or a persistent defect of character) or an "error in judgment." Cedric Whitman sums up the controversy:

There are two fundamental ways of explaining the tragedy, corresponding in general to the two possibilities involved in hamartia. One is to attribute Oedipus' fall to the rash, self-willed temper already mentioned. But others maintain that no such moral failing is involved, but rather an intellectual slip, an error, entailing no moral guilt, but merely the well-known cataclysmic sequel. This error—"trifling," as Aristotle said— occurred when Oedipus slew his father and married his mother. He was innocent, in that he acted in ignorance, but he was wrong in that he did these things. . . . The relative significance of these two views for tragedy itself is, of course, immense. But the important question for the present is, which did Aristotle mean? Did he intend us to find a morally culpable act or merely a mistake as the cause of tragic catastrophe? [16]

An either-or dilemma again. Whitman quite rightly decides that neither theory is adequate and rejects a *hamartia* explanation altogether. But instead of answering "Neither" it is possible to answer "Both." Possession of knowledge or the lack of it, exercise of reason or the failure to exercise it, are never ethically neutral in all their aspects. Modern thought, with its fundamental neglect of the will, or rather its submergence of the will into desire, leads to a mere ethics of custom, *mores* instead of morality, which is impersonal and does not truly engage the individual will. Surely the relationship between the parts of the soul is more complex; there are an ethics of epistemology and an ethics of logic. *Hamartia* may possibly be neither mere intellectual error nor misconduct; it is blindness to a whole phase of universal reality, blindness to such a degree that it affects all of a man's attitudes and all of his behavior.

What is Oedipus' *hamartia* then? Obviously it is not bad temper, suspiciousness, hastiness in action—for his punishment does not fit these crimes; nor ignorance of who his parents are—for ignorance of this type is not culpable; [17] still less murder and incest—for these things are fated for him by the gods. [18]

No, Oedipus' blind spot is his failure in existential commitment; [19] a failure to recognize his own involvement in the human condition, [20] a failure to realize that not all difficulties are riddles, to be solved by the application of disinterested intellect, but that some are mysteries, not to be solved at all, [21] but to be coped with only by the engagement, active or passive, of the whole self. [22] Oedipus' punishment, then, is not really punishment at all, but the only means by which the gods may enlighten blindness of such density. Sophocles was not concerned to tell a crime-and-punishment story; this is shown by his leaving the "crimes" out of the action. [23]

Of course certain critics contend that after all Sophocles was not really concerned to do anything but tell a good story well. [24] "The play's the thing," they say. Admittedly, but what kind of thing? And why is it a good thing, a better thing, say, than the detective play on the television set? To evade the task of answering such questions is to posit the impossibility of criticism altogether. Yet the advocates of silence babble on. The last word on such negativism has been said by Charles Williams, in regard to similar non-interpretation of Dante: "It is a tender, ironic, and consoling view. It is consoling because it shows us that, though we cannot write like Dante, yet we shall not be taken in by Dante. It is also consoling because it relieves us from the

necessity of supposing that Dante may be relevant to us." [25]
Such critics, in short, are blind with Oedipus' own brand of
blindness: they do not wish to be involved.

The action of the play begins when the King undertakes
a project, the discovery of the murderer of Laius, and binds
himself with the most solemn promises to carry this project
to its completion. The concept of the project and the promise is dear to the existentialists: [26] only Man can so engage
himself, for only Man, unlike the other animals, has knowledge of past and future as well as present.[27] Yet the celebrated irony of the scene, as has been obvious to every
reader, consists in the fact that the engagement is far more
real than Oedipus knows. From the audience's point of
view, therefore, this commitment has something of falsity
about it, of incompleteness; it becomes to them a symbol of
our common human failing to look for evil everywhere but
in ourselves. (Tragedians love this ironic device; one thinks
of Clytemnestra prating about justice, rash Hamlet com-
mending the stoical Horatio, and Lear praying for Heaven
to give him patience, which Heaven does by letting fall on
his own top all the stored vengeances he wants poured on
his daughters.) This failure to commit oneself fully is the
prime temptation of the intellect, which in its essential direction points from the self to the exterior world.

Oedipus is willing to avenge the death of Laius as
though Laius were his own father (264–65); he is willing to
suspect even a member of his own household (249–51):
these ironies are obvious. He says that the griefs of his people are his own, that he feels them even more deeply than
others do (59–64), speaking more truly than he knows. He
undertakes to solve the riddle as a father would resolve a
difficulty for his children,[28] little realizing that, as Teiresias
warns him, this very day is to make him and his children

equal (425).[29] But even as he begins his denunciation of the unknown murderer, he emphasizes his own non-involvement (219–20): "But what I am about to proclaim I shall proclaim as a stranger to this tale and a stranger to all that has been done." [30] The project therefore has an air of dissociation about it, because it lacks the last full measure of personal commitment; a promise may not be a real promise, cannot in fact, be a real promise unless a person stakes on it a real share of his existence as a creature who is in time but who transcends time. That at the end Oedipus fulfills his project to the letter is the measure of his moral grandeur.

It may be objected that Oedipus *is* personally interested in solving the murder. This is true, but not because he feels any real involvement of himself in the general human condition. Rather he feels his own external fortune affected by the threat to his power. "The man who did this to Laius has reason to do this to me" is a quite different attitude from "What Laius's murderer did I may have done." "We must punish criminals in order to protect ourselves" is only the beginning of morality, the end of which is "There, but for the grace of God, go I." [31] Oedipus is involved only as regards his self-interest, not as regards his own self; hence his quickness in directing his suspicion toward Creon.[32]

The person who wholly projects morality into the outer world loses his own selfhood in the process. Sophocles does not waste his time and the reader's patience by making Oedipus lament at the last that he could not help doing what he did or being what he is.[33] To look upon oneself as the mere product of external causes is to make oneself a thing instead of a person, as the existentialist philosophers never tire of pointing out. Oedipus is horrified at having been his own self-accuser, but he does not therefore retract the accusation. He realizes that he is a scapegoat; he does not complain that he is a goat. Determinism, theories of heredity and environment, fatalism: all are devices, not for explaining guilt and evil, but for explaining them away, away from ourselves, at all costs; Oedipus disdains to avail himself of these devices. Rather he reaches his true moral stature at the end of the play. For a man is never more conscious of being a person and less conscious of being a thing than when the self is accusing itself and accepting its own guilt. The willingness to accept guilt is an indispensable step toward the goal of self-knowledge; an animal or a child cannot fully grasp the concept of guilt; similarly an adult who falls into deterministic excuses for his behavior shuts the door on the possibility of self-development. But a person reaches his greatest intensity of self-consciousness when he simultaneously plays the part of both the accuser and the accused. To such intensity the individual will not rise as long as his external fortunes are in a state of prosperity; herein lies the necessity of tragedy. Albert Camus remarks: [34] "The human heart has a tiresome tendency to label as fate only what crushes it. But happiness likewise, in its way, is without reason, since it is inevitable. Modern man, however, takes the credit for it himself, when he doesn't fail to recognize it." Sophocles, needless to say, knew better than the "modern men" of his day.

Even the recognition of an unpleasant truth is a moral act; if a man is hideously ugly, he deserves some praise for taking an honest and steady look in the mirror.[35] Morality is not merely a matter of putting some goodness or wickedness into a slot and receiving in return a proportionate package of pleasure or pain. *Oedipus Rex* is only externally a crime-and-punishment play; internally it is a moral drama of self-recognition.[36] That the recognition is neither prompt nor willing is natural, and increases our feelings of pity and fear. The view that represents Sophocles as an advocate of mere religious conventionality and ethical conformity is inadequate. Oedipus as a scapegoat is singled out,[37] but, by accepting the role, he singles himself out and differentiates himself from the mass, the Chorus. It is his acceptance of the wretched creature that he is that makes him a hero.[38] In Kierkegaard's terms, Oedipus chooses to live his own life, to become what he is. His life is henceforth to be unique, a life set apart, as he well recognizes, and in this respect it is to become the being of a Person in contrast to the existence of a Thing.[39]

The Chorus, however, are quite willing to dissociate themselves from him and to withdraw into the anonymity of convention, a withdrawal which, as Heidegger [40] repeatedly emphasizes, is one of the chief methods of evading human freedom. The Chorus say that they take Oedipus as their *parádeigma*, their model from whom they may learn a lesson, but their wish never to have known him shows that his is a lesson that they are not actually prepared to learn. Thus they fall into the same error from which Oedipus is emerging.

It is ambiguous, therefore, to say that Sophocles does not offer a solution to the problem of evil such as Aeschylus gives. This is usually taken to imply an attitude of pessimism on his part, at worst marked by befuddlement or bitterness, at best stoical or pietistic.[41] Granted that he discovered that evil is irrational, what does such a discovery mean?[42] Evil is of course "irrational" in the same way that any datum of experience is, which is only to say that evil exists. Occasionally, too, the evil that befalls us appears to be the work of a malevolent demon, of a subhuman intelligence, "whatever brute and blackguard made the world":

criticism that calls *Oedipus Rex* a tragedy of irrational evil seems to be toying with this sense of the word. But this can hardly have been Sophocles' final attitude toward the matter, since he goes to such pains to show that he has limited esteem for human intelligence itself. In his thinking, then, evil must be irrational only in the sense that its meaning is beyond the scope of human reason. It is something to which there is no ultimate "solution"; it is a mystery. For even evil that seems remote always has indissoluble connections with the self. Any evil that seems outside myself, once it is recognized, immediately offers a challenge to me that I cannot elude; if I refuse to act or react—and strictly speaking I can only apparently refuse—I compound it. And evil that strikes nearer home, the evil of my own limited nature and destiny, is the precondition of my action or reaction.

Let it be said again that Oedipus' prime *hamartia*, his blind spot, his moral ignorance, is precisely his tendency to suppose that evil is a problem rather than a mystery, a something unrelated to the self that can be solved without involving the self.[43] Though such ignorance can be instructed only through the most awesome suffering, the tragic finale is like the rolling of a weight from the soul: the insignificance and foulness of man as embodied in *Oedipus* implies the greatness and purity of the divine powers that have brought him low.[44] Ultimate humiliation frees the man from his imprisonment in his petty ego and points out to him the only proper object of his reverence.[45] In direct contrast to the humanists of today, Sophocles seems to be saying in this play, "Thank God there is something in the universe worthier of worship than Man!"

Sophocles found in the Oedipus myth the perfect material for his purposes; he it was, perhaps, who converted the peripety from a mere penalty for transgressing a taboo into a means of moral enlightenment. Doubtless already in the myth as he received it the solution of the Sphinx's riddle was the cause of the King's prosperity and intellectual pride. Sophocles' contribution was to bring out the fact that Oedipus' apparent success at explaining away the evil of the Sphinx was to mislead him into supposing that he could similarly explain any evil away.[46] But the answer to the Sphinx's riddle is a simple abstraction.[47] "What is it that goes on four feet in the morning, two feet at noon, and three feet at eventide?" The answer is "Man," but Man in General means nothing to the Individual Man. The whole play is thus richer in tragic irony than has ever been realized, perhaps—than ever, in fact, can be realized, for the play itself says that its own message can be driven home only by personal experience, and not simply by viewing or reading.[48] The distinction between theoretical and experiential knowledge is everywhere made evident. Since irony, on one side, depends on the disclosure of ignorance that thinks itself to be knowledge, the spectator, watching Oedipus' folly in cursing the murderer of Laius, must uneasily perceive that here is a symbol of every man's situation; Aristotle's tragic fear should strike into his soul when he realizes that just as from his superior position he views the antics of a wise fool, so there may be other still higher beings who are similarly audience to his own play.[49]

Oedipus' encounter with Teiresias is, from beginning to end, a clash between such degrees and types of cognition. Oedipus heralds the arrival of Teiresias as of a "godly prophet, in whom alone of men truth is innate" (298–99), and greets him (330–331) as "You who have known all and been all and contemplated all,[50] all things that can be taught, all things that cannot be put into words, things of

heaven, and things that make their way on earth!" Yet
Teiresias' first words on being appealed to for a revelation
are simply (316–17), "Alas for intelligence! How fearful
and slippery (*deinòn*) a thing it is when it brings no profit
to him who has it!" [51] Among other considerations, he is
thinking here about the fact that Oedipus' cleverness in
solving the riddle of the Sphinx, his greatest success, has
led inevitably to the kingship of Thebes, the marriage with
Jocasta, and the present obligation to track down the murderer of Laius. Teiresias knows also that all knowledge,
and all intelligence that is the basis of acquiring it, are gifts
of the gods and of chance.

This is precisely what the priest has said to the King in
the Prologue, reminding him that the riddle was solved "by
the assistance of gods" (cf. 37–39). But Oedipus tends to
forget this; he taunts Teiresias (391 ff.): "How was it that
you chanted no way of deliverance for your fellow-citizens
when the riddling hound was here? . . . But you were unable to speak out; neither birds nor knowledge from the
gods helped you. But I stopped her, I, Oedipus, knowing
nothing, prevailing by sheer intelligence, learning nothing
from the birds." His arrogant skepticism here, reinforced
later by his own and Jocasta's impieties,[52] is nothing but the
pride of intellect untrammeled by the embarrassing par-
ticularities of actual existence. But Teiresias knows that
Oedipus' abstractive intelligence is foolishness compared to
the wisdom that accommodates itself to the unique "this-
ness," the *haecceitas*, of reality. The contrast between the
two is a contrast between such knowledge as solves problems and such wisdom as plumbs mysteries. And so Teiresias actually cannot tell Oedipus anything; all his prophe-
cies and revelations provoke in the King merely the
reaction: "This is a mistake. This is a plot." The calamitous

nature of existence is always seemingly intended for someone else and overwhelms oneself only by wicked error. But
the same fortune that brings a man to greatness proves a
man's undoing (cf. 441–42); and man, like Oedipus, is
truly the Child of Chance (1080).

As the drama unfolds, Oedipus finds himself doomed in
his own person to live out his abstractions; his own day's
journey is to be the journey that the Sphinx's riddle hinted
at; [53] the Sphinx has her revenge. "This day shall bring you
to birth and destroy you," Teiresias tells him (438); and
this day, at the height of his manhood, he shall first truly
learn what he was as an infant and what he shall be as an
old man (454–60):

> Of the man of sight shall be made a blind man, of the rich
> man a beggar, and he shall make his way into an alien land
> testing the ground ahead of him with his staff. And he shall
> be shown to be in like case with his children, brother to them
> and father; to the woman from whom he sprang he shall be
> seen to be son and husband; the seed of the father shall have
> sown seed where the father sowed,[54] and he shall have cut his
> father down.[55]

The solver of all problems is himself the problem beyond
all solution. What appeared to Oedipus as a riddle—Man—
is in reality a mystery—Myself.

5

The Gateway of HIPPOLYTUS

M ANY Greek tragedies are likely to trouble and baffle the
reader by the apparent fatalism of their plots: *Prometheus
Bound, Oedipus Rex,* and *Hippolytus* are obvious examples. Certainly the Greek tragedians seem to be saying
much of the time that mankind has not a chance—"As flies
to wanton boys are we to the gods," in effect [1]—and at least
a good third of the Chorus's lines carry the burden: "Life is
painful; death is best" or "Knowledge is evil; 'tis better not
to know." The natural reaction to all this is to take the plays
as paeans of irrationalism, in one sense or another, and this
line of interpretation—we may call it the Irrationalist
School—has evoked reams of fine ratiocination. So far
things are troubling, but not baffling. Bafflement sets in
when we listen to the tragedians' equally frequent exhor-
tations to lead the upright life, advice which is pointless in
a deterministic context, and ask ourselves on closing the
book what we are supposed to have got out of all this. For
the irrationalist view is essentially undidactic, teaching us
that there is nothing to be learned, and is ethically costive
in its effect rather than purgative of pity and terror. Are we

to o'erleap ourselves, then, and fall on the other? Is the
Euripidean corpus, for instance, a cento of late-nineteenth-
century agnostic-liberal opinions, sometimes expressed directly, sometimes implied by the absurdity of their denial? [2]
This is too fantastic; conformably to common sense and
common taste, we are much more comfortable if we suppose ourselves spectators of ethical demonstrations, perhaps the working out of a "tragic flaw" in one or more of the
characters: the Rationalist School.[3]

As with the *sententiae,* so with the plots. If we look for
the powers which motivate the action of *Hippolytus,* for
instance, we are immediately embarrassed by riches.[4] The
ancient summary of the play is one of the fullest *hypotheses*
we have:

King Theseus of Athens, son of Aethra and Poseidon, married
Hippolyta, one of the Amazons, who bore him Hippolytus, a son
wonderfully handsome and chaste. On the death of this first
wife, Theseus then wed a Cretan woman, Phaedra, daughter of
King Minos of Crete. With her he went into exile in Troezene
after killing Pallas, one of his kinsmen. Now, it so happens that
Troezene is where Pittheus, Theseus' grandfather, has agreed to
take Hippolytus into his home and bring him up. When Phaedra
sees the young man, she immediately falls in love with him, not
out of mere wanton passion, but in fulfillment of the wrathful
design of Aphrodite, who has determined to destroy the youth in
punishment for his chastity. Phaedra conceals her affection for a
while, but when her old nurse promises to help her, she reveals
the whole truth. On her own initiative the nurse carries the story
to the young man. He is outraged, and when Phaedra learns of
his reaction, she showers the nurse with reproaches, and then
hangs herself. At this point Theseus appears. Hastily cutting
down the body of his dead wife, he discovers on her person a
writing-tablet on which there is written a message accusing
Hippolytus of an attempt on her virtue. Theseus believes the

evidence, banishes Hippolytus, puts curses on his head, and calls on Poseidon to fulfill them. The god gives heed; Hippolytus is destroyed. But Artemis discloses the truth of the matter to Theseus, absolves Phaedra from blame, and comforts him for the loss of wife and son. And she orders a local cult to be instituted in Hippolytus' honor.

This is the well-known Potiphar's-wife story; the first Greek version to appear in literature is the tale of Bellerophon and Queen Anteia recounted by Glaukos in Book Six of the *Iliad*. These two narratives, the Biblical and the Homeric, are good demonstrations of how myth, even in very early times, could be transformed into mere romance. In the plot of *Hippolytus*, too, no student of comparative mythology would have difficulty in recognizing an ancient and multiform mythical scheme: a mortal lover spurns the advances of a female deity, suffers abasement or death, and afterwards is raised to glory.[5] The most familiar form of the myth, and the one nearest to ritual, is of course that involving Venus and Adonis, or their Near Eastern counterparts.[6] But Artemis also figured in some of the versions; she was more or less responsible for the death of her lover, the great hunter Orion, for example. In fact, the Ugaritic *Poem of Aqhat*, in which the goddess Anat, Queen of the Chase, contrives the death of the huntsman Aqhat because he refuses to yield her his divine bow—the affair finally concluding with the reassemblage and resuscitation of the pieces of Aqhat's body—is a variation that quite closely suggests the relationship between Artemis and Hippolytus.[7] So the original formula can be stated: Aphrodite-Artemis-Phaedra is offended by her lover Hippolytus, causes his death, and procures his apotheosis. We can hardly guess what shape the myth was in when it came into the hands of Euripides; apparently his original material was the simple romance of Hippolytus and Phaedra and the results of her guilty love. Probably the goddess Aphrodite took no part in the story as tradition handed it down to the author; she must have been an addition of Euripides' own.

Why did he add her? To point up his indictment of religious belief, the older critics answered, to show that if the gods are as ruthlessly vengeful as this, they are unworthy of reverence. This theory might account for Aphrodite, but scarcely does justice to the unobjectionable Artemis. Actually, if Artemis is presented in a bright light and Aphrodite looms in the dark background in *Hippolytus*, it is not because one goddess deserves worship and the other does not, but rather because Aphrodite is the dark side of Artemis. Euripides certainly understood, and his audience perhaps less certainly apprehended, that Aphrodite and Artemis were ultimately one. The play gives many intimations to this effect. Both were Queens of the Night, and if we did not know that Hippolytus is rejecting Aphrodite in the Prologue, we might think he was referring to the moon-goddess Artemis when he says (106): "No deity who must be adored in the night pleases me." [8] Immediately afterward, Phaedra's affliction, due to Aphrodite, is attributed by the Chorus to Artemis, who is said rather surprisingly to "roam by the strand of the sea in the wet swirls of the brine" (148-50)—where we would sooner expect an association with the goddess who rose from the sea-foam. And not long after that the one function of fertility-goddess that remained to Artemis in popular belief, her status as a helper of women in pregnancy and child-birth, is emphasized by the Chorus (cf. 161-69).[9]

Finally, to make the parallelism unmistakable, Euripides refers to the myth of Adonis (cf. 1416-22); Artemis is made to promise the dying Hippolytus that she will avenge his

death by shooting down whatever man is dearest to Aphrodite. As Adonis was traditionally said to have been done to
death by a wild boar, Euripides obviously used a less familiar version in order to even the balance between his
twin goddesses.[10] Thus Artemis' hard words about Aphrodite, and her explanation that Zeus allots to each lesser
deity a sphere beyond which there may be no transgression,[11] are mere attempts to smooth out the complications
occasioned by the one primitive Maid-Mother's dissolution
into a Virgin-phase and a Matron-phase.[12] Similarly, as
Adonis was yearly serenaded by the hymns of women, so
Phaedra's love and Hippolytus' are to be celebrated by
maidens in song; brides-to-be will dedicate their hair on
Hippolytus' altar, and he will become, in effect, a satellite
of Aphrodite, goddess of marriage.

Such is the supernatural machinery. But the plan of
Aphrodite would seem to have been sufficient for all dramatic purposes; what then is the importance of Phaedra in
the play as we have it? It is as though our vehicle were being pulled to its end by two ill-yoked teams, a divine and a
human, where one would be quite enough. Aphrodite's
opening speech, foretelling revenge on Hippolytus and incidental disaster to Phaedra, seems entirely sufficient to im-
pel the play along its course; every development that follows is only a further attestation to the goddess's relentless
potency. Poseidon sends the bull-like sea-monster to cause
the death of Hippolytus, who, dying, is comforted and
vindicated by the appearance of Artemis. All is fated,
destined, doomed, it would seem; men are puppets of the
gods.

Yet the human characters are blameworthy, too. Hippolytus need not have been so priggish and proud, so full of
self-admiration and self-pity, or so vulgar and brutal in his

rejection of Phaedra's love.[13] Perhaps for Phaedra suicide was the only escape from the shameful situation into which Aphrodite had led her, but surely to leave behind the note alleging that Hippolytus had assaulted her virtue was a totally unnecessary posthumous crime. And it was hardly honorable of Theseus ostensibly to send his son into exile, while actually arranging for his death. Wholly eliminate the gods from the plot, then: there is still enough human malefaction to culminate in tragedy. "No," the irrationalist might say, "an error. These misdeeds are themselves manifestations of numinous forces; they result either from passion or from ignorance. Passion is, so to speak, the welling-up into the human soul of that sea-flood of nature which is the domain of Aphrodite, Artemis, and Poseidon. Whereas ignorance is inseparable from the divinely ordained condition of man: 'The gods have bestowed on men a propensity for making mistakes,' Artemis contemptuously remarks (1433–34). Therefore considerations of will and intellect have no place in an explanation of Euripides' story; it is a tale solely of natural, god-given, uncontrollable passion."

Of course this entire dilemma of mortal responsibility versus divine determinism could be easily resolved if we took the Greek gods to be only symbols of human passions and human habits. This solution has attracted numbers of critics, who have no belief in the divine themselves and no desire that Euripides should have had any either. But if Aphrodite was only a symbol of sexual desire and Artemis only a symbol of asceticism, the reader would find it impossible to say what Poseidon was a symbol of in this particular play.[14] A mythic interpretation, on the other hand, would assert that though the particular Aphrodite on stage was a representation of the real goddess, the real Aphrodite to the ancient Greek was not a "symbol" of anything. He would rather have reasoned from the divine to the human than vice versa: to him sexual desire was a sign of the power of Aphrodite, just as the sea-beast would have been a sign of the power of Poseidon. Aphrodite to him was not a generalized projection of human emotion; each instance of desire was a piece of her handiwork.

It was for this reason that the classical languages so frequently referred to emotions as coming into the individual from the outside; the affective phenomena were looked on as *data*—they were sufferings, *páthe* · and *passiones*. It was observed that they arise from our bodies, which are our links with the external world, and that they are unlikely to manifest themselves on summons.[15] It was not, then, that the human sexual appetite was hypostatized as the goddess Aphrodite; it was rather that Aphrodite *was* the procreative urge, human, non-human, or biding her time somewhere out of sight. She was often pictured as having a beautiful female form precisely because, to the Greeks' observation, she often enters into and clothes herself with such a form. The sexual urge was personified because it so often personifies itself. Aphrodite, of course, might take on the forms of animals; she might take on a thousand forms at the same time in a thousand different places. Wherever there is the sexual urge, Aphrodite is there. She cannot die, and she cannot be successfully flouted.[16] Taking these attitudes into consideration, it seems improbable that Euripides meant his play to be taken only on the human-psychological level.

The same attitudes considered, it would appear that such gods should be viewed as pre-ethical, beyond good and evil, not to be called either good or bad in themselves.[17] Yet the natural power that Aphrodite essentially is, is not itself

a matter of indifference to ethics; whether a human being
treats it with scorn or reverence is what gives it its ethical
aspect: [18] this must be remembered when we contemplate
Aphrodite's spite toward Hippolytus. We think too easily
of the classical gods as static conceptions, fixed in the Greek
religious consciousness once and for all; we picture these
anthropomorphized forces of nature as amoral, hedonistic,
"pagan;" yet even in Homer, where much of this picture
comes from, they are by no means unacquainted with grief.
And we speak too glibly of these gods as being immanent
in the world and not transcendent.[19] Yet Zeus at least, by
the greater writers' indications, was sometimes thought of
as partly independent of nature, directing it and unaf-
fected by it. Lastly, we sometimes fall into the way of
imagining that these happy, "pagan" gods were wish-pro-
jections of their happy, "pagan" worshipers. Nothing
could be less true. Immanent, transcendent, or, as is more
probable, confusedly both, the gods were universally
acknowledged to require and to deserve reverence. However much some commentators may admire the anti-sexual
Hippolytus, the Greek spectator could only have looked on
the youth as a rebel against heaven and on his catastrophe
as deserved retribution. Aphrodite could do no other than
crush him.

With this discussion we seem to circle back to the former
question: Are men only puppets of fate? The issue of fate
versus free will will undoubtedly be debated in connection
with Greek tragedy as long as it will be debated in philosophy
and theology—and that may very well be forever.[20] But it is
possible that Euripides in *Hippolytus* reveals that he understands these ethical complexities better than his modern
critics do. "Are human beings ever really guided by their
intellects, or are they rather always swept along by their

passions?" is a false either-or proposition. "Rationalism, or Irrationalism?" begs the very question that it attempts to answer. We are still prone today to be crushed beneath the dead hand of neo-classic theory, with its doctrine of separate human faculties, the doctrine itself being a misconstruction of classical psychology, in which Plato and Aristotle analyzed the human soul [21] into the intellect, the passions, and the will. But Euripides was fortunate in one respect to have lived before the two philosophers, in that he was never exposed to the risk of being unable to put the soul together again. The irrationalist view of human nature is based on the premise that we cannot act better than we know; from this perfectly reasonable beginning it goes on to draw the conclusion that if we act badly we must have known no better, and to proceed on the assumption that knowing itself is not a form of action. This view is similar to that of the later Greek philosophers, who in identifying knowledge with virtue treated the will quite inadequately.

But the problem of the relationship between knowledge and virtue is the central theme of *Hippolytus:* innocence, the virtue with which the plot is mainly concerned, is hard to distinguish from ignorance. And ignorance is not presented as ethically neutral, as something for which the ignorant person is never to blame.[22] Euripides shows that the human soul is a mystery, that there is no simple cause-and-effect relationship among its interacting parts.[23] Knowledge confines and conditions choice, but choice in turn determines the amount and quality of our knowledge. Appetite presses toward its realization through the will, but the will intensifies one appetite, immobilizes another. Knowledge increases the range of appetite, but the appetite for knowledge may be a precondition of such increase. Human beings cannot choose what they do not know, but their failure to know may be a chosen ignorance. They cannot will when they have not learned, but they may have willed not to learn. Not all reprehensible behavior results from a simple surrender of the intellect to the affections; equally pernicious is willful ignorance, whether it takes the form of a mere refusal to learn, or of confusing negativism with virtue, or of deliberately repressing what one already knows. In *Hippolytus* Theseus rejects investigation; Hippolytus renounces adult experience; Phaedra forswears her own better knowledge.[24] The play is a study of intentional blindness.

Theseus' behavior exhibits a type of culpable ignorance that is easily analyzed.[25] His approach to the whole question of intellection and morality is blunt and actualistic, cynical but not profound: "Oh, human beings! So foolishly missing the mark! Why do you teach unnumbered skills, work out, uncover every trick, but never know, never track down one little thing: how to teach thinking to those who have no brains (916–20)?"

In other words, like some modern psychologists, he assumes that human intelligence is a fixed and measurable quantity, a conception that allows the will no place. As for the use of language, the tool of the intellect, the only complication that he can recognize is that words may be used for downright deceit: "Every man ought to have two voices, one truthful and the other fitted to the occasion, so that the honest voice would confute falsity, and we would not be deceived (928–31)."

The double meaning of language, the true and false, that Theseus here alludes to is an easily avoided snare compared to the semantic net in which Phaedra finds herself entangled, to whom, as we shall see, words themselves, almost apart from their human users, appear potentially deceitful.

Because of his crudity Theseus not surprisingly falls into the sin of rashly jumping to a conclusion without full investigation.[26] He glories in his precipitate action, obviously fearing that any wavering may seem a reflection of some infirmity in his character, or of a lack of integrity in the grief he has expressed at the loss of his wife, or of simple naïveté. And in answer to Hippolytus' plea that his defense be tested by an appeal to soothsaying, Theseus to obstinate unenlightenment adds a dash of impiety: "To those birds that flit overhead, goodbye and goodbye again, say I" (1058–59), thus echoing Hippolytus' disastrous rejection of Aphrodite in the first scene.[27] For all this Theseus is sharply rebuked by Artemis (1320 ff.). So much, then, for the stubborn refusal to learn, willful not-knowing at its lowest level.

Theseus glories in his ignorance; Hippolytus glorifies his. Theseus makes a virtue out of his repudiation of knowledge; Hippolytus makes such repudiation a virtue from the outset.[28] At his first entrance he lays a garland on the shrine of Artemis that flanks the palace gateway on one side (the shrine of Aphrodite being on the other), saying that he has culled the flowers from a meadow where *Aidos*—call her Innocence, Reverence, Modesty, Chastity, Awe, or Shame [29]—keeps her well-watered garden only for those to whom "nothing has been taught, but to whom has been allotted in the course of nature complete self-control" (79–80). And he ends with the prayer that he may round the final turn of life's race as he began. His prayer is granted, but only at the cost of his destruction.

Every living creature comes into existence pure and virginal, knowing nothing; it is Hippolytus' boast that he has

preserved his being in its pristine ignorance.[30] He is therefore devoted to Artemis, the great virgin-goddess herself,
the protectress of animals and presider over child-birth, the
spirit of fertility, but only of its unconscious and guiltless
phases. But "Nature by nature in unnature ends," as Auden
says. In exalting one nature-goddess, Hippolytus degrades
another; natural virginity clashes fatally with natural sexuality. Artemis speaks of Aphrodite as the "divinity most
hateful to all of us whose delights are virginal" (1301–2);
certainly Hippolytus belongs to this group, since his chief
pleasure seems to consist in boasting of his purity. But what
would be spontaneous innocence in a child is in a mature
young man something offensive and unnatural; it leads him
to a coarse contempt for one half of the human creation and
to a puerile wish that the operation of nature itself may be
changed.[31] Denouncing all women in Phaedra's presence,
he exclaims (616 ff.): "O Zeus, why did you domicile in the
light of day these women, this false thing, this bane to mankind?" [32] and concludes with the resolve to trample them
under foot forever (668). But, ironically, when he comes to
be deified, he is forever to be associated with women; he is
to reap a harvest of maidens' tears (cf. 1427) and become
little more than a minion of Aphrodite.

Hippolytus will not surrender this ignorance which is his
very being; therefore his only chance to preserve it is to die,
to go out of nature, and to be apotheosized.[33] This is the
boon Artemis grants him: girls before their marriage will
cut off their hair for him and weep for him, and his and
Phaedra's story will be material for song (1423–30). So he
never really learns, as Phaedra threatens that he shall, the
true meaning of *sophrosyne* (730–31); "he shall have a
share of my disease, and shall learn *sophrosyne*," are her
last words.[34] But instead he persists to the end in supposing

that this virtue is merely negative—"intactness of mind"—
whereas the audience may learn from the action of the play
that it rather connotes "whole-mindedness and wholesome-
mindedness."

As for his sharing Phaedra's disease, it would perhaps be
more accurate to say that she shares his, to a greater degree. For Phaedra knows, and knows that she knows, but
nevertheless chooses not to know.[35] In her much-debated
monologue beginning "Women of Troezene" she reveals
herself as by far the most thoughtful and self-conscious
character in the play (373 ff.):

> Women of Troezene, through the long stretches of the nights,
> I have often pondered, and wondered how it is that the life of
> us human beings comes to be corrupted. And I have reached
> the conclusion that we sin not because of the natural limitations
> of our intellects—for most of us have adequate mental powers—
> but rather on closer examination I have decided that we have
> knowledge of the good and recognize it, but we fail to work it
> out to its consummation, sometimes from apathy, sometimes be-
> cause we are seduced by pleasure in one form or another. Life
> affords many pleasures: long dinners and idle hours—entice-
> ments to mischief!—and *Aidos,*

she says, in substance. *Aidos,* then, the sense of innocence
and the sense of guilt, the keeper of Hippolytus' virginal
garden, is emphatically included by Phaedra among life's
pernicious pleasures. Certainly Hippolytus' career proves it
to be so. Yet the notion that *Aidos* might be a pleasure has
struck some editors as so odd that they have resorted to the
favorite solution of "solid" scholarship and expunged the
whole passage as an interpolation.[36] *Aidos* can also mean
"reverence," and it has been suggested [37] that Phaedra's
words may refer to a clash between two different moral
obligations: the reverence due to a suppliant's request, and

a woman's duty to preserve her modesty and chastity. By this reasoning, when the Nurse appeals as a suppliant to Phaedra to save her own life (325 ff.), Phaedra is duty-bound to grant the request, even at the sacrifice of her virtue. But all of this is extremely dubious. Why should such reverence be considered a pleasure? And would a Greek suppose that one is obligated to accede to any petition whatever, if only the petitioner has assumed the role of suppliant? On the contrary, this duty was thought to be owed only to those in dire straits who cast themselves on one's mercy, and even then the obligation was to be discharged only after careful consideration of all the circumstances. Several other tragedies, Aeschylus' *Suppliants* for instance, are illustrations of this.

No, Phaedra is probably thinking rather of the pleasure to be derived from the respect accorded a virtuous married woman, the enjoyment of a good reputation, since later in her speech she denounces promiscuity and marital deceit. A more profound and subtle character than Hippolytus,[38] she perceives that *Aidos*, "innocence," becomes *Aidos*, "shame," once innocence is lost, that the desire for virtue becomes in the unvirtuous the desire to keep up the appearance of virtue at all costs; to preserve her good repute she prepares herself for a deception more monstrous than mere concealment, feeling herself betrayed by a word. Already she has tried to stop the mouth of the Nurse, from whose lips flow "fine-sounding words that destroy the well-peopled cities and households of men" (486–87). And so, immediately after mentioning *Aidos* among life's pleasures, she goes on to say: "*Aidos* is a twofold thing, in one of its phases harmless, but in the other a bane to family life; if it were possible to know which to use on which occasion, we should not have the identical word for both."

Euripides seems here to be facing the mystery that gave
rise to Platonism, that has beset every thinker since man
began to think, and that still embroils our contemporary
linguistic philosophers: the fact that language is transcendental and protean, being the superficies, one may say, of
the fluctuating human soul. Aristotle, in his *Politics*
(1.1.10–11), says: "Speech is designed to indicate the ad-
vantageous and the harmful and therefore also the right
and the wrong: for it is the special property of man, in distinction from the other animals, that he alone has perception of good and bad and right and wrong and other moral
qualities." [39]

Aristotle does not bother to develop what might be called
the latency of ethics in logic, perhaps because his master
Plato had already abundantly shown that logically every
concept tends toward purity and consistency in definition,
and this consistency of definition in turn exercises a prescriptive effect on human behavior. What Phaedra seems to
be saying in her reflections on language is that when one's
behavior has offended against the pure concept (*Aidos*—
"modesty") one is tempted to have recourse to deceit and
to shift to a related concept (*Aidos*—"respectability")
with which one's behavior can be reconciled. But all this is
not to eliminate free will; on the contrary. Phaedra says
that she will never succumb to this temptation, but she
does—in the most abominable way. So that she may die
"respectable," she commits her heinous crime.

Therefore, only as long as words refer to natural objects,
processes, and behaviors, are they relatively manageable,
but when we cross the border into the realm of human conduct, we find that they may slip, expand, and even turn
into their opposites. It is on this dichotomy that King Lear.
for instance, is broken; he struggles with the meanings of

the words "nature" and even "daughter," and loses reason in the fight.[40] But if the meaning of "daughter" shifts, as its reference passes from the actual to the ideal, how much shiftier is the meaning of a quality and an attitude such as *Aidos!* Phaedra realizes that mortals are doomed to approach the mystery of sexuality with mingled feelings of reverence and obscenity, of awe and shame; that lack of shame among animals becomes shamelessness among humans; that innocence in a child is either ignorance or hypocrisy in an adult.

Phaedra knows all this, but in the end she chooses not to know it. She harkens to the Nurse's saying that "it is not necessary for human beings to work life out to its conclusion" (467). She surrenders to the attractions of ignorance, having already pointed out soon after coming out of her delirium (247–49): "To keep one's thinking straight is painful, and though insanity is bad, it at least has the advantage that one is destroyed without knowing it." Accordingly she confounds the truth by leaving the note behind accusing Hippolytus of an attempt on her virtue.

Here, then, we have three different patterns of relationship among will, passions, and intellect; all three characters, Theseus, Hippolytus, and Phaedra, in their different degrees, willfully permit their passions to preclude the exercise of their reason.

Is the key to an understanding of *Hippolytus* rationalism or irrationalism therefore? It is neither and both: it is myth.[41] A myth is the linguistic concomitant of mystery; a mystery is a pattern of spiritual reality that finds repeated and multi-level expression in literal-historical events. When confronted with such a mystery as the operation of the human soul, where passion, will, and intellect may each be simultaneously both cause and effect of the others, the human mind must have recourse to myth, if only in order to grasp the complexity of the ethical-psychological issues involved.[42] In the tale of Hippolytus there are suggestions of the interpenetration of innocence and experience, of the rejection and subsequent acceptance of full humanity and hence of divinity, in short of the fall and the redemption of man. Phaedra, whose name means "The Radiant One," is only another form of the Great Goddess; demoted to mere human status, she yet reveals, vacillating between maidenly shame and matronly voluptuousness, the contrasting aspects of procreation that were deified as Artemis and Aphrodite.[43] We may picture the two latter, not as being whisked on and off the stage by the machine, but rather as standing in visible symbolism on either side of the palace gateway throughout the play: [44] Artemis, in her niche above her altar, coming to life at the end, overseer of innocent animal reproduction; [45] Aphrodite, in her corresponding shrine, after her opening speech lapsing into an aloof immobility, instigator of guilt-involved human sexuality. Between the pair, through the gateway, lies the difficult path of morality for mankind. As the Nurse says (189–97):

Painful is the whole life of man; there is no surcease from struggle. But whatever else there may be that is dearer than life, darkness hides it and envelops it in cloud. So we seem doomed to love this thing that gleams on earth's surface, because of the hiddenness of all the rest under ground. We are swept on our way merely by myths.[46]

6

Euripides' BACCHAE

The Stranger Within Us

A CERTAIN mid-Victorian Englishwoman, after a performance of *Antony and Cleopatra*, is said to have been so disconcerted by the passionate antics of the Siren of Old Nile that she went home and observed in her diary: "How unlike the home life of our own dear queen!" Similarly, the usual modern critic of Euripides' *Bacchae*, reading about how Queen Agave leads a band of Maenads in tearing to bits her own son Pentheus and how she carries off his gory head as a trophy—all this in the name of religion—seems to produce his criticisms under the dominating but unconscious impression: "How unlike the church life of my own dear mother!" [1] For even after almost two hundred years of Romanticism the modern mind has so little shaken itself free from the eighteenth century's strictures against "enthusiasm" that it cannot fully join in Euripides' celebration of Dionysianism. [2] So convinced are we that there is something naughty about the emotions, something reprehensible about the whole affective side of man, that we can even condemn certain uses of language with the pejorative epithet "emotive," can toy with the notion of codes of communication completely devoid of all the rich suggestiveness of living speech, and, as a culture, can indulgently relegate religion, art, and poetry to the realm of the merely therapeutic.

The wholesome mind is passionless: such a proposition is congenial to us; it is at once so modern and so "Greek." [3] Yet in the *Bacchae* one of the greatest of the Greeks in one of the greatest expressions of the Greek genius flatly disagrees. For in the *Bacchae* Dionysus, emotiveness incarnate, wholly triumphs, whereas Pentheus, the pitiless opponent of passion, suffers the ultimate Passion in his own flesh. This is the inescapable fact about the plot: Pentheus, the Puritan, is not merely defeated; he himself literally and his ethical position figuratively are both torn to shreds. Yet modern commentators, of our modern Puritan persuasion by and large, cannot really accept the fact that Euripides meant his play to end this way, with a mother recognizing the bloody head of her own son whom she has just helped to rend asunder, and with the glorification of the god who has caused it all. No, the critics tend to approach Pentheus' disembodied head as gingerly in print as they would in reality.[4] None of them wants to pick it up and look it in the eye. Perhaps they are uneasily mindful of Nietzsche's advice: "Gaze not too long into the abyss; else the abyss will gaze into thee."

Even the most sympathetic of Euripidean scholars suppose that a shift of sympathy is intended at the end of the play. They intimate that Dionysus goes too far, that the audience can only experience revulsion at the excessive vindication of the god. "Yet Euripides does not take sides" —this line of criticism usually proceeds—; "he is an artist

primarily and a realist, and with his matchless skill he simply
portrays the orgiastic Dionysiac religion as he saw it in his
last years of exile in Macedonia, incidentally giving us an
unforgettable picture of how loathsome Dionysus is." [5]
We should be on our guard against the latent moralism of
such "purely aesthetic" criticism, to which it should be
answered that no artist ever painted a picture without
painting it from one side. [6] Actually, after all, Euripides may
be assumed to have meant what he says: Pentheus is
punished, and Pentheus has been at fault. The crucial question is then, as always: What is the fault for which the opponent of Dionysus deserves to be, not exactly decapitated,
but decorporated? (For it is not so much that Pentheus
loses his head as that his head loses him.)

Some say that he is punished for not opposing the god
with sufficient rigor; these critics seem not to understand
Dionysus more, but Pentheus less, and they want nothing
better than to wash their hands of both the god and his
victim. According to these—and this is really Puritanism
compounded—the king who opposed the god of wine and
joy falls victim to the god not really because of his opposition, but because of weakness within himself, because
he already nourishes within himself those emotions of
which Dionysus is the theomorphic representation. [7] According to this line of thought, then, the moral of the play
would presumably be: Become utterly unfeeling, utterly in-
human, and you may escape the unhappy fate depicted
here.

At this point the blind spot of Pentheus seems
coterminous with the blind spot of his critics. Blindness
and hostility toward the affective side of human nature can
be carried no further.

Now, the alleged prurience and irascibility of Pentheus

are not so extreme as to shock anyone but a mid-Victorian. Pentheus suspects the Maenads of illicit sexual behavior during their orgies; no one who knew anything of these all-night festivals would deny that he had good grounds for his suspicions. Pentheus wishes to peep at their carousings unseen. He rants when his orders are outrageously flouted. He waxes hysterical when his royal power seems to evaporate like a wisp of smoke in the wind of the god's omnipotence. The Theban king, in short, has a dirty mind, a stubborn will, and an inadequate faculty of self-command.

But so, alas, do we all. Dionysus' victim is a human being.

Yet it would be a mistake—and the fundamental mistake of the above-mentioned commentators—to read the *Bacchae* as merely a study in naturalistic psychology.[8] We are slowly coming to realize that great tragedy is always much more than that. Greek drama, at any rate, is nothing if it is not mythic and symbolic.[9] Certainly with the story of the conflict between Pentheus and Bacchus we enter the very heartland of myth and mystery.[10]

The argument of the play is summarized as follows in the *hypothesis* that has come down to us:

Since Dionysus' divinity has been denied by his relatives, he proceeds to exact appropriate punishment by driving the Theban women mad and making Cadmus' daughters lead the rioting bands of females out to Mount Cithaeron. Pentheus, son of Agave, has ascended the Theban throne and casts a very cold eye on these proceedings; he captures some of the Bacchic women and puts them under lock and key, and sends another search party out after the god himself. Dionysus willingly gives himself up and is brought before Pentheus, who has him bound and thrown into prison. For Pentheus is not content with the mere denial that Dionysus is divine; he strives to prove his point by daring to maltreat him, exactly as he would behave toward a mortal. Dionysus, then, having brought on an earthquake and laid the palace low, persuades Pentheus to don female dress and follow his lead to Cithaeron to spy on the women there. These latter, led by Pentheus' mother Agave, tear the king to pieces. Cadmus learns of the matter and gathers up the scattered members, coming on the head last of all, still cradled in the mother's arms. There is then an epiphany of Dionysus, who makes certain pronouncements to the company in general and then explains to the individuals concerned their future destinies, making it clear that by their actions they are to serve as a warning to others not to be guilty of scornful words toward the god on the assumption that he is merely human.

Aristophanes the Grammarian adds that this story was to be found in an earlier play of Aeschylus entitled *Pentheus;* Euripides' play was also sometimes called by the name of the Theban king.

Most of our knowledge of the Pentheus myth comes from the *Bacchae* itself. But some features from the original mythic store seem to have survived independently, unused by Euripides. According to certain authors there were three bands of Maenads that joined in the rending of the king, one led by Agave, one by Ino, the nurse of Dionysus, and the third by Autonoe, the mother of Actaeon.[11] Some versions fail to mention the mysterious stranger who figures throughout the drama under the title of "Dionysus" which all the manuscripts give to him; other versions make no mention of the perch on the tree from which the Bacchantes pull down their victim, though this whole episode is a high point of Euripidean description. One treatment of the material, apparently a late and pietistic revision, insists that the Bacchanalian women prayed to Dionysus to convert them into leopards and Pentheus into a bull,

which being done, the slaughter was accomplished by
merely animal media without the shedding of human blood
by human hands.[12] We also know some details about the
principal characters' later careers apart from the fragmentary Dionysian prophecy with which the *Bacchae* ends: it
was said that the oracle at Delphi ordered the female murderers to make two wooden images of Bacchus from the
tree whence King Pentheus had been dislodged; these gold-
covered, red-faced *eidola*, called Lysios and Baccheios, were
set up in the market-place at Corinth and worshiped.[13] It
was also said that Agave persisted in her man-killing ways;
she went on to marry the Illyrian king Lycotherses, but
dispatched him in order to hand the kingdom over to her
father Cadmus.[14]

It is familiar knowledge that the Pentheus story was only
one of a number of myths that depicted the dire consequences of human resistance to the power of Dionysus.
King Lycurgus, of the Thracian Edonians, paid for his opposition to the god by going mad, killing his own son, and
by being further, according to varying accounts, stricken
blind, or chained on a mountain, or torn to pieces by horses.
The daughters of Proitos in Argos were also driven to insanity and the murder of their children; so were the daughters of Minyas, in Boeotia, who cast lots to see whose offspring they should dismember. Infanticide appears as a
common motif in many of the tales having to do with
Dionysus. Athamas, Ino's husband, is made to kill his child
Learchos, while his second wife Themisto kills her own
children by mistake. Athamas also chases Ino and another
son, Melicertes, into the sea, where they are metamor-
phosed into sea deities, just as the Lycurgus mentioned
above is related by Homer to have pursued Dionysus himself and his nurses into the waters, where Thetis gave them

refuge. These would all seem to be variants of the most famous Dionysus-myth of all, in which Hera, jealous of Semele's pregnancy by Zeus, inveigles the latter into consuming Semele with heavenly fire, whereat Zeus snatches up the unburned and unborn Dionysus and pins the fetus into his own thigh for the remainder of the gestation period; Hera, still at work, coaxes the Titans to tear the infant to pieces, but these parts are reassembled and resuscitated; or, according to another variant, Hera is fobbed off with a phantom Dionysus, whom she holds captive; or else she persuades the Theban king Cadmus to throw Semele and the new-born babe into the sea in a chest. And so forth. The kernel of it all seems to be:

A god or goddess or mother or wife or king is offended and persecutes a god or goddess or mother or wife or king or child; murder or near-murder is the result and, afterwards, transfiguration and apotheosis. So Hera and Dionysus, Ino and Melicertes, Agave and Pentheus, *et al.*, are parallel. And not only these, but Cybele and Attis, Aphrodite and Adonis, Isis and Osiris, Artemis and Hippolytus, the divine wife-mother and the divine husband-son: the Pentheus-story turns out to be only another form of the primal myth of all.[15]

In view of all this, it is difficult to see how there could still be those who cleave to a belief in an historical basis for the material used by the author of the *Bacchae*.[16] There certainly must have been opposition in Greece to the cultivation of the more extreme forms of Dionysus-worship; there must have been many respectable burghers who were as outraged over these Bacchanalian manifestations as the Senators of Rome were later to be. Nevertheless it would seem to be a mistake to posit a euhemeristic origin for Pentheus' story,[17] even as a symbol of the clash between a

purely Greek "Olympianism" and an indigenous "chtho-
nianism"; and the belief that the myth represents merely
a reminiscence of a collision between a traditional religious system and an imported foreign cult not only is
dubious on historical grounds,[18] but tends to diminish the
spiritual content. There were orgiastic elements in the worship of the Olympians, too, sometimes fossilized and half
forgotten in classical times, as in the cult of Zeus or of
Artemis, sometimes very much alive, as in the mysteries of
Demeter.[19] The entire invasion-motif of the Dionysus-
saga probably signalizes primarily an irruption from below,
socially and psychologically speaking, into a Greek religious consciousness which may periodically have been
lulled to complacent conformity with regard to the official
deities.[20] As anthropologists and archaeologists enable us to
peer further back into the mists of primitive religion, we
perceive that all divinities merge into one another and as-
sociate with themselves barbarities that more rationally inclined cultures are bound to palliate or suppress. Dionysus
was known to Homer and to the Mycenaeans, even if not
as a member of the higher pantheon; it may have been that
after Zeus was tamed and Artemis converted into a lady,
Dionysus still exerted the call of the wild, exerted it, perhaps, all the more forcefully because most of the other gods
had modulated their voices to decorous hymns. In a similar way Christendom has repeatedly seen some recondite
germ of Scripture spawn a new orgiastic sect.[21]

But the point is not an important one. The real danger
of dismissing the Pentheus story as a transmuted bit of generalized history is that one thereby loses its mythical significance.[22] Frazer and Murray long ago maintained that
the traditions concerning Pentheus might well be distorted
memories of the custom of sacrificing human beings, and

especially divine kings, in the character of Dionysus—in sum, that Pentheus, far from having originally been an opponent of Dionysus, had been the god himself, in a sense. Ample evidence for this exists in Euripides' play.

Furthermore, that the orgies celebrated in Dionysus' honor were not essentially different from those rendered to the "older" Olympian gods can be shown from the context of the *Bacchae* itself. Not only are the rituals of the Kouretes and the other ceremonies attendant upon the commemoration of the birth of the Cretan Zeus closely associated by the poet with the cult of the wine-god,[23] but also there is pointed up in the play a distinct parallel between the fate of Pentheus and that of Actaeon, who fell a victim to Artemis.[24] Actaeon was the son of Autonoe and was therefore Pentheus' cousin (cf. 230); his sad end furnishes the theme for the warning that the aged Cadmus gives the King (337–340): "You see Actaeon's wretched lot: whose raw flesh his own cubs—the cubs that he himself had reared—mangled and scattered across the mountain woodlands, because he boasted that he was better at the chase than Artemis."[25]

Pentheus also was killed on Mount Cithaeron, the site of Actaeon's death (1291). Now, according to the more usual version Actaeon was changed into a stag, to be run down and rent to pieces by his own hounds for having glimpsed, though purely by accident, a sight unholy and unlawful for mere man, namely the nude Artemis at her bath in a spring. It is hard to see why Euripides ignored this form of the story, so much more closely resembling the actions of Pentheus when he went to spy on the exclusively female Bacchanalia. Yet the significance of both myths was certainly lurking in the back of the poet's mind. Actaeon, like Pentheus, must surely have been a temporary god-king, the chosen spouse of a priestess impersonating the fertility goddess. The modesty-idea, and the boasting-idea too for that matter, must have been later accretions; originally, no doubt, Actaeon was represented as being a man privileged to behold the goddess's purification ritual, i.e. her bath, and to view her unclothed, i.e. to go in to her as her sacred consort. Afterward, like Pentheus, he must have been torn to pieces as the climax of some sort of totemistic dance involving animal costume. The fact that his dismemberment occurred in the same locality as the sacrifice of Pentheus seems to indicate the existence in prehistoric times of a spot on Mount Cithaeron sanctified to the observance of such a periodically recurring ceremony.

An understanding of this substratum of mythic significance should prevent the reader from falling into the error of interpreting the *Bacchae* as an essay in modern psychological realism. Toward the end of the play, after the mother Agave comes to full recognition of the fact that she had led the pack to her son's disintegration, she is horrified, grieved, and overwhelmed, but she is not particularly conscience-stricken. All emphasis is placed on her sorrow for her son's death, not on her regret for her own actions. And the god Dionysus, who is responsible for it all, makes no apology whatever, needless to say, when he appears at the end, but busily sets about imposing still further penalties on the late-repentant Cadmus and his guilty daughters.

All this should have given some pause to those commentators who have supposed that Euripides packed his denouement so full of horror and cruelty as to transform the entire play into an indictment of Dionysus, or of the gods, or of religion in general. Did the Greek spectator really lose sympathy with the persecuted god from the point where the "Asiatic Stranger" gains ascendancy over the mind of Pentheus and proceeds to expose the King to ridicule and subject him to disaster? Apparently not, for the Greek sensed what the action really signified and gave his interest to matters far more profound than the working out of a mere melodramatic peripety. Is the play down to the scene of Agave's recovery of her senses only an objective presentation and vivid description of repulsive contemporary worship, at which juncture it turns into a study of normal human revulsion against such bizarre and bloodthirsty zoolatry? Certainly not, for Agave never ceases to fill her symbolic role of mother-goddess and priestess of the earth.

Pentheus' domination by the god Dionysus begins at Line 810,[26] where the Asiatic Stranger, himself perhaps at this point feeling a sudden pneumatic onslaught, emits a ringing cry and proceeds to solicit the king to go out spying on the activities of the Bacchanals. Pentheus is persuaded to don female clothing, ostensibly as a disguise, but symbolically, since the disguise is singularly ineffective, so that he may simulate the Dionysian priesthood and the epicene god himself.[27] The Stranger's announcement to the Chorus, as he prepares to follow Pentheus into the palace to dress him, suggests the ritual investiture of a candidate for immolation (857–59): "I go now to bestow the robe on Pentheus (*kósmon prosápso·n*), the adornment in which he shall depart to Hades' house, slaughtered by the hands of his mother." Every detail of the female costume must be exactly so; every hair must be in place beneath the snood; every fold of the gown must flow in symmetry: Euripides uses these instructions to enhance the Stranger's jeering humor while Pentheus is being decked out as a woman, but there is a definite suggestion, too, of the meticulous attention traditionally given to ceremonial attire. Nor is the mockery itself without religious point. Pentheus, whose name means "the Sufferer," [28] once he is properly accoutered, begins the march to his *Agon*, his trial and his struggle, and in this procession the mock-king, who has so far been revered, is loaded with ridicule and revilement.[29] "Stretch forth your hands, Agave; stretch forth your hands, fellow-seed of Agave, daughters of Cadmus!" the Stranger intones (973 ff.). "This young man I bring to his great trial! (*eis agô·na mégan*)." We must picture Pentheus led humbly across the *orchestra*, while the Chorus of Maenads pours curses on his head.

He is, of course, the Scapegoat. "Thou, thou alone sufferest in behalf of this nation," the Stranger tells him (963 ff.). "And verily trials await thee such as must needs be. But follow: I go thy guide and savior. And from thence another shall lead thee back . . . to be a sign unto all men." Pentheus accepts, honored and willing, as most such sacrificial victims must have been honored and willing, being assured that he will return cradled in the arms of her who bore him, that his agonies will end in a reversion to the luxurious helplessness of infancy: the Return to the Womb, the Rebirth.[30] "Terrible art thou (*deinòs sù*), terrible," the Stranger says (971 ff.), "and to terrible passions thou goest (*kàpì deín' érchei páthe·*), so that thou shalt find a fame rising to heaven."

The pair then exit on their way to what the Second Messenger calls a *theoria* (1047),[31] which is to say not merely a "watching" or a "viewing," but a beholding of such a spectacle as was destined in historical times to take the form of either a drama or an oracular deliverance or one of the athletic games sacred to some god (*agones*).[32] Pentheus, like the initiate into the mysteries, is to be inducted first as witness, then as protagonist.

Of the climactic rite, the dreadful tearing to pieces of the living Pentheus in the wilderness, we learn from the speech of a Messenger (1043 ff.)—the same sort of emissary who appeared to the devotees of Attis, for instance, to announce the death of the god. Exhibiting the usual syncretistic reconciliation of variant cult observances, the plot hints at provision for the death of Pentheus in at least three different ways. He is first elevated upon a fir or pine (*eláte·*), the tree sacred to Dionysus, which has been drawn down to earth by the Stranger in an access of preternatural strength.[33] In a similar way certain deities, or their representatives, were either fastened to trees to be killed (e.g. Marsyas) or exposed on trees after death (e.g. Attis). Next Pentheus is stoned, then pierced with javelins of firwood and with the holy thyrsi used as missiles: Dionysus is, so to speak, slain with his own weapons. The final method of dispatching him is of course the *sparagmos,* the rending to pieces of the victim while still alive; his mother Agave, called here the Priestess of the Slaughter (1114),[34] begins the fray by frenziedly planting her foot on her son's side and wrenching his left arm from the shoulder-socket.

Agave's description of her child as a "beast" (*thé·r—* 1108) and the frequent references to the ceremony as a "hunt" (*ágra*) cause the reader to hear in this "wild rout that made the hideous roar" echoes of some totemistic animal dance connected with a prayer for good hunting. Just before the end Pentheus makes what sounds like the formulated appeal of the trembling initiate before the Great Mother (1118 ff.): "Behold me, mother; I am thy child, Pentheus, whom thou borest in the house of Echion. Pity me, O mother, and do not for these my blindnesses kill thy seed." Needless to say, the plea falls on ears deafened by ecstasy; the immolation proceeds; Agave, high priestess of the Wild Women, bears off as her own particular booty the head of her son, which is by this time (cf. 1170 ff.) referred to as a lion's head or a bull's head or a fresh-cut vine-twig or ivy-tendril; the queen-mother intends to affix this prize to the palace roof. (We remember that Orpheus, after an identical contretemps, landed bodiless in Lesbos and was there enshrined.) And the Chorus of Bacchantes sing appropriately as they greet Agave on her return (1153 ff.):

> Let us dance Bacchus as our dance.
> Let us lift up as our cry the fate undergone
>   By Pentheus, serpent's child,
> Who wore the wear of woman,
> And bore the rushy thyrsus, trustful death!
>   And the bull was his guide to his fate.
> Daughters of Cadmus, women of Bacchus,
> You have fulfilled the glory of your victory
>   To groaning and to tears.
> O rare ordeal and fair, when the hand dripping with
>   the blood of one's child
>   Embraces him as well!

"Trustful death" (pistòn Haídan) [35] and the mother's blood-dripping, child-caressing hand have caused the commentators no end of mystification. Critics should have surrendered to Dionysus, as Pentheus finally did. Their initial error seems to have been that in a spirit of utter sobriety they have set about interpreting a paean to the god of intoxication. Hades is "trustworthy" or "obedient, faithful" in the hymn precisely because the Dionysus-rite was a resurrection-rite, and the maternal hand of the Earth-goddess is at once murderous and comforting because the Mother was thought by meting out death to confer immortality.

A greater difficulty remains. Why is the narthex-thyrsus,

the Bacchic staff crowned with a bunch of vine-leaves, or later with a pine-cone, equated with "faithful Death"? [36] For an answer to this, even a conjectural one, there must be a plunge into the depths of mystery. To be sure, the bearing of the narthex turns out to be certain death for Pentheus in this particular case, but *pistós* means "trustworthy," not "certain," and the words of the Chorus seem to indicate rather a general characterization of the magic wand.[37] Besides, all the phraseology of this chorus is strongly reminiscent of mystery-formulae; it seems probable that the Dionysus-worshiper might have boasted, "I have worn the female costume; I have carried the thyrsus," just as the Attis-worshiper proclaimed, "I have undergone the *taurobolium* (the customary baptism of blood beneath a slaughtered bull); I have carried the *kernos* (the compartmented tray containing products of the earth)"—which was to say, "I have been through; I have come out on the other side; I am one of the saved." [38]

Frazer, Murray, and others long ago taught us to discern the origins of these rites in primitive agriculture, arboriculture, and the quest of beast and fish.[39] But they were almost all ensnared by that "genetic fallacy" that William James isolated as the particular foible of the scientific-minded, which supposes that if a silk purse can be proved to have really been made from a sow's ear, a sow's ear it is and a silk purse no longer. Not necessarily so. However barbarous Dionysianism may have been in its beginnings, and however barbarous it may have remained in Euripides' day, to it there had undoubtedly accrued a many-layered symbolism of spirituality. In fact, it would not be too much to say that many of the spiritual principles of our civilization are outgrowths stemming from this cult and similar cults, and that it is highly problematical whether our spiritual life would not wither away if severed wholly from the mythic stock.[40] Perhaps the spiritual symbolism was there from the start. At any rate in Euripides' time the mind of an initiate into Dionysiac or similar mysteries must have already been toying, more or less obscurely, with such fancies as these:

The thyrsus, the reed topped with a cluster of ivy or with a fir-cone, had a manifold significance in the neophyte's hands. By its resemblance to a spear it symbolized death —and it was tentatively used as an instrument of death against Pentheus. Because of its phallic shape, it symbolized fertility, the instrumentation by which the seed of life is planted, apparently dies, and lives anew. By its utilization of the evergreen ivy or the evergreen fir, it became a symbol of everlasting life. By bearing the thyrsus, the male emblem, and simultaneously arraying himself in woman's clothing, the initiate became, like Teiresias, one who has done all things and suffered all things. In himself he personified the whole mystery of reproduction, and in this state of exalted consecration his life was taken by the Earth-Mother priestess, and through the *omophagia*, the cannibalistic Banquet of Raw Flesh,[41] which was sequel to the *sparagmos* and in which Agave vaguely invites her sister-Bacchae to participate, his physical substance was taken into her and her votaries. He thus lived again, in all senses of the word: the male's seed in the female earth sprouted anew; his germ and his flesh grew to new flesh in her body; and his spirit rose to new life in eternity.[42]

Thus Agave, whose name means "the Shining one," doubtless originally a goddess of the moon, whom Briffault argues to have been the most primitive of fertility deities, destroys and preserves her son Pentheus, "the Sufferer, the Man of Sorrows." Nor do the elements of ritual disappear from the drama at this point; she still continues to play her role of priestess. The much-admired psychological verisimilitude of her recognition scene after the murder, the *anagnorisis,* indicates only one level of meaning to be found there. It was the regular part of the celebrant portraying the Mother Goddess to come upon the body of the slain one and to mourn over him.⁴³ Shortly after Cadmus comes in bringing the recovered bits of Pentheus' body, there is a great lacuna in our text of the play. If the late rhetor Apsines is correct in saying that the gap was originally occupied by Agave's speech of lamentation over each of the reassembled limbs in turn, then these actions also seem typically ritualistic.⁴⁴ So Cybele came upon the body of Attis; so Aphrodite mourned for Adonis' disaster; and so Isis searched for and brought together the dismembered body of Osiris.

Cadmus, of course, shares these duties with Agave in the *Bacchae,* even joining in the formal threnody (1302 ff.); one is reminded that Zeus re-created Dionysus himself after the latter had been torn to shreds by the Titans. Furthermore, if we can trust the parallels in the Byzantine play, *Christus Patiens,*⁴⁵ much of which scholars have long believed to have been imitated from the *Bacchae,* then Agave's actions and expressions took a rather stereotyped form: "How shall I lament?" she presumably chanted, proceeding then with Cadmus' help to fit Pentheus' head and limbs together, to weep over them, and to cover the whole with a veil.⁴⁶ There followed the epiphany of Dionysus, the reappearance of the former victim as a god indeed, and the drama-ceremony drew to a close.

All the foregoing is more or less familiar ground; if it is still out of bounds to the sober, one can only repeat that they are ill equipped to house the Dionysiac spirit.

Perhaps more interesting than the roles played by
Pentheus and Agave is that of the Asiatic Stranger. He is
called Dionysus in the manuscripts, obviously to be
identified with the god who appears *in propria persona* in
the prologue and epilogue, but he does not seem to be
Dionysus, or at least he does not always seem to be
Dionysus, during the episodes of the play. A couple of generations ago the eminent classical scholars Norwood [47] and
Verrall [48] raised a scandal by maintaining that the Asiatic
Stranger is simply a stranger, nothing more, and that, since
Euripides is doubtless a good modern agnostic quite devoid
of any primitive religiosity, the character can only have
been intended to represent a trickster, a peddler of oc-
cultist quackery. The theory was deservedly trounced. And
yet it would not appear to have been wholly wrong, after
all. Not that the miracles attendant on the Stranger's release from Pentheus' dungeons midway in the play are
bogus, as the two rationalist critics asserted; it was well
pointed out in rebuttal that no such rigidly realistic standards can be applied to the happenings on the Greek
stage. No, it is the Asiatic Stranger's behavior itself that
raises some doubt about his undeviating divinity. On the
basis of the words that Euripides puts into the character's
mouth one can only conclude that the Stranger is intended
to be Dionysus at times, but that at times he is only a human being.

For if we proceed on the assumption that the Stranger
is never anyone but Dionysus, we find ourselves in difficulties. It is not only that he represents himself to Pentheus,
his enemy, as being distinct from the god. This we should
expect him to do, the better to victimize the king. But why
should he maintain this distinction before his own Maenad-

band when Pentheus is offstage? Yet this is precisely what he does on two different occasions.

Once, while Pentheus is still inside the palace, exhausted from his fight with the god-sent phantom and dazed from the collapse of the building, the Stranger emerges unbound and addresses the Bacchantes (605–606): "Did you perceive how Bacchus, it seemed, shook the house?" It is certainly odd that he refers to himself in the third person before those with whom no concealment is necessary, but even odder words are to ensue. While describing the antics of the deluded Pentheus binding an hallucinatory bull, the supposed Dionysus remarks (621–24): "And I sat quietly by and watched. And at that moment came Bacchus, and he set the house to swaying and kindled the flame on his mother's tomb. . . . And then Bromios, so I suppose—for I merely relate the event as it appeared to me—created a phantom and set it down in the quadrangle. And Pentheus attacked it, darting his foil at it and piercing the gleaming air, thinking he was butchering me." And the Stranger continues to speak of the god as entirely distinct from himself until Pentheus staggers on the scene.

It might be possible to assume—dubiously—that there are supernumeraries about, representing Pentheus' soldiers and townsmen, and that it is for their benefit that the Stranger maintains his deception. But later, when Pentheus has been persuaded to array himself as a woman and has retired into the palace for the purpose, the Stranger confides in the Maenad-band alone; as the King retreats into the house, the Stranger passes sentence (cf. 847 ff.): "He goes to the Bacchae, where justice will be done to him by death," turns to his followers, saying, "Women, the man is in the net," and then prays: "Dionysus, now thine is the task; for thou art not afar," continuing to apostrophize the god for several lines.

If the Stranger, therefore, is not always identical with Dionysus, it is unnecessary to assume that he is dissembling in his dialogues with Pentheus when he speaks of the god as of someone far distant. The Stranger claims to be from Lydia, where he learned the Bacchic rites under the very tutelage of Bacchus and whence he has been inspired by the god to bring these orgies into Greece. When Pentheus asks what Dionysus is like, the Stranger replies (478), "He took what shape he pleased. It was not for me to say." And he goes on to assert that he is growing a special lock of hair sacred to the god (cf. 494 ff.) and that the thyrsus he carries he has received from Dionysus himself. We are not surprised, then, to hear him allege that his deity will come to his rescue and already is traveling invisibly by his side. And this colloquy ends with the Stranger's assurance to Pentheus that (516–17) "Dionysus, whose existence you deny, will make you pay dear recompense for these blasphemies." Similarly there is no reason to disbelieve his assertions that he has been saved by the god (649–51), that he has made a pact with the god (808), or that he is inspired by the god (825). And so, finally, he is telling only the truth when he reassures Pentheus (923–24) to the effect that "the god walks beside us step by step; ill-disposed before, he has entered into a truce with us. Now you see what see you must." [49]

Beside these proofs that the Asiatic Stranger and the god Dionysus are separate personalities must be ranged proofs indicating the essential identity of the two. In view of the Stranger's narrative about the supernatural advent of Bromios-Bacchus detailed above, it would be rash to assign to any human frame the Voice that calls from the depths of the palace while the Stranger is still imprisoned there (cf. 576 ff.). It is rather to be likened to the Voice from the upper air that later on incites Agave and her sisters to wreak vengeance on Pentheus as he perches in the tree (1078 ff.).[50] But when the Stranger emerges from the palace he is greeted by the Chorus in terms proper only to deity (608, 612): "O greatest light of our Bacchic revels! . . . Who would be my guardian, if you met with misfortune?" And he goes on to claim an almost exclusive role in his own deliverance: "I, myself, easily, without effort, extricated myself."

None of these citations, admittedly, offers proof of the identity of the man with the god. Rather, such identification rests mainly on two bases: the fact that the undoubted Dionysus twice announces in the prologue that he has come out of Asia to have satisfaction of the infidel Thebans and that to do so he has taken on human form (4, 53–54), and the fact that the Stranger, after conducting Pentheus to Mount Cithaeron, bends down a tall pine tree with perfect ease to the ground (1063 ff.), "performing," in the words of the Second Messenger, "deeds by no means mortal." This seems to be the reason why manuscripts and editors concur in supplying the speaking part of the Stranger with the tag "Dionysus" throughout the play.[51]

The Asiatic Stranger is therefore both a human being and the god Dionysus, or rather, sometimes human being, sometimes god.

This is not too surprising. There have been many discussions of the phenomenon of "possession" in connection with this play and with the Dionysian religion in general. The Stranger is a mortal; he comes from Asia; probably all that he tells Pentheus about himself is intended as circumstantial truth. Ovid, retelling the Euripidean story in the

Metamorphoses, and perhaps following a dramatic tradition still current in his day, even gives us the Stranger's name: " 'My name is Acoetes,' he said; 'my native land is Maeonia; my parents of humble stock.' " [52] This, then, is the man Dionysus "possesses" when it suits his purposes to do so, just as he "possesses" Pentheus in the ultimate scene of the king's life. For it was expected that the leader of the *thiasos,* the band of Bacchanals, should "become the god" when the orgies reached their height and should be looked upon by the dancing Maenads as their divinity incarnate. [53]

There were various ways by which Dionysus might be invited into the individual psyche: he might be induced to enter consequent upon the dizziness, fatigue, din, and communal rapture that marked the Bacchanalia, or more commonly, he might enter in the simple form of wine. [54] "There are two principles basic in human beings, my young friend," the prophet Teiresias tells Pentheus early in the play (274 ff.), "the goddess Demeter—and she is the earth; call her by whatever name you like—and she nourishes men in the domain of the Dry; and then he came, Semele's child, Demeter's moist counterpart, who found the liquor of the grape and poured it into men. . . ." [55] So in this way, he goes on to say, "much god might come into the body." More strikingly, however, the divinity might assault with less palpable preliminaries and invade an unwilling self, as Dionysus takes Pentheus over, breaking down resistance, overcoming defenses, often achieving complete occupation in an instant. [56] If Dionysus was, as Plutarch and Euripides call him, the principle of all that is Wet, [57] then his onslaught upon the reluctant soul may be likened to a tidal wave from the realm that the psychoanalysts, with modern mythopoeic ingenuity, have dubbed the Subconscious.

Just as Dionysus was an intrusive and disconcerting out-
sider to his ancient victims, so he has proved to be to later
interpreters of the Greek spirit. The fact that he existed and
the manner in which he was worshiped have been upsetting
to many cherished theories, though the theories have
flourished for all that. He struck Pentheus as barbarous and
un-Greek, as he has struck many a philhellene since. The
Enlightenment had its calm and classical Greeks; the
Romantics had their pagan, sun-drenched Greeks; the scientists and would-be scientists have had their level-headed,
rationalistic Greeks; and all these branches of the Hellenic
tree are still very much alive. Perhaps it is time for the
darkening twentieth century to engraft thereon its Greek
mystics, even its Greek obscurantists. There is possibly no
more obscene and absurd collection of narrative grotes-
querie in existence than the monstrous corpus of Greek
mythology, but there are not lacking commentators who say
that the god Dionysus is out of place there. He is supposed
to jar with the serene and detached Olympianism of the
Homeric pantheon.[58] He offends most grievously because of
his unwillingness to respect the bounds between the human and the divine that we are told the Homeric gods
were so scrupulous about.

Now, this depends on which Homer, and how much
Homer, one reads. In the *Iliad* and the *Odyssey* that most
of us read the gods are stubbornly unaware of a sharp
dividing line between human and divine; they fight with
mortals and are wounded by them, make love to them,
have children by them, are shut up in bronze vessels by
them, trick them, go to banquets with them, and pull them
by the hair. Furthermore, they take human forms, the
forms of specific familiar human beings, and thus bend
other human beings to their wills, precisely as Dionysus

takes the Stranger's form and dominates Pentheus in the *Bacchae*.[59] It would not be too much to say that the Olympic pantheon was anthropomorphic because of the universal belief that the gods could enter, and did enter, into human bodies and souls at their own sweet will.[60]

Let it be remembered that in the *Bacchae* the great transgression of Agave and her sisters and her son is that they cannot bring themselves to believe that a human being can become a god. Therefore to prove them wholly wrong, the god enters into them and destroys them, as Zeus entered into and destroyed Dionysus' mortal mother Semele.[61]

Dionysus cannot expect to find many believers today, but he has surprisingly failed even to find interpreters who know what the Greeks were believing in when they believed in him. Even the most sympathetic of modern observers seem to assume that Dionysianism is a kind of "letting oneself go." Yet surely, whatever opinion the Greeks may have had of Bacchic behavior, they never thought of it as a release of forces *within* the personality. If Bacchus was *Lyaeus*, the Roman *Liber*, "the Liberator," it was rather because he made the individual free and open to psychic invasion from without.

But our disesteem for the message of the *Bacchae* is due perhaps not so much to a misconception of the nature of the Greek god as to a conception differing radically from the Greek one as to the nature of man. We still suffer from Descartes' disease: "Here am I, essentially a mind," we think; "closely bordering, yet distinct from, the circle of the Me is my body, and beyond that is the world." It is likely that the ancients drew no such circle around their essential selves, or that, if they did, it was drawn more narrowly than ours, or encompassed a different psychological area.

To us nothing seems more intimate, more personal, more a part of ourselves, than our emotions. Remarkable then to note how often in ancient language and literature an emotion is viewed as a something external, a something that comes from without and that is regarded as alien throughout the period of its persistence. This line of thinking seems to have been ingrained in the Greek mind. Dodds says in *The Greeks and the Irrational:* [62]

When Theognis calls hope and fear "dangerous daemons," or when Sophocles speaks of Eros as a power that "warps to wrong the righteous mind, for its destruction," we should not dismiss this as "personification": behind it lies the old Homeric feeling that these things are not truly part of the self, since they are not within man's conscious control; they are endowed with a life and energy of their own, and so can force a man, as it were from the outside, into conduct foreign to him.

Dodds analyzes along this line the interference of the Homeric gods into the affairs of men, and seems to regard this "psychic intervention," as he felicitously calls it, as something comparatively occasional and extreme. [63] But on the contrary, according to his own testimony it would seem to have been the usual approach of ancient psychology to emotive phenomena. To quote the same book again (p. 185):

The Greek had always felt the experience of passion as something mysterious and frightening, the experience of a force that was in him, possessing him, rather than possessed by him. The very word *pathos* testifies to that: like its Latin equivalent *passio*, it means something that "happens to" a man, something of which he is the passive victim.

Only recently in English have we begun to speak of a man's psychological "reaction" to an external situation; far older in our language are expressions that run parallel to the classical: "to be seized with panic, to be filled with fury, to be smitten with desire, to be touched by pity." [64] And often English represents the feelings as though they were external obstacles: "to fall in love, to fall into a rage, to come to grief." But we are not likely to say of a person, as the Greeks often did, that he is "outside of fear" or that "love falls into him" or that "courage seizes him." In English one at least "reacts" to the external action; in Greek one regularly "suffered" it (*páschein*). No wonder then that in ancient metaphysics *pathé·mata* "emotions" could easily be classified as *pathé·mata* "accidents" and looked upon as mere incidental appurtenances of the soul, or that in ancient ethics, especially in Platonism, Stoicism, and Epicureanism, *páthe·* "emotions" could easily be regarded as *páthe·* "calamities." So that there was always implicit in the Greek vocabulary a germ of potential puritanism. The *ê·thos* was the "usual haunt" of the soul, its "habit," its fixed character; the *diánoia* was the purposive intellect; the only desirable psychical state was a *harmonía*, in Latin *aequus animus*, a natural placidity from which those "disturbances" and "disorders" that constitute the affective life of man were to be fended off as far as possible. This ethical psychology of the ancient—post-Euripidean—sages was revived in the seventeenth and eighteenth centuries, was corroborated by the very assumption that scientific method can be applied to human behavior, and remains as an invisible ally in all attempts to belabor Mythos with Logos.

The myth of the *Bacchae* embodies a mystery, the one ubiquitous mystery, the mystery of the human soul. At what point does the outer World leave off and the inner Ego begin? Just as the winds of philosophical controversy have whirled about the subjectivity and objectivity of

ideas, about the relations between the outer Logos and
the inner Logos, so the myth of Pentheus focuses our attention on questions even more vexing, so vexing that they
are seldom even asked: Just how subjective and just how
objective, in the epistemological sense, are emotions? Is
there no such thing as emotional truth? Are not some feelings false to the objective situation to which they are reactions? Is this not what is meant by neurosis and psychosis?
Can we draw a sharp dividing line between our intellection and our affection? If we cannot, does it not follow that
there can be a logic of the emotions? Are there in external
situations objectively existing values that emotions are our
modes of apprehending? Is it the function of art and
poetry to school us in the correct apprehension of such
values?

Modern thought shies away from these questions, by and
large, and it is not the province of an interpreter of the
Bacchae to attempt an answer to them. It is enough to
point out that Euripides and his hearers approached the
questions with assumptions far different from ours. In the
first place, for all the rationalism imputed to them by modern thinkers, they had no word for "reason." "Logic" was
simply a systemization of that part of the soul's activity
which finds direct expression in words. In the second place,
in Euripides' time no cleavage had yet been made between
the intellectual part of the soul and the other parts. There
was merely an awareness that the soul's topography in-
clines indefinably from the clearly communicable to the
wholly ineffable, and that even these latter areas, the domain of *sophía*, "true wisdom," may be compassed by the
circumlocutions of the seers and poets. And thirdly, there
was in their belief no gulf between the soul and the world;
the circle they drew around the Self to distinguish it from

the Not-Self was narrower than ours, more shifting than ours, and fainter than ours. Around the soul and in the soul itself were felt the tides of the universal ocean of inter-mingled and indistinguishable Natural and Divine.

Rationalism calls these assumptions primitive, but can reason disprove them? Modern thought takes off on a dif-ferent career: starts with an hypostasis of "Reason"—a myth in miniature, but a poor one—, conjures up hostilities between this reason and the emotions, erects a kind of Manichaean barrier between this whole complex of reason-emotion and the rest of reality, proceeds to go stark mad from its self-created "alienation," and ends with delirious praises of passionlessness and denunciations of "value-judgments." Because a false emotion can cause a false understanding, we banish emotion from the soul. Our cure for astigmatism is to put out the patient's eyes.

This, one may suspect, would have made no sense to the reputedly "logical" Greek of the fifth century B.C. He would have realized that, conversely, a false judgment may equally well produce a false emotion. He would have realized, too, that false emotions and false judgments can-not be separated one from the other nor arranged in any completely satisfactory sequence of cause and effect, both being equally inadequate responses of the subject to the Objective that surrounds him. On the contrary, the Greek cured the kind of madness in which the self is disoriented from its environment, or attempted to cure it—and we do no more today—by an application of the Corybantic madness leading to complete self-oblivion.[65] This was not mere homeopathic psychiatry; the two types of madness were looked on as being poles apart. One was a withdrawal from reality, and a simultaneous misvaluation of it; the other was a reestablishment of contact. Allowing one-

self to be wholly "possessed" could be thought of as reach-
ing a temporarily more nearly complete awareness of the
demonic forces that were always active both within and
without the soul in the ordinary course of events. Dionysianism was only a heightened recognition of one's kinship
with nature.[66] To nature the Greek did not pay lip-service
only; nor did he "love" it; nor did he strive to "master" it.
These are modern attitudes, never adopted by him because he never conceived of himself and nature in such
subject-versus-object terms. He did not degrade his relationships with nature to the level of problems; he felt it right
to leave such things to remain the mysteries they are.

Pentheus' offense, therefore, is not that he has his share
of natural human passion. Rather, his *hamartia* is one of
those blindnesses to a whole phase of reality, one of those
willful ignorances that are defects more fundamental than
any character trait or overt misdemeanor. His offense is
precisely what Euripides says it is: he does not acknowledge Dionysus as divine.[67] By exalting a wisdom that is self-
based and over-cerebral, he shows that he possesses no true
sophía at all. By fighting shy of the wild joy that Dionysus
is, he digs a moat between man and nature; by scoffing at
the proposition that his own relative has become a god, he
creates a gulf between the human and the divine. This is
his hybris. His only salvation is to become a god himself.
And that means death.

And the most enlightened man of the twentieth century
is guilty of the same offense. He might well take the message of the *Bacchae* to heart. Instead of deprecating "emotive" uses of language, instead of eschewing "value-judgments," instead of praying for "freedom from fears" and
paying for "peace of mind," he might do well to recognize
the divine in Dionysus, acknowledging that emotional life

in modern times is liable to be too impotent rather than too intense, and realizing that there are right occasions for all feelings, even the most full-blooded. Instead of banishing our emotions to a mythical subsconscious, nursing the "yelling monsters" there in a kind of psychic womb, where, as Milton's Sin pathetically says, they "howl, and gnaw / My bowels, their repast; then bursting forth / Afresh, with conscious terrors vex me round, / That rest or intermission none I find," we might better contemplate the line of Jacopone da Todi that Dante affixed as epigraph to his *Purgatory: Ordina questo amore, O tu chi m'ami!* "Set Thou my loves in order, O Thou that lovest me."

7

Hamlet and the Strumpet Fortune

IN EXTANT literature Hamlet makes his first appearance, in a passing reference, as the proposer of a riddle: the sea is called "Hamlet's mill," presumably because its ebb and flow grind even the rocks to bits. In the earliest surviving full-scale treatment, that of Saxo Grammaticus, Hamlet "puts an antic disposition on" as part of his campaign to kill the usurping king, but occasionally dumbfounds his hearers by the shrewdness of his riddling comments. And in Shakespeare's definitive portrait, not only does Hamlet play the role of a madman, but he defies his observers to "pluck out the heart of his mystery."

Is it possible that the heart of the mystery is mystery itself? [1] In view of the general lack of agreement about the play's meaning, this proposal may seem a counsel of desperation. Yet could not Shakespeare deliberately so have balanced his mighty opposites that our final judgment must be that a final judgment is impossible? As we contemplate Hamlet's fate, are we not advised by the play itself to agree, "And how his audit stands who knows save heaven?" (III.iii.82). *Hamlet,* as may perhaps be shown, is a study of the supernatural virtue of Charity, and charity warns us in one of its primary precepts that a judgment on another is *ipso facto* a judgment on ourselves. *Hamlet* is also a play about spying; [2] it might almost be subtitled, "The Mystery of the Observer Observed." In the climactic scene, the audience watches an audience on the stage which is in turn watching a play within a play; two of the members of the stage audience, Hamlet and Horatio, are watching the King to see whether, as he watches, he will betray his knowledge that the things he watches are not merely "actions that a man might play," but have "that within which passeth show." Nor are the audience the only spectators of these spectators. Shakespeare wants us to know that he "sees a cherub that sees" our purposes; Heaven's face does not merely glow, grow thought-sick, and weep with burning eyes at the acts referred to on the stage, but it is turned toward the audience itself; Heaven is the audience of us, *Hamlet's* audience, and watches our earthly play. [3]

In the same way the representative of Heaven in the soul, our conscience, the Self as It Ought to Be, watches the Self as It Is, and urges the latter to identify itself with the role composed for it by God. [4] And so that the virtue of Charity may not be offended by a temptation to pass judgment, Shakespeare contrives to leave Hamlet's eternal destination in obscurity. [5] The raging controversy over the Prince's "regeneration" in the last act may indicate to us that the author intends no verdict to be decisively pronounced. [6] No sooner are we edified there by some Christian, or Christian-Stoical, expression of resignation from Hamlet's lips than we are jolted to dismay by the recollection of his abominable behavior at Ophelia's grave or by the revelation of his callousness at the trick played on Rosencrantz and Guildenstern. ("Why, man, they did make love to this employment," [V.ii.57] is Shakespearean for the gangsterese, "The suckers asked for it.") This suspension of certainty in outcome is taken to be a fault by some critics; it may be a greater virtue than they know. Perhaps Charity has its inception in the willing recognition of mystery.

The mythical character of the matter of *Hamlet* needs no elaborating.[7] Gilbert Murray long ago pointed out many parallelisms with the Orestes myth;[8] some resemblances had been noted centuries before him.[9] Dr. Ernest Jones, doubtless misguidedly but nevertheless cogently, revealed to the *Hamlet*-reader's attention that the Oedipus story is lurking in the background.[10] Saxo Grammaticus himself tells how Hamlet's father, King Horwendillus, or Orwendel, a personification of Spring, slew King Collerus, "King Cold," in a "spring-tide wood," [11] and wedded Queen Gerutha, or Gertrude, who is none other than Mother Earth. Saxo also details his Hamlethus' assumption of the role of Fool in avenging his father's death,[12] and involves his hero in adventures leading to marriage with other Earth goddesses.[13] Additionally, there are suggestions of the Hippolytus myth,[14] with all that that implies, in the episode where Hamlet carries a sealed commission to England enjoining his own execution; the tale of "Fortune's Child with the Letter of Death" is widespread.[15] So those who have noted that the black-suited Hamlet in Shakespeare's play is a kind of emissary from the Land of Death to the Land of the Living,[16] and that he bears an intimate relationship to the Goddess Fortune, have only brought to light mythical motifs that lay concealed in the primal matter.[17]

To see what Shakespeare is about, let us begin with Aeneas' tale to Dido, the Player's Speech (II.ii), which has been so truly "caviare to the general" as to have been judged an interpolation from another writer's hand. Not so, of course; the lines are thoroughly relevant; the speech is as important as the following "Rogue and peasant slave" soliloquy that it inspires.[18] "It begins with Pyrrhus"—a blood-soaked Pyrrhus, a hellish Pyrrhus, seeking out King Priam; it describes his attack on the king, the momentary arrest of his arm as he hears the crash of collapsing Troy, and the resumption and completion of the slaughter; it concludes with the grief of the "mobled" Queen Hecuba, which "Would have made milch the burning eyes of heaven / And passion in the gods."

What's Hecuba to *Hamlet* that Shakespeare should weep for her? Obviously, she is Queen Gertrude—not the happy queen who has posted with such dexterity to incestuous sheets, but the widow who would sincerely mourn if King Claudius, the husband she loves, were murdered. Priam then becomes, not so much the Elder Hamlet, but Claudius, the present monarch, for Shakespeare does not make these parallels except as profound ethical commentaries on the main action.

The hellish Pyrrhus must accordingly be Prince Hamlet.[19]

True, Pyrrhus is also Fortinbras, the ruthless invader; [20] as a king-killer, he may be Claudius himself; as a man mad to revenge his father, he may be the counterpart of Laertes. But, in all these aspects, destroyer of the state, murderer of a ruler, unscrupulous avenger, he is Hamlet, the Hamlet of the play's final scene, "Horridly trick'd / With blood of fathers, mothers, daughters, sons"—Polonius' blood, Claudius' blood, Gertrude's blood, Ophelia's blood, Rosencrantz' and Guildenstern's blood, Laertes' blood. For it is Hamlet's desire to avenge his father that leads to all this carnage.

Pyrrhus is portrayed, though repulsively, as a mighty warrior and knight in discharge of that duty most sacred to a man of honor, the avenging of the greatest of all wrongs to his family and his name. The Warrior, the Knight, the Man of Honor was the ideal man of the Renaissance; [21] this ideal might embrace, and indeed was supposed to embrace, courtier and scholar, "glass of fashion" and "mould of form" as well, but it was the aristocratic sense of honor that was the wellspring of his being.[22] *Hamlet* is Shakespeare's pointing-up of the ideal's shortcomings; Hamlet fulfills the requirements of the code of honor, but, for all his good qualities, in this fulfillment the fulfillment of his real self is called into question.[23]

His class-consciousness has something unpleasant in it to begin with. He is capable of abusing his rank to make sport of Polonius (Yonder cloud is a camel—a weasel—a whale) and Osric (The wind is cold—is hot, and so forth), apparently forgetting his own advice to use men after one's own "honour and dignity" (II.ii.563–64). Worse yet are his comments on the dead Polonius, "I took thee for thy better" (III.iv.32), and on the dead Rosencrantz and Guildenstern, " 'Tis dangerous when the baser nature comes / Between the pass and fell-incensed points / Of mighty opposites" (V.ii.60–62), in both remarks ranging himself with Claudius. (In short, to Hamlet the killing of underlings is no crime; it is sport, or, at worst, regrettable error.[24]) Here he shows the seamy side of the Aristocrat.

As a Man of Honor, Hamlet has "examples gross as earth" to exhort him (IV.iv.46 ff.), the phrase referring specifically to Fortinbras, the "delicate and tender prince," with spirit "puff'd by divine ambition," who is about to risk the lives of twenty thousand men for a patch of dirt not sufficient to bury them in, and all "for an egg-shell." Such foolishness elicits from Hamlet the familiar confused bit of sophistry: "Rightly to be great / Is not to stir without great argument, / But greatly to find quarrel in a straw / When honour's at the stake." One would like to apply to Fortinbras Hamlet's question about the lawyer's bones: "Is this . . . the recovery of his recoveries, to have his fine pate full of fine dirt?" (V.i.114–15).

Also in the procession of Men of Honor comes Osric, who has "much land, and fertile; let a beast be lord of beasts, and his crib shall stand at the king's mess; 'tis a chough, but, as I say, spacious in the possession of dirt." (V.ii.87 ff.) Young Osric is a caricature, an unfinished sketch of the Courtier; he has "only got the tune of the time and outward habit of encounter," but with age he should become what Hamlet feels a compulsion to be.

Third is Laertes, in whose cause even Hamlet sees the "portraiture" of his own. It is as fitting, according to the custom of revenge, that Laertes kill Hamlet at the last as that Hamlet kill his own father's murderer. Laertes, who wishes "no reconcilement / Till by some elder masters of known honour," he has "a voice and precedent of peace" (V.ii.261 ff.), is a rasher, cruder, more blatant Hamlet, though at Ophelia's funeral, when Hamlet feels challenged, he manages to outdo Laertes in crudity too. ("Woo't drink up eisel? eat a crocodile? / I'll do't."—V.i.298–99.) Laertes is useful in putting into words what Hamlet's conduct implies (IV.v.130 ff.):

> To hell, allegiance! vows, to the blackest devil!
> Conscience and grace, to the profoundest pit!
> I dare damnation. To this point I stand;
> That both the worlds I give to negligence,
> Let come what comes; only I'll be revenged
> Most throughly for my father.

Like most of Shakespeare's "Men of Honor," he, with his poisoned sword point, is replete with dishonesty. And, in

sum, his heart, like Hamlet's perhaps, becomes so brass'd
by the "damned custom" of the code of honor "That it is
proof and bulwark against sense" (cf. III.iv.37–38).

A second basis for identifying Hamlet with the hellish
Pyrrhus is the fact that Pyrrhus, in so atrociously murdering
King Priam and devastating Troy, was not only wreaking
vengeance for his father's death, but also emulating his
father's martial prowess. Hamlet's much-quoted speech ex-
pressing disapproval of the Danes' excessive drinking, the
"custom more honour'd in the breach than the observance,"
must be quoted yet once more in this connection
(I.iv.23 ff.): [25]

> So, oft it chances in particular men,
> That for some vicious mole of nature in them,
> As, in their birth,—wherein they are not guilty,
> Since nature cannot choose his origin,—
> By the o'ergrowth of some complexion,
> Oft breaking down the pales and forts of reason,
> Or by some habit that too much o'er-leavens
> The form of plausive manners; that these men,
> Carrying, I say, the stamp of one defect,
> Being nature's livery, or fortune's star,
> Their virtues else, be they as pure as grace,
> As infinite as man may undergo,
> Shall in the general censure take corruption
> From that particular fault: the dram of eale
> Doth all the noble substance of a doubt,
> To his own scandal.

Whatever the notorious "dram of eale" may be, the gist
of the passage is clear: just as one bad custom can ruin the
reputation of a nation, as drunkenness has "soiled the addition" of Denmark, so in a particular individual, who has
many good qualities, one fault, native or habitual, may be-

come a stumbling-block and source of general corruption and disrepute.

By talking so, is Hamlet simply whiling away the time, biding the appearance of the Ghost? The principle of presumptive unity, which must be allowed to be operative in any work of art unless definitely shown not to be there, would induce us to say, on the contrary, that Shakespeare inserts this apparent digression for good reason, that Hamlet is saying something of vital significance to a complete understanding of the play. For of whom is he speaking, if not of himself?

The present-day, sociologically conditioned reader would be inclined to say that the particular fault which threatens corruption to Hamlet is either hereditary or environmental. This seems to be confirmed by the alternatives: "some vicious mole of nature"—a mole being an inborn defect that later in life may become tainted—or "some habit that too much o'erleavens the form of plausive manners"—that is, some mode of action, conformable to the ideals of the time, that becomes excessive, thus effecting the "scandal" —not only loss of reputation, but the risk of spiritual damnation (the Biblical use of the word)—of the actor. But perhaps those are not so much alternatives as different phases of the same thing, for at the next mention, the distinction is blurred: "one defect, being nature's livery, or fortune's star." "Nature's livery" suggests the physiognomy with which we are clothed from birth, as well as the uniform of that social class in which our birth has placed us ("for he himself is subject to his birth," says Laertes of Hamlet—I.iii.18); "fortune's star" calls to mind not merely the sphere in which Hamlet is destined to move ("Lord Hamlet is a prince, out of thy star," Polonius says he told Ophelia—II.ii.141) and the accidents which may befall

him throughout life ("fortune's star" being the moon, from
which the Goddess Fortune capriciously directs all sub-
lunary affairs), but it also suggests a scar or brand, a birth-
mark. Hamlet is right in pointing out that a man is not
guilty of these things, but wrong in assuming that he is
not responsible for the way in which he reacts to them,
for precisely here lies the whole domain of ethics.

Though the hereditary and environmental defects from
the moral point of view are the same, for convenience they
may be considered separately. The corrupting factor in
Hamlet's social milieu is the compulsion of the code of
honor already discussed. But what is the "vicious mole of
nature"? This must refer to certain psychological traits inherited from his parents. Hamlet resembles Gertrude in
being passionate, sensitive, volatile, and sympathetic. But it
is his emulation of his father that chiefly motivates his behavior. What was the elder Hamlet like?

He appears in the play indirectly and directly, through
the reminiscences of other characters and in person (perhaps) as the Ghost. Disregarding Hamlet's complimentary
but vague descriptions, we can see from what others say of
the former king that he was martial, combative, hot-tem-
pered, a paragon of chivalric conduct in its grosser aspects.
Undoubtedly in so fulfilling the ideal of the age he aroused
widespread admiration. His attitude toward his wife would
seem to have been that of a perfect knight, but it is on his
warlike accomplishments that most emphasis is laid. His
combat with the Elder Fortinbras must have been the
epitome of the code duello: two princes, for the mere honor
of the thing, fought to the death, all in approved chivalric
style, the stakes being parts of their territories. Even when
the Elder Hamlet broke the rules he did so in manly fashion: "in an angry parle, / He smote the sledded Polacks

on the ice" (I.i.63)—a vexed line, which may possibly mean that while in a discussion during a truce, he lost his temper and struck the Polish envoys.

Hamlet is conscious, or partly conscious, that he has inherited his father's passionate, rash, and resentful nature. The ghost of the father is already in Hamlet's mind from the beginning. Horatio, after his first glimpse of the apparition, says, "A mote it is to trouble the mind's eye" (I.i.112), and then a little later, about to reveal his news to Hamlet, he is startled to hear the latter say, "My father— methinks I see my father" (I.ii.184 ff.).

> HOR. O! where, my lord?
> HAM.   In my mind's eye, Horatio.
> HOR. I saw him once; he was a goodly king.
> HAM. He was a man, take him for all in all,
>   I shall not look upon his like again.

Hamlet's admiration for his father is the mote in his mind's eye, and in the context of the play and as a reminder of the Biblical injunction it becomes a portent of his own corruption and of the fall of Denmark.

This brings us to the Ghost.

It is an ambiguous ghost: we can say this if nothing else.[26] Catholic or Protestant? Redeemed spirit or devil? Hero or villain? Genuine revenant or hallucination? "Oh, there has been much throwing about of brains" in the attempt to settle these matters. And yet, should the questions be settled at all? All answers tend to convert the play from an internal drama of morality into an external melodrama of incident. The domain of ethics lies in a man's reactions to his circumstances. "For there is nothing either good or bad, but thinking makes it so," Hamlet says himself

(II.ii.259 ff.). Shall a man react with charity, or otherwise? That is the question.

Does the Ghost, in its turn, pour poison into Hamlet's ear? [27] Shakespeare, by sounding the note again and again, seems to have intended us to suspect this; the story of the Ghost, against which Hamlet's ear is not fortified like Horatio's, becomes a "leprous distillment" to infect the Prince's soul, to "freeze his young blood," and "deprive his sovereignty of reason." And yet it is Hamlet's reception of the tale which gives it this poisonous power, and not the substance itself.[28] For though the Ghost counsels revenge, it nowhere counsels murder—on the contrary, it expressly condemns it ("Murder most foul, as in the best it is"— I.v.27),[29] and solemnly warns Hamlet against the possibility of infection: "But, howsoever thou pursu'st this act, / Taint not thy mind" (I.v.84–85). But Hamlet the son, daring "hell itself" to "gape," and confident that the Ghost cannot harm his soul, "Being a thing immortal as itself," courts damnation, showing a recklessness echoing Horatio's "I'll cross it, though it blast me," and forgetting that it may bring with it "airs from heaven" as well as "blasts from hell." With uncharitable intent, a "fool of nature," he lets his disposition be shaken horridly "with thoughts beyond the reaches of his soul." (Vengeance is mine, sayeth the Lord; leave Claudius to heaven.) His "flaming youth" naturally takes the Ghost's adjuration, "If thou hast nature in thee, bear it not" (I.v.81), to be a demand of murder for murder; youth, of course, is generally liable to "savageness in unreclaimed blood" (II.i.34—i.e. blood unredeemed as yet by the Atonement) and "taints of liberty." Laertes puts it neatly: "And in the morn and liquid dew of youth / Contagious blastments are most imminent" (I.iii.41–42). Not

strangely then Ophelia, after Hamlet plays the part of
poisoner in his turn, and, "As if he had been loosed out of
hell / To speak of horrors" (II.i.83–84), has started her on
the road to destruction, bemoans that his "unmatch'd form
and feature of blown youth" is "blasted with ecstasy." Yet
there is always the possibility that the Ghost is out to "catch
the conscience of the king" rather than the king himself, a
possibility of which Hamlet seems dimly aware on its
second appearance, when he says to it (III.iv.126 ff.): "Do
not look upon me, / Lest with this piteous action you convert / My stern effects: then what I have to do / Will want
true colour; tears perchance for blood": if the Ghost were a
"spirit of health," it would be satisfied with Claudius' tears
of repentance; Hamlet himself is responsible for taking it as
a "goblin damn'd," to be appeased only by the blood of the
murderer.

From the moment that Hamlet learns of his uncle's crime
he is "like the owner of a foul disease," who, "To keep it
from divulging," lets "it feed / Even on the pith of life"
(IV.i.21 ff.). The "vicious mole of nature," the natural pro-
pensities of his youth and his inheritance from his father,
"infects unseen." We may legitimately suspect a pun,
therefore, when, in swearing his friends to conspiracy, he
responds to his father's encouragement: "Well said, old
mole!" (I.v.162).

Two things corrupt Hamlet, then: one, the influence of
his father's example, the heritage of his father's tempera-
ment, and the exhortation of his father's ghost, which are
all the "vicious mole of nature" implanted in his earth by
the "old mole"; and two, the pressure on Hamlet to conform
to the courtier's code of honor, which is "the habit that too
much o'erleavens / The form of plausive manners."

To return to the Player's Speech: immediately after de-

scribing how Pyrrhus' bleeding sword remorselessly falls on
old King Priam, the actor suspends his narration to de-
nounce Fortune (II.ii.523 ff.): [30]

> Out, out, thou strumpet, Fortune! All you gods,
> In general synod, take away her power:
> Break all the spokes and fellies from her wheel,
> And bowl the round nave down the hill of heaven,
> As low as to the fiends! [31]

The notions about the Goddess Fortune, here and elsewhere in the play, were widespread.[32] She, of course, turns
a wheel, often having bound to the rim four figures super-
scribed *Regnabo* "I shall be king," *Regno* "I am king,"
Regnavi "I have been king," and *Sum sine regno* "I am
without a kingdom." [33] She is a strumpet, a harlot, as the
conversation between Hamlet and his schoolfellows shows
(II.ii.237 ff.):

GUIL. On Fortune's cap we are not the very button.
HAM. Nor the soles of her shoe?
ROS. Neither, my lord.
HAM. Then you live about her waist, or in the mid-
         dle of her favours?
GUIL. Faith, her privates we.
HAM. In the secret parts of Fortune? O! most true;
         she is a strumpet.

She often makes faces at men; hence, Young Fortinbras,
"Exposing what is mortal and unsure / To all that fortune,
death, and danger dare, / Even for an egg-shell" (IV.iv.51),
retaliates and "Makes mouths at the invisible event." She
is closely associated with the moon, symbol of mutability,
and has been granted some sort of power by God to regu-

late all affairs beneath the lowest, lunar, Heaven. She is disdained by Poverty; the poor Horatio is sublimely indifferent to Fortune. She sometimes plays dice, chess, or bowls with men; sometimes she fishes for them; sometimes, with limed twigs, she captures them like birds. (So King Claudius is kept from repenting by the double fortune of his stolen bride and kingship: "O limed soul, that struggling to be free / Art more engaged!"—III.iii.67–68.) She is involved in all matters of reputation and scandal. She lives on a mountain—which may have suggested the "hill of Heaven," though Shakespeare's idea of the descent from that hill "to the fiends" adds the thought of damnation—and she keeps a garden, perhaps the "unweeded garden" of this world. She is often connected with the perilous, shifting sea, and she is at continual war with men, darting arrows at them, which raises the question in the Soliloquy, of "Whether 'tis nobler in the mind to suffer / The slings and arrows of outrageous Fortune, / Or to take arms against a sea of troubles / And by opposing end them." In short, an answer to the problem of how best to fight the war with Fortune constitutes one of the central meanings in *Hamlet*.[34]

One of the possible defenses against Fortune's "slings and arrows" is the natural virtue of fortitude, Stoic self-sufficiency, by which one suffers nobly in the mind, but reacts not at all outwardly. Horatio, "more an antique Roman than a Dane" (V.ii.355), with his well-known philosophy that fails to dream of as many things as there are in heaven and earth (neglecting doubtless among others those "bad dreams" that may come in the sleep of death) is the type of this.[35] Here are Hamlet's familiar words to Horatio (III.ii.61 ff.):

   Nay, do not think I flatter;
For what advancement may I hope from thee,
That no revenue hast but thy good spirits
To feed and clothe thee? Why should the poor be flatter'd?
No; let the candied tongue lick absurd pomp,
And crook the pregnant hinges of the knee
Where thrift may follow fawning. Dost thou hear?
Since my dear soul was mistress of her choice
And could of men distinguish, her election
Hath seal'd thee for herself; for thou hast been
As one, in suffering all, that suffers nothing,
A man that fortune's buffets and rewards
Hast ta'en with equal thanks; and bless'd are those
Whose blood and judgment are so well co-mingled
That they are not a pipe for fortune's finger
To sound what stop she please. Give me that man
That is not passion's slave, and I will wear him
In my heart's core, ay, in my heart of heart,
As I do thee.[36]

   Hamlet, it must be noted, only "wears" such a man in his
heart's core, for if he has any thought of becoming one, he
definitely "recks not his own rede." Actually, till his dying
voice, his dear soul's "election lights on Fortinbras," the
fiery Man of Honor. But Hamlet's creator seems always to
have admired the self-sufficient man, though with a limited
and grudging admiration. We think of Sonnet XCIV, often
quoted in this regard:

> They that have power to hurt and will do none,
> That do not do the thing they most do show,
> Who, moving others, are themselves as stone,
> Unmoved, cold, and to temptation slow,
> They rightly do inherit heaven's graces,
> And husband nature's riches from expense,

which might almost be called the "Hamlet-Sonnet," so accurately does it echo some of the keynotes of the play: discretion, husbandry, stewardship, thrift, slowness to action, the shielding of the flower of nature's sweet riches from infection. In fact, voices throw this advice to the audience from all quarters of the stage—some indirectly, some hypocritically, some, like Hamlet's, with sincerity but no true comprehension.

King Claudius says to the council, of his brother's death: "Yet so far hath discretion fought with nature, / That we with wisest sorrow think on him, / Together with remembrance of ourselves." And a little later his phrase, "In equal scale weighing delight and dole," suggest the "man that Fortune's buffets and rewards / Hath ta'en with equal thanks." Hamlet's exhortation to his friends to "Give it an understanding, but no tongue," is paralleled by Polonius' advice to his son to "Give thy thoughts no tongue, / Nor any unproportion'd thought his act," whereas the further maxim, "Neither a borrower nor a lender be, / For loan oft loses both itself and friend, / And borrowing dulls the edge of husbandry," might better have been taken to heart by Ophelia, whose ultimate groaning may perhaps have been due to her having taken off Hamlet's edge.

No one in the drama accepts any of this sage advice, however; there is reason to believe that Ophelia may not have heeded her brother's and father's injunctions to practice thrift: "Keep you in the rear of your affection," and "The chariest maid is prodigal enough / If she unmask her beauty to the moon" (I.iii), and the warning "When the blood burns, how prodigal the soul / Lends the tongue vows." For "it is common for the younger sort / To lack discretion"; consequently Hamlet, too, who can advise the actor (III.ii.6 ff.), "in the very torrent, tempest, and—as I may say—whirlwind of passion, you must acquire and beget a temperance, that may give it smoothness," pays no attention to his mother's "O gentle son! / Upon the heat and flame of thy distemper / Sprinkle cool patience" (III.iv.121–22).

Hamlet is an uncomfortable play for busybodies, for all "extravagant and erring spirits." [37] Rosencrantz and Guildenstern "make love to" the "employment" that leads them to their deaths. Poor Polonius, having boasted that he has not "play'd the desk or table-book, / Or given my heart a winking, mute and dumb" (II.ii.136 ff.), but has gone "round to work," receives as his final accolade from his slayer: "Thou wretched, rash, intruding fool, farewell! / I took thee for thy better; take thy fortune; / Thou find'st to be too busy is some danger" (III.iv.31 ff.). True it is that, as Hamlet and Polonius fear, fortitude may degenerate into a variety of sloth (IV.iv.33 ff.):

> What is man,
> If his chief good and market of his time
> Be but to sleep and feed? a beast, no more.
> Sure he that made us with such large discourse,
> Looking before and after, gave us not
> That capability and god-like reason
> To fust in us unus'd.

But of course the chief function of "god-like" reason is to foster prudent, and inhibit imprudent, action, not to expend the self in rash adventure. This Hamlet does not realize, nor does he realize either that fortitude may sour into fatalism, finding expression in an inertia relieved only by sporadic frenzy. At the time when he says, "If it be now, 'tis not to come; if it be not to come, it will be now; if it be not now, yet it will come; the readiness is all"

(V.ii.233 ff.), he may be already corrupted. Not surprisingly he praises rashness (V.ii.7 ff.):

> And prais'd be rashness for it, let us know,
> Our indiscretion sometimes serves us well
> When our deep plots do pall; and that should teach us
> There's a divinity that shapes our ends,
> Rough-hew them how we will.

This divinity may well be none other than the Goddess Fortune; at this point Hamlet seems ready for the dizzy whirls of Fortune's wheel that constitute the action of the final scene.

But even as the natural virtue of fortitude may descend into fatalism, so it may rise into its complement, the Christian virtue of Charity, the recognition of the good of one's self and one's fate, the good of others, and the good of the world.[38]

As every close reader since Dr. Johnson has discovered, the best-known soliloquy in dramatic literature is not as simple as it sounds. What after all *is* the question? If "to be or not to be" means merely "to live or to die," is it not strangely rephrased immediately afterward as "to suffer in the mind or to take arms against a sea of troubles"? Or is the latter quite a different pair of alternatives? No doubt "not to be" embraces the project of suicide, but does it embrace anything more? "The fear of something after death," which is a factor in "conscience," quite plainly deters us from suicide, but what are those "enterprises of great pith and moment" that "with this regard" "lose the name of action"? They can hardly be self-slaughter only.[39] It would seem that the celebrated monologue is either a verbal ramble through utter confusion, or else it has a consistent meaning, which may be summed up as: True being is to suffer one's fortune nobly in the mind; [40] on the other hand, suicide, murder, and all rash and splenitive reactions against one's destiny end in not-being, the full horror of which the sinner encounters when at death he passes from "nature to eternity." [41] There at the Judgment, "when we have shuffled off this mortal coil," there is no more "shuffling," as King Claudius knows (such as the "shuffling" by which, as he advises Laertes, Hamlet is to be attacked with the poisoned sword); "there the action lies / In his true nature" (III.iii.61–62). For there is in every human being a real self more ideally natural than the ordinary natural self; the realization of this "inmost part" of one's nature is the task of morality: "this above all: to thine own self be true." [42]

"Poor Ophelia" in her madness, "Divided from herself and her fair judgment, / Without the which we are pictures, or mere beasts" (IV.v.84 ff.), has a dim inkling of the human plight, lamenting, "Lord, we know what we are, but know not what we may be" (IV.v.43–44). So she drowns "herself in her own defence" . . . "*se offendendo;* it cannot be else" (V.i.7 ff.), according to the grave-digger—for to defend one's native self by a passionate self-assertion ending in self-destruction is to attack and offend one's real self.

True realization, real Charity, on the other hand, is to save the soul by losing it, or giving it away. Here "thrift" changes from its Stoic-naturalistic meaning of parsimony, implying self-containment, to its Christian-supernatural meaning of growth. To thrive and advance truly is to grow in love and charity. [43]

> For nature crescent does not grow alone
> In thews and bulk; but as this temple waxes,
> The inward service of the mind and soul
> Grows wide withal (I.ii.11 ff.).

"The inward service" that grows wide within "this temple" of the body can only be the joyful acceptance of one's nature and destiny, which is charity toward one's self, and the love of the good of others, which is charity directed outward: Use every man "after your own honour and dignity; the less they deserve, the more merit is in your bounty" (II.ii.563 ff.). Charity seeketh not her own: "Most necessary 'tis that we forget / To pay ourselves what to ourselves is debt" (III.ii.204–205), warns the Player King; instead we must, as the people do Hamlet's, dip all our fellows' faults in our "affection" and convert their "gyves to graces" (IV.vii.19 ff.), thereby turning our own fetters into means of salvation.[44] Thus we refine our natures (IV.v.160 ff.):

> Nature is fine in love, and where 'tis fine
> It sends some precious instance of itself
> After the thing it loves. . . .

and overcome Fortune (III.ii.214–15):

> For 'tis a question left us yet to prove
> Whe'r love lead fortune or else fortune love.

To Hamlet, who from the very beginning does not set his "life at a pin's fee," the question ultimately takes the form of whether "that within which passeth show" is material or spiritual. Is the reality beneath the skin the soul or the skull? "Now get you to my lady's chamber, and tell her, let her paint an inch thick, to this favour she must come; make her laugh at that" (V.i.211 ff.), he tells the skull, as he had formerly told the "beautified" Ophelia, "I have heard of your paintings, too, well enough; God has given you one face, and you make yourselves another" (III.i.150 ff.). But after all, to a man without charity, women are only "breeders of sinners" as the "sun breeds maggots in a dead dog, being a good kissing carrion," [45] and "We fat all creatures else to fat us, and we fat ourselves for maggots" (IV.iii.23 f.), so that Hamlet inevitably arrives at the query, "Did these bones cost no more the breeding, but to play at loggats with 'em?" (V.i.97 ff.)—skulls, one supposes, being finally as futile playthings as that nave of Fortune's wheel which is to be bowled down the hill of heaven as low as to the fiends.

This is a far cry from "the inward service of the mind and soul." Though it may always be true that "Virtue cannot so inoculate our old stock but we shall relish of it" (III.i.120 ff.), still "use almost can change the stamp of nature / And either master the devil, or throw him out / With wondrous potency" (III.iv.168 ff.). These "actions that a man might play" can eventually "denote" him truly if they are virtues which, having them not *in esse,* but only *in posse,* he assumes long enough and earnestly enough to fix permanently in his character.

But quite a different play within the play of life is the role that the sinner must assume who, unless he repent, can never again know honesty or sincerity.[46] His actions can never be real; he must forever betray his true self, which, being created for him in potentiality by God, cannot jibe with evil; he must carry forever the "heavy burthen" of hypocrisy. King Claudius knows well the torment of being always an actor, never a real person; in his agonized hour of facing that fact—"O! my offence is rank, it smells to heaven . . ." (III.iii.36 ff.)—Hamlet, whose idea of utter disaster is to meet his "dearest foe in heaven" (I.ii.182), brings the irony of the play to a climax by reserving him for future slaughter, ignorant that there is "no relish of salvation" in Claudius' prayers and that by catching "the conscience of the king" the Ghost's revenge is actually already complete. Claudius' punishment has of course begun long before; Polonius' comments on hypocrisy cause the king to say to himself (III.i.50 ff.):

> How smart a lash that speech doth give my conscience!
> The harlot's cheek, beautied with plastering art,
> Is not more ugly to the thing that helps it
> Than is my deed to my most painted word.

This speech, contrasting the painting with the reality, immediately precedes, and sets the mood for, "To be or not to be." [47]

Both Hamlet in his cowardice and Claudius in his false repentance should have heard and harkened to Ophelia's comments on "rue," with its connotations of penitence and charity:

> . . . there's rue for you; and here's some for me; we may call it herb of grace o' Sundays. O! you must wear your rue with a difference (IV.v.180 ff.)

instead of which both prefer to be "o'ersized with coagulate gore" like the "painted tyrant," Pyrrhus, and wear the "more dismal heraldry" of "total gules."

Though Charity may be considered the opposite of almost any one of the seven deadly sins, it is perhaps most properly ranged against the sin of *Acedia,* or Accidie. In the first scene in which he appears, Hamlet, although, psychologically speaking, he is in a state of melancholy, is from a moral point of view under the influence of this deadly sin of Sloth. *Acedia,* somewhat misleadingly translated "sloth," is the sin of indifference to one's own good.[48] It has its origin in dissatisfaction with the good of one's own fortune; it is initially a deficiency in that phase of charity which is joyful acceptance of the will of God. Claudius is right, when he first addresses Hamlet, in calling Hamlet's conduct (I.ii.93 ff.)

> a course
> Of impious stubbornness; 'tis unmanly grief:
> It shows a will most incorrect to heaven,
> A heart unfortified, a mind impatient,
> An understanding simple and unschool'd:
> For what we know must be and is as common
> As any the most vulgar thing to sense,
> Why should we in our peevish opposition
> Take it to heart? Fie! 'tis a fault to heaven,
> A fault against the dead, a fault to nature,
> To reason most absurd. . . .

All this is a perfectly just description of *Acedia*, though the description itself proceeds from the mouth of a hypocrite.[49] The sin is one of treason against the natural law; it is a fool's attempt to flout Fortune by petulant withdrawal from the game of life. Springing from a wounded vanity and a thwarted self-love, it distends into a world-disgust, a deliberate blindness to all the good of God's creation (I.ii.133 ff.):

> How weary, stale, flat, and unprofitable
> Seem to me all the uses of this world.
> Fie on't! O fie! 'tis an unweeded garden,
> That grows to seed; things rank and gross in nature
> Possess it merely. . . .

and into despair, a longing for annihilation (I.ii.129 ff.):

> O! that this too too solid flesh would melt,
> Thaw and resolve itself into a dew. . . .

a temptation to suicide.

Having thus sunk to the bottom level of moral indifferent-ism, regarding all else as defiled, the individual in a state of *Acedia* is quite ready to excuse his own defects. Hence Hamlet in the closet scene expresses to his mother what has probably been in his mind from the first (III.iv.82 ff.):

> Rebellious hell,
> If thou canst mutine in a matron's bones,
> To flaming youth let virtue be as wax,
> And melt in her own fire: proclaim no shame
> When the compulsive ardour gives the charge,
> Since frost itself as actively doth burn,
> And reason panders will.

In other words: let my flesh melt; let my virtue melt—it is all the same!

Ophelia too, being a woman, must be a strumpet, and is to be treated, even before the assembled court, as one. But, more horribly, Ophelia is actually treated so not out of resentment, but out of indifference. The man under the sway of *Acedia*—"not-caringness"—inevitably passes from disgust with his own and the world's good to complete insensibility wherever the good of others is concerned. Once the Ghost has given a motive for action, Hamlet, having wiped away from the table of his memory "all trivial, fond records," is prepared to regard his friends, his mother, his lover, her father, and his old schoolfellows not as human beings, but as mere instruments or obstacles to the attainment of his designs; this is perhaps the most dangerous aspect of his corruption. Polonius, murdered, be-comes "guts;" Rosencrantz and Guildenstern, put out of the way by a grisly practical joke (and without a word in the text of the play to convict them of anything worse than an over-zealous interest in Hamlet's welfare), become oc-

casion for a chuckle; and Ophelia becomes the topic for
a contest in ranting between brother and lover, after they
have finished scuffling at her grave. (Yet the false and
loathsome words, "I loved Ophelia; forty thousand brothers / Could not, with all their quantity of love / Make up
my sum" [V.i.291 ff.], have moved generations of sentimental critics and playgoers to tears.)

No doubt with respect to all of them Hamlet behaves as
though "They are not near my conscience"—a self-damning
conclusion. In fact if we consider his actions at the last, the
callous rodomontade marring the obsequies of his dead
victim Ophelia, the lie to Laertes ("Then Hamlet does it
not; Hamlet denies it. Who does it then? His madness.
. . ."—V.ii.250 ff.), the supercilious baiting of Osric, the
willful morbidity in the grave-digging scene, we can almost
say of him (III.ii.33 ff.):

O! there be players that I have seen play, and heard others
praise, and that highly, not to speak it profanely, that, neither
having the accent of Christians nor the gait of Christian, pagan,
nor man, have so strutted and bellowed that I have thought
some of nature's journeymen had made men and not made them
well, they imitated humanity so abominably.

Hamlet begins amid a scene of warlike threats and political forebodings, and ends as Denmark passes under alien
domination. In other words, the play is a study of social as
well as individual catastrophe.[50] The fall of the tyrant,
Claudius, involves the fall of the city. All the premonitions
and misgivings expressed in the first act—"something is
rotten in the state of Denmark"; "This bodes some strange
eruption to our state"; Horatio's address to the Ghost, "If
thou art privy to our country's fate, / Which, happily, fore-
knowing may avoid, O, speak!"; and Claudius' contradic-

tion of Fortinbras' thinking "by our late dear brother's death / Our state to be disjoint and out of frame" (Hamlet also thinks the time is "out of joint" and he has been born to set it right)—all these are amply justified by the last scene, when Fortinbras, heir to Norway, marches in to add Denmark to his dominions. The working out of Hamlet's vengeance involves the destruction of his country.[51]

The classic literary example of the Fall of the City was of course the capture and burning of Troy; hence the further relevance of the Player's Speech.[52] Pyrrhus' ear, while his sword is "declining on the milky head / Of reverend Priam," is taken prisoner by the "hideous crash" as "senseless Ilium, / Seeming to feel this blow, with flaming top / Stoops to his base." And Pyrrhus stands "as a painted tyrant" and "like a neutral to his will and matter" does nothing—for the moment. There is no indication that Hamlet ever consciously draws back from his vengeance for fear of involving the city in ruin; but that such an idea is insinuated into the Pyrrhus episode shows that it was present to Shakespeare's mind.

Richard the Second, Henry the Fourth, Julius Caesar, Coriolanus all illustrate Shakespeare's disapproval of rebellion against constituted authority, however tyrannical or inefficient or originally usurpative. The reminiscences in *Hamlet* of its near predecessor *Julius Caesar* have often been noted; the assassination of Caesar was the classic historical example of the Fall of the Tyrant. Yet every reader realizes that Brutus, though he kills from the noblest of motives, is somehow refuted and condemned. We have proceeded only a little over a hundred lines into *Hamlet* when we are reminded of the dismal portents that went before the death of Caesar and of the general disaster that befell "the high and palmy state of Rome." Heaven, as

Horatio makes clear, was then aghast at the misbehavior of
earth's denizens, and the moon, Fortune's habitat, "the moist
star, / Upon whose influence Neptune's empire stands, /
Was sick almost to doomsday with eclipse." In the light of
this we may read self-condemnation into Hamlet's exchange with his future victim, Polonius (III.ii.108 ff.):

> HAM. And what did you enact?
> POL. I did enact Julius Caesar; I was killed i' the
>   Capitol; Brutus killed me.
> HAM. It was a brute part of him to kill so capital a
>   calf there.

So it is a beastly act for Hamlet to sacrifice the one whom
he takes for the tyrant ("I took thee for thy better") and,
finally, the tyrant himself.

But it is not necessary to go outside of the play for con-
firmation of the author's attitude. Granted that King Claudius' opinion (IV.v.123 ff.),

> There's such divinity doth hedge a king,
> That treason can but peep to what it would,
> Acts little of his will,

has been invalidated by his own actions and is to be invalidated by Hamlet's final attack, yet there is no reason
to doubt that Shakespeare subscribed to Rosencrantz'
speech (III.iii.15 ff.):

> The cease of majesty
> Dies not alone, but, like a gulf doth draw
> What's near it with it; it is a massy wheel,
> Fix'd on the summit of the highest mount,
> To whose huge spokes ten thousand lesser things
> Are mortis'd and adjoin'd; which, when it falls,
> Each small annexment, petty consequence,
> Attends the boisterous ruin.

Keeping in mind also that Shakespeare spares no pains to
represent Claudius as a capable administrator, it is with a
new perspective that we turn back to the lines about breaking all the spokes and fellies from Fortune's wheel and
bowling the round nave down the hill of heaven as low as
to the fiends. Evidently the man who in this way " 'Gainst
Fortune's state would treason have pronounced" is headed
for damnation. By Rosencrantz' lines we are reminded that
rulers were bound to Fortune's wheel: *"Regnabo, Regno,
Regnavi*—I shall be king, I am king, I have been king." But
it would seem that an attempt to take away Fortune's
power by substituting on the throne one treasonous murderer, Hamlet, for another of the same kind, Claudius,
would be but to confirm the goddess's triumph.

And the last scene of *Hamlet* is indeed a triumph of Fortune. That accidents are so prominent in the plot is not
accidental. Coleridge commented: "This is almost the
only play of Shakespeare in which mere accidents, independent of all will, form an essential part of the plot;—
but here how judiciously in keeping with the character of
the over-meditative Hamlet, ever at last determined by accident or by a fit of passion."

Coleridge's perceptions were right; his interpretation, if
one may say so, mistaken. The determination of Hamlet's
character by luck or passion is the tragic meaning of the
play; Fortune's final victory, ending in the "feast of death"
that Fortinbras walks in upon, is the demonstration that
Hamlet and the other characters have lost their war with
the goddess by opposing her wrongly. From the moment
when the prince has the luck to board the pirate ship alone,
Fortune is the divinity that shapes his end. He who has
boasted to Guildenstern (III.ii.387 ff.), "You would play
upon me; you would seem to know my stops. . . .

'Sblood, do you think I am easier to be played on than a pipe?" becomes a "pipe for Fortune's finger / To sound what stop she please." Nor is he alone. Laertes, thanks to the accidental exchange of rapiers, "as a woodcock" to his own springe is justly killed with his own treachery (V.ii.320–21); the murder of Claudius seems almost fortuitous; and, most accidental of all, Gertrude reaches for the poisoned cup: "The queen carouses to thy fortune, Hamlet." Truly, as the Player King says (III.ii.223 ff.):

> Our wills and fates do so contrary run
> That our devices still are overthrown,
> Our thoughts are ours, their ends none of our own.

Gertrude's carousing recalls the King's rouse in the First Act, which "the heavens shall bruit again / Re-speaking earthly thunder" (I.ii.127–28), and in Act Five, when "The king shall drink to Hamlet's better breath [his afterlife?]; . . . And let the kettle to the trumpet speak, / The trumpet to the cannoneer without, / The cannons to the heavens, the heavens to earth" (V.ii.284 ff.). Thunder is a symbol both of accident and of punishment; the triumph of Fortune is also a triumph of heaven's justice. So we note that thunder and other celestial phenomena roar and flash from the wings throughout the play, as it were: in the description of the omens preceding Caesar's death; in the "dreadful thunder" that "rends the region" as Pyrrhus butchers Priam; in the "burning eyes of heaven" that look on the bereaved Hecuba; in Gertrude's interview with her son (III.iv.48 ff.):

> HAM.   Heaven's face doth glow;
> Yea, this solidity and compound mass,
> With tristful visage, as against the doom,
> Is thought-sick at the act.

QUEEN.   Ay me! what act,
        That roars so loud and thunders in the index?

The outside universe mirrors the conscience within by being "sicklied o'er with the pale cast of thought," the thought of the dispensation at doomsday. So in the last scene "is doomsday near" for Hamlet. To him, as well as to Claudius and Laertes, Horatio's words are applicable (V.ii.394 ff.):

> So shall you hear
> Of carnal, bloody, and unnatural acts,
> Of accidental judgments, casual slaughters;
> Of deaths put on by cunning and forc'd cause,
> And, in this upshot, purposes mistook
> Fall'n on the inventors' heads. . . .

For the idea of *hamartia*, etymologically "the missing of the aim," is omnipresent in this tragedy. Hamlet has correctly predicted to his mother, concerning Rosencrantz and Guildenstern (III.iv.204 ff.):

> They must sweep my way,
> And marshal me to knavery. Let it work;
> For 'tis the sport to have the enginer
> Hoist with his own petar: and it shall go hard
> But I will delve one yard below their mines,
> And blow them at the moon.

But this speech has an irony that he does not discern, for all the while the ghost of his father, whose abilities as sapper he himself has commended ("Canst work i' the earth so fast? A worthy pioner!"—I.v.162–63), with "rank corruption, mining all within," prepares to blow Hamlet up to "Fortune's star." The Ghost's poison has done its work in Hamlet's earth.

Hamlet's dying remark (V.ii.367), "The potent poison

quite o'er-crows my spirit," takes us back to the crowing of
the cock in the opening scene, when his father's spirit
"started like a guilty thing / Upon a fearful summons"
(I.i.148–49). Cock-crow was not only the harbinger of day,
but was of course God's reminder to Saint Peter that he
should return to his duty. One thinks of Ophelia's song
(IV.iv.59 ff.),

> By Gis [i.e. Jesus], and by Saint Charity,
>   Alack, and fie for shame!
> Young men will do't, if they come to't;
>   By Cock [i.e. God], they are to blame,

of the legend that (I.i.158 ff.)

>   ever 'gainst that season comes
> Wherein our Saviour's birth is celebrated,
> The bird of dawning singeth all night long;
> And then, they say, no spirit can walk abroad,

and of Horatio's words immediately before,

>   I have heard,
> The cock, that is the trumpet to the morn,
> Doth with his lofty and shrill-sounding throat
> Awake the god of day; and at his warning,
> Whether in sea or fire, in earth or air,
> The extravagant and erring spirit hies
> To his confine. . . .

Whether for Hamlet, mixture of good and evil as he is,
the o'er-crowing poison is a herald of eternal day or a sum-
moner to fast in fires is left a mystery. The reader, however, as the "extravagant and erring spirit," the spendthrift
and straying soul, is recalled to its proper bounds, must
wish for Hamlet and for every man, with Charity equal to
Horatio's, that "flights of angels sing thee to thy rest!" [53]

8
=

Lear's Equations

IN OUR observation and systematic study of nature, we shall take
as our starting-point the following basic principle: that nothing
whatever is produced from nothing by agency of the divine
under any circumstances.

So says Lucretius in beginning his exposition of the prototype of all materialisms and scientisms, *On the Nature of
the Universe* (I.148 ff.). And he continues:

For we mortals are hedged about by feelings of dread and awe
because we are spectators of multiform phenomena in earth and
sky to which we are unable to assign visible and comprehensible
causes and for whose explanation we have recourse to some concept of deity. But when once we have perceived the principle
that nothing can be created from nothing, then the road to the
goal of our inquiry lies clear and straight before us, and, discarding all notions of divine intervention, we are enabled to
understand the origins of particular things and the workings of
the universe.

In all literature, Lucretius' is the noblest and most im-
pressive statement of human despair precisely because he

does not blink the fact that, according to his lights, for one particular thing in the universe, namely Man, the road that leads to the goal of inquiry is a road that leads to death, to nothingness. If nothing can come from nothing, it follows that all things, save only the blind and unfeeling atom, the imperishable and unliving, purposeless and meaningless atom, go their way in time to certain annihilation. Nature, too, or all that we may sense of Nature, is similarly doomed. "O ruined piece of Nature!" Gloucester exclaims when he comes upon mad King Lear on the heath: "this great world / Shall so wear out to naught (IV.vi.138–39)" —a thought that Lucretius had in his time found most congenial.[1]

But unlike the Roman poet, Shakespeare was no philosopher, we have been repeatedly told. True, perhaps, yet happily voices have recently been raised to assert that this by no means prevented his being a thinker, and a profound one.[2] Instead of attempting to solve the problems of existence, he symbolized life's mysteries; instead of working analytically, he worked mythically. The mythic quality of such a play as *Lear* impresses every reader and every spectator.[3] The ceremonious implausibility of the opening scene has been remarked upon from a time at least as far back as Coleridge.[4] And equally formalistic and unnatural elements have aroused critics' ire or approbation: the final duel between Edmund and the Unknown Challenger, the leap of Gloucester over an imaginary Dover cliff, Lear's mad monologues, and the mock trial of Goneril and Regan in the hovel, to name only a few. It is as if Shakespeare, by choosing to construct his plot out of such wild improbabilities, had deliberately flouted all the canons of naturalism.[5] Could he have done so? Was naturalism abroad in Elizabethan England that it need be flouted?

Perhaps the profoundest significance of that rebirth of antiquity that we call the Renaissance was not that the European mind became reacquainted with classical art and literature and science, not even that by recovering a knowledge of the ancient world in true perspective it reacquired a sense of history. Rather, as we look back through subsequent intellectual development, we may see that of gravest import was the reemergence of a system of philosophic thought—naturalism, Stoicism, atomism, scientism—which in its nobility and complexity could constitute a serious rival to Christianity.[6] In late antiquity and in the High Middle Ages the Christian world-view had been able, by and large, to assimilate paganism, Platonism, and Aristotelianism. But the newly revived naturalism it could not assimilate. There were attempts during the Renaissance to do so, of course. There was, for instance, the Christian Stoicism of such men as Chapman and Justus Lipsius.[7] Even more indicative, however, of the course of thought in future centuries was the experiment of Bacon in compartmentalizing religion and science; relegating religion to a limbo of occasional faith, Bacon transferred human hopes from Supernature to Nature.[8] With this severance of Faith from Hope, already, one or more generations before Hobbes, Descartes, Newton, and Gassendi, philosophic mechanism was set in motion and had only to follow out its predestined way.

This was the intellectual atmosphere in which *King Lear* came to birth.[9]

It has often been called a pagan and a secular play; its Christian elements have also often been emphasized.[10] It would seem that to classify *Lear* either way calls for much qualification. It certainly is a Christian play, but its Christianity is mainly a matter of negative proof. It begins with the assumptions of secularism and bears these out to their

conclusion. And the conclusion is despair, horror, nothingness.[11] "As flies to wanton boys are we to the gods" (IV.i.36)
is the Q.E.D. of the naturalistic demonstration. With
Gloucester tormented and dead, Cordelia hanged and
dead, Lear maddened and dead, the curtain falls. "Is this
the promis'd end? Or image of that horror?" (V.iii.265–66)
is the ultimate question posed to the audience. Which is to
say: the Last Judgment is your judgment; you may believe
that it is this way if you will; but there are not lacking intimations of a better view.

It has been noted that when Shakespeare brings the villains of the drama on the stage he presents them as naturalists; Gloucester and Lear also begin their reasoning in a
naturalistic way. Lear's initial axiom is "Nothing can come
from nothing." [12] Lear's corollary is, "All things end in nothing." From these principles the play proceeds to draw certain equations and to show that they are invalid.

Equation One is the Equation of Logic: "Words equal
things."

Equation Two, the Equation of Causality, states that
"Things equal things," which is to say, "Effects equal their
causes."

Equation Three, the Equation of Analysis, maintains that
as far as mankind is concerned "Human beings equal
things," i.e. that "What a human being really is is the sum of
the things of which he is made."

Logic, causality, and analysis are the foundation-stones
of the scientific structure. (I take measurement and classification to be varieties of analysis.) Naturalism is that
philosophy which excludes consideration, and sometimes
denies the existence, of all reality that is not amenable to
approach by the scientific method. "Where there is no
mathematics, there is no science": naturalistic thought is

therefore necessarily equational thought. Opposed to this is
transcendental thought, which deals with mystery, which,
in turn, can be adequately symbolized only in terms of
myth.

To expose the insufficiency of these fundamental naturalistic equations, Shakespeare has resort to three myths, at
least: the Ordeal of the Riddle, the Debasement of the
King, and the Duel with the Unknown Champion.[13]

(An apology is doubtless in order here for this over-
schematic analysis of such a unified work of art as *King
Lear*. One can only plead in defense that such is the nature of criticism; if it is not to compete in kind with the
art work to which it is applied, it must employ a radically
different method of discourse. In short, it cannot escape
from those very limitations of language which we shall see
Shakespeare expose. Besides, the reader will note that the
three equations are basically one, stemming from a circular
concept of reality, in the same way that the three myths are
basically one, symbolizing the impingement of the transcendent on the actual.)

Words equal things: at first glance it may seem grossly
unfair to impute such an assumption to naturalists, since
they have been most careful in rejecting any hint of hypos-
tasization, being in fact the very group who have assigned
to a fictive "primitive mentality" such confusion of words
with the entities to which they refer. The proposition, however, does not state that words are identical with things,
but that they are equivalent, that, to put it otherwise, language, though somehow not a part of reality, can truthfully
reflect it. The inadequacy of this naturalistic assumption is
revealed most glaringly in the utter failure of logicians to
define "truth" itself. Every such attempt has come to grief
because "truth" is a mystery, being a term in language that

refers exclusively neither to language nor to non-language, but to a certain ethical relationship between the two. But naturalists assume that truth can be the more nearly approached the more narrowly circumscribed the area of non-verbal reference to which each single word is applied. This does not work very well, or at least does not get us very far into those realms of meaning that are most meaningful. Not even in the physical realm, disconcertingly enough, is accuracy always desirable. One recalls Pierre Duhem's discussion of the difficulties attendant on ascertaining the temperature at which a block of ice will melt under a certain pressure.[14] As the practical facts in the situation can be translated into any of a range of theoretical mathematical facts, it follows that the more precise the mensural terms are, the less accurate is the description. It would seem that there are innumerable situations where accuracy is inaccurate; Aristotle knew this, but the Neo-Aristotelians have forgotten it.

And at the beginning of the play, King Lear has never known it. The test that he sets for his daughters in the first scene is of course an impossible one.[15] Goneril, even in the midst of her falsehood, has an inkling of this; certainly words cannot "wield the matter" of love. But Cordelia, though she knows the right course to follow, to "love, and be silent" (I.i.64), is forced by her father to fall into that very mathematical bias that is his besetting intellectual sin. Little attention need be given to such efforts as have been made to justify Cordelia's later misfortunes by considering them the consequences of a tragic flaw of pride and obstinacy. The fact is, when Lear insists on words, words then she must produce, though knowing that all language must go wide of the mark.[16] And in the search for greater linguistic precision she offends against her own truth. "I love you according to my bond, no more nor less," "I return to you the duties you performed for me," "I shall give you half my love, and my husband the other half": these are indeed frigid mathematical computations in a sphere where mathematics should not enter. But, as has been said, she has been compelled to such hair-splitting, and she knows better.[17] She knows that words are not a mere reflection of reality, but that, by slipping into the realm of the ideal, they can anticipate reality and induce it to follow in their wake. So at the end of the scene she will not call her sisters' faults as they are named (I.i.270–74). Kent also, Cordelia's counterpart, apparently hopes that Goneril and Regan will bring their behavior into line with their protestations, wishing "that good effects may spring from words of love" (I.i.188).

On the other hand, Lear's linguistic madness is deeply ingrained and not easily curable. It is his trust in the equivalence of words and things which prompts him in the first place to his foolish enterprise of surrendering parts of his kingdom which shall reproduce proportionately in physical wealth and extent the expressed affections of his daughters. He is obviously accustomed to having his words converted immediately into things; throughout his presumably long reign, to command has been for him tantamount to having his language take instant shape in reality. He has thus become blinded to the slippery behavior of words, their tendency to glide away from the particular to the universal, to rigidify that universal into an ideal, and, in reversion, to force actual non-verbal particulars into this ideal mold.

He should not have been old before he had been wise, as the Fool reminds him (I.v.49–50); his tardy education commences with the word "daughter." A daughter who is a daughter yet who is not what a daughter should be is no daughter at all. Lear is shocked at the inappropriateness of applying the term to a person who so little fulfills the definition. In the scene where he is reprimanded by Goneril for the misconduct of his knights, his first reaction is to ask, "Are you our daughter?" (I.iv.241); "I should be false persuaded I had daughters," he continues, and, when Goneril suggests that he "a little disquantity" his train, he posts away in fury to Regan, exclaiming, "Yet have I left a daughter." Simultaneously he begins to doubt the identity of "Lear" with the Lear now being so un-ideally abused, and the identity of Goneril with the abuser. "Does any here know me? This is not Lear," he rants, and of Goneril he inquires, "Your name, fair gentlewoman?"

Consequently, when he runs across the Dover plain "fantastically dressed in flowers" (IV.vi), the discrepancy between words and ideal reality drives him to the depths of his madness. Swinging to the opposite extreme, he weighs nature in the balance and finds it wanting; the word "adultery" is only a word, no more, and "justice" is a mere mocking sound.[18] Because the natural does not correspond to the ideal always, he concludes that it never does so: there is no ideal ("None does offend, none, I say none"— IV.vi.173) and nature, which is all that exists, is rotten. And yet his perception of this discrepancy is his first step back on the road to sanity. In his recovery scene (IV.vii), when he awakens in Cordelia's camp, he doubts that his hands are his hands, that Cordelia is his child, that her tears are wet, but his doubt is exactly the opposite of that outraged indignation before Goneril which was poured out when his word was not instantly translated into the deed, being rather at this point a realization that things are not always as they are named.

Shakespeare symbolizes this refutation of the equation "Words equal things" by using a folklore motif, the "Love like salt" story, that appears in many versions in many parts of the world.[19] The story, in brief, is that a daughter is asked by her father how much she loves him. She replies, "I love you as I love salt." Angered, he banishes her from his presence, but in the ensuing days he learns how necessary salt really is. He therefore admits his mistake, and there is a reconciliation.[20]

Obviously the tale is an example of the well-known primitive delight in riddles; and riddles and similar nonsense formulae, we may suspect, were not originally mere amusements of children. Along with other arcane lore, they must have figured in initiations into *rites de passage*, or into secret phratries, or into professional shamanism itself.[21] Riddling ordeals were among the barriers that the initiate had to surpass before he could undergo the rebirth into a higher order of being. Acquiring the answer to the riddle gave him insight into the hidden nature of the world and bestowed on him powers that he had not previously possessed. In the usual form of the "Love like salt" stories the riddling test leads to double suffering, for both father and offspring. One is reminded, too, of how Siegfried, after fathoming Wotan's riddles, is able to break the god's spear and enter the magic circle of fire unscathed, and of how Oedipus, after replying to the Sphinx's question, which had meant death to so many before him, automatically becomes a man above the common level of men. Shakespeare's more immediate sources had already dropped the answer, "I love you like salt," but had kept the question intact, thus retaining the essential feature: that there is a lack of one-to-one correspondence between words and things. Yet the philosophical insight into the vagaries of language, into what one may call the Mystery of the Word,[22] since it reflects the mystery of man's mind itself, was implicit even in the primitive initiatory ceremony.

One cannot help remembering in connection with this line of thought about language that one of the problems troubling philosophers of science is the suspicion that mathematics, the quintessential scientific language, may be only a vast and elaborate tautology, and that all of scientific theory itself may be only a "logical construct." This is not surprising, once we realize that mathematics is intended to describe a natural universe which for practical purposes must be thought of as a closed equilibrium, in which nothing can disappear without being replaced by its equivalent. From the assumption that reality is stable enough to be described it is easy to proceed to the assumption that its stability is constant beneath its apparent multiformity. Hence we arrive at the second naturalistic equation: things equal things; or effects equal causes, causes equal effects. Form succeeds form; the younger generation crowds out—in fact, devours—the old ("age is unnecessary"); nothing comes from nothing, nothing can be produced from nothing; but all things change into all other things as the circle of nature, that Heraclitean fire, ceaselessly turns and burns.[23]

So the great image of the Wheel of Fire dominates *Lear*.[24] And the result for a human being, who must from this viewpoint be regarded as a thing made up of things which are doomed to disintegrate and reintegrate into different things, is despair and meaninglessness. For in the over-all tautology he is only a term whose meaning is to be found only if he is redefined in other terms, which in turn may be redefined in others, and so on *ad infinitum*. All mortals, then, like Lear, are bound upon a wheel of fire which their

poor tears scald like burning lead (IV.vii.46–48). Lear's
first equation then merges into the second, for not merely
did he wish to have his daughters' love reproduced in
words, but he also wished to compensate their love by a
proportionate amount of his physical domain.

Here, of course, the equating process breaks down. However necessary a principle the conservation of matter and
energy may be for our manipulation of the physical, it is
obviously inadequate when we proceed to the realm of the
ethical. Yet if this world and this life are all that exists,
which is the basic assumption of naturalism, it is reasonable
to suppose that our deserts should be rewarded with this-
worldly satisfaction and our demerits punished with this-
worldly pain. Since the plot of *Lear* is contrived in such a
way as to negate emphatically that this is so, many critics,
who take Lear's second equation for granted, are reduced
to reading the drama as a celebration of despair. Like Lear,
they are loath to be parted from the naive notion that
Nature's compensatory principle is a matter of visible
reciprocation. Lear begins to learn his lesson when his acts
of bounteous giving are reversed by his two elder daughters, who progressively reduce the size of his retinue; yet
the pattern of his former thinking persists: when Regan
allows him but twenty-five knights, he pitifully turns again
to Goneril, whom he has cursed, with the words: "I'll go
with thee: / Thy fifty yet doth double five-and-twenty, /
And thou art twice her love" (II.iv.262–63).

That such equational reasoning is inadequate the critics
might have perceived from a careful scrutiny of two juxta-
posed speeches at the end of the play, where Albany, "with
easy, unthinking optimism," [25] promises (V.iii.303 ff.) that
"All friends shall taste / The wages of their virtue, and
all foes / The cup of their deservings"—a hint that he is

about to repeat all the errors that the old King had made before him—only to be interrupted, and contradicted, by Lear's lament of inequality: "And my poor fool is hang'd! No, no, no life! / Why should a dog, a horse, a rat, have life / And thou no breath at all?"

For Nature, viewed as the All, as the naturalist views it, is not a system of smooth replacement and recompense, but a kind of balanced chaos in which things devour and obliterate one another "like monsters of the deep" (IV.ii.50). It is not a child's game of handy-dandy, but a war to the death, in which no creature may subsist except on the slain bodies of his fellows.[26] So Gloucester says, naturalistically if erroneously, about astrology: ". . . though the wisdom of nature can reason it thus and thus, yet nature finds itself scourged by the sequent effects. . . ." (I.ii.116 ff.). Nature annihilates itself: "Is it not as this mouth should tear this hand / For lifting food to't?" (III.iv.15–16), Lear says of his "pelican daughters."

It follows that good and evil are obtrusions into Nature; they strike the circle of natural causation, as it were, at a tangent.[27] ("Some good I mean to do / Despite of mine own nature" [V.iii.245–46], says Edmund at the last.) [28] According to Occam's Law, they should to naturalists be dispensable concepts, provided of course the naturalists could ignore the ethical and personal aspects of their own experience.[29] That good and evil are superfluities from the standpoint of causation can easily be seen from the consideration that an evil action is, and has to be, just as adequately caused as a good one, even as an erroneous conclusion, to the logicians' embarrassment, is as fully caused as a truthful one. Nevertheless, ethical conditions are obviously operative in the stream of cause and effect, striking it, as said before, at a tangent and altering its direction or intensity: Edmund means to *do* some good, despite of his own nature.

The explanation seems to be that causality may be viewed externally and impersonally, as the scientist views it, whereupon it becomes a sheer supplantation of things by other things, but that this is not the only possible way to view it. Schopenhauer and Nietzsche were quite right to point out that the genesis of our whole concept of causality probably lies in a personal and internal approach, since we most intimately perceive the working of one action's leading to another when the spiritual decisions of the will eventuate, through an uninterrupted continuum, in physical consequences: we say silently to our right arm, for instance, "Rise up," and it rises; the intention passes imperceptibly into its fulfillment. This is what gives us that indelible impression of causality as a current of power streaming through a series of events, an impression that no amount of Humean argument about mere sequentiality can eradicate. T. H. Huxley used to dumbfound his hearers into acquiescence with his own determinism by posing the question: "I ask you, gentlemen, can you change your constitutions?;" one can only regret that no Schopenhauerian in the audience ever countered with the obvious reply, "Of course I can, to a limited degree, by the way I choose to eat and sleep and exercise." Similarly opponents of free will love to quote Spinoza's remark (*Epistle* 58) to the effect that a falling stone, if it had a conscious mind, would think it was going toward the ground because it wanted to. But Spinoza's observation is manifest nonsense: my own body has often been tripped and thrown to the ground, but I never at any time supposed I wanted to fall. Possession of a conscious mind implies by definition that one knows the difference between occasions when one is acting freely as a person and those when one is being acted on as a thing.

The upshot is that man may be less logically justified in transferring the impersonal analogy to his own inner life than he would be in transferring the personal analogy to the outer universe, thus picturing the latter as primarily an interplay of personal wills.[30] According to such a world-view, life then becomes a confrontation of an I with a Thou, or with several Thous, which by the rationalist is regarded as an aberration of the primitive and mythic mentality, but which such philosophers as Martin Buber and certain existentialists have shown can perfectly well be entertained by a sophisticated modern thinker.[31] King Lear, admittedly, is never without the conviction that natural phenomena are set in motion by a will; he begins, however, as does Edmund, by identifying the will with Nature itself ("Hear, Nature, hear! Dear Goddess, hear!") and proceeds with an attempt to subdue this will to his own (with his orders to the winds in the storm scenes). Only gradually does he approach the conception that these phenomena are expressions of a Will infinitely superior to himself ("as if we were God's spies" [V.iii.17]—or "gods' spies": it makes little difference), and only perhaps at the very end, if then, does he arrive at the height of realization (which Gloucester reaches after his failure at suicide) that this transcendent Will is "opposeless" and through its working on the individual human being has purposes for him which are not his own purposes.

Enid Welsford showed a generation ago that Lear is the Mock-King, the Fool-King, the Holy Fool, the Scapegoat.[32] By his travails and humiliations, throughout the central part of the drama, he shows himself to be the same sort of figure that Pentheus is in Euripides Bacchae or Oedipus in Sophocles' *Oedipus Rex*. It is needless to elaborate on the implications of this theory; for Shakespeare uses this myth to counter and confute a mere mechanical concept of causality, what we have called Lear's second equation. When the personal element enters into considerations of causality, then the equational balance is upset: causes may be less or larger than their effects, effects less or larger than their causes.

Just as the Mock-King in the ritual was loaded with honors that he did not merit, so he was subsequently afflicted with sufferings that he did not deserve. In the same way Lear and his companion figure Gloucester become "more sinned against than sinning." [33] As the Fool, or Lord of Misrule, Lear reaches his apogee in the Mad Scene on the heath (IV.vi): [34] like the Christ-surrogate and fertility-deity that he is, he enters crowned with "all the idle weeds that grow / In our sustaining corn" (IV.iv.5–6); he proceeds, like the Fool Bishop, the *episcopus stultus*, to proclaim a general leveling of status, to indulge in talk calculated to incite sexual license, to preach on the "great stage of fools," and to parody the Christian remission of sins, since he himself is the atonement-sacrifice who wipes all slates clean. He exits in a chase that suggests the *Regifugium*, the ritual Chase of the King. [35] Finally, after the scene, he undergoes a symbolic death and resurrection, and, as in the Mummers' Play, is brought back to life by a physician. [36]

To make clear the superfluity of the factors of good and evil, it is of interest to behold how Shakespeare has played off two of the sisters, Goneril and Cordelia, against each other. Goneril is a perfect illustration of the Biblical text: "It must needs be that offences come; but woe to that man by whom the offence cometh!" (*Matt.* 18:7). She is the embodiment of the superfluity of evil; she anticipates the wickedness of other men and strikes her blow first. She "must do something, and i' the heat" (I.i.312); she instructs her steward Oswald to "put on what weary negligence you please," as she would "have it come to question" (I.iii.13–14); and she informs her husband, "Fools do those villains pity who are punish'd / Ere they have done their mischief" (IV.ii.54–55). One might say that Goneril, assuming a balanced circularity of natural causation, thinks that it is a small matter whether a man requites an injury before or after it is tendered, except that in the former case he shows himself more clearly not to be a "moral fool" and except that to "fear too far is safer than trust too far." No wonder, then, that when Lear is informed that she and her tigerish sister Regan "desperately are dead," he merely replies, "Ay, so I think" (V.iii.294), as though they could have died in no other way than "desperately" and "untimely," as Cornwall and Oswald and Edmund do, dying without that hope which none of them has ever possessed.[37]

On the other hand, Cordelia represents that superfluity of good which goes the second mile and which, when sued for a coat, lets one have the cloak also. What she "well intends, she'll do't before she speaks" (I.i.228–29). Because of what France calls her "tardiness in nature / Which often leaves the history unspoke / That it intends to do" (I.i.238–240) she is "most rich, being poor; / Most choice, forsaken; and most lov'd, despis'd" (I.i.253 ff.), and she seems to fulfill the prophecy of the Fool in having "more / Than two tens to a score" (I.iv.140–41).[38] She moreover interrupts the chain of cause-and-effect by ignoring and nullifying the precedent actions that might have been of offence to her; her response to Lear's "If you have poison for me, I will drink it. / I know you do not love me; for your sisters / Have, as I do remember, done me wrong: / You have some

cause, they have not," is the ineffably poignant "No cause,
no cause" (IV.vii.72 ff.). She is Forgiveness incarnate, and
from her Lear learns the lesson: "When thou dost ask me
blessing, I'll kneel down, / And ask of thee forgiveness"
(V.iii.10–11). In Cordelia the natural reciprocal law of Justice is completed in the transcendent principle of Grace.[39]
She is a "soul in bliss," who redeems "nature from the general curse," a sort of personified intervention of Super-
Nature into the natural scheme of causation, escaping the
Wheel of Fire precisely because she confounds natural re-
ciprocity by returning good for evil, love for hatred.

We come to the last of the naturalistic equations, the one
that states that "Human beings equal things." This assumption took its most pernicious form in the Stoic-Cynic doctrine of *autarkeia*, "self-sufficiency." [40] It was believed that
the essential self is a composite of simple and easily satisfied needs, that these few needs can be ascertained with
the aid of reason, that the self thus stripped of superfluities
can constitute itself independent and self-sufficient, and
that in this way its particular place in nature can be defined
and its particular natural duties discharged. Far from regarding the self as a transcendent *infinitum* of potential development, the dominant thought of pagan philosophy
worked in the opposite direction, toward a diminution, a
retrenchment, a cutting down.[41]

Lear's journey through the storm is, from this point of
view, a symbolic exposition of the inadequacies of this philosophy.[42] Forcibly stripped of the enjoyment of luxury and
the prerogatives of power, the old king not unnaturally supposes that he is to be taught a lesson in Stoic self-sufficiency; for the Stoic sage, having cut himself down to the
bare essentials, could be calm amid the vicissitudes of external fortune.[43] So when the tempest breaks upon him,

Lear tries "with presented nakedness" to "outface / The winds and persecutions of the sky" (II.iii.11–12) and "Strives in his little world of man to out-storm / The to-and-fro conflicting wind and rain" (III.i.10–11). And having encountered Edgar (III.iv), Lear mistakes him for a pagan philosopher, noting that in all respects Edgar fulfills the requirements, since he wears only a ragged cloak, lives in a hovel or in the open, drinks ditch-water, and eats "rats and mice and such small deer." [44] Hence Lear addresses him as "noble philosopher," "learned Theban," and "good Athenian," and wishes to discuss "the cause of thunder" with him,[45] having already apparently recognized in him the model of the natural way to live: "Is man no more than this? Consider him well. Thou owest the worm no silk, the beast no hide, the sheep no wool, the cat no perfume. Ha! here's three on's are sophisticated." Yet there are notes of disillusionment in this discovery of the Stoic *autarkeia*, for Lear continues: "Thou art the thing itself; unaccommodated man is no more but such a poor, bare, forked animal as thou art." [46]

It is a philosophy of reasoned despair that Lear is approaching, and though he is willing to signalize his embracing it by tearing off his clothes, he has already prefaced his conversion with the observation that Edgar would "be better in his grave than to answer with his uncovered body this extremity of the skies." That this retrenchment to essential needs is ultimately no way to live, but merely a way to die continually, Lear should have recollected from his treatment by his elder daughters, whose cutting down of his knights from fifty to twenty-five to ten to five to one to none symbolizes just such a process of reduction, and who provoke him to his great speech beginning, "O reason not the need; our basest beggars / Are in the poorest things superfluous: / Allow not nature more than nature needs, / Man's life is cheap as beast's" (II.iv.267 ff.).[47]

The truth is that reason cannot arrive at a natural minimum to which a human being can be reduced.[48] The minimum that reason leads to when it tries to ascertain the necessities of a man's existence in the scheme of nature is precisely nothing; for there is no reason why a man should exist at all.[49] Thus the symbol of man in the natural universe is Lear tearing "his white hair, / Which the impetuous blasts, with eyeless rage, / Catch in their fury, and make nothing of" (III.i.7–9) and running unbonneted through the rain, bidding "what will take all" (III.i.14–15). The Stoic compromise, to be contented with little, is a false one, because Nature takes all, takes even that little away. Edgar's misfortunes typify this truth; betrayed and disinherited, he comforts himself with the thought, "To be worst / The lowest and most dejected thing of fortune, / Stands still in esperance" (IV.i.2–4), only to be straightway harrowed by the spectacle of his blinded and persecuted father and forced to concede, "The worst is not, / So long as we can say, 'This is the worst.'" Just as "the clearest Gods, who make them honors / Of men's impossibilities" (IV.vi. 74–75) can lift a man from plane to plane of transcendent being, each level unimaginable before, so the strokes of fortune can debase him from depth to depth of misery, to fling him away into final nothingness.

Nor is mere endurance the answer. The Stoics made much of the virtue of fortitude, and many a critic has found in *Lear* the preachment of a Stoical sermon. Yet it would seem that Shakespeare took some pains to show that patience is not enough. Patience may indeed be the "true need" as far as one's attitude toward Nature is concerned: this Lear intimates, as has been noted more than once, when he breaks off his "Reason not the need" speech with "But for true need,— / You heavens, give me that patience, patience I need!" And this patience he seems to have acquired in large measure by the time he delivers another climactic speech, the one beginning, "Come let's away to prison" (V.iii.8 ff.), with all its essentially pagan-philosophical implications of withdrawal from the harsh realities and troublous involvements of the world. Yet by a supreme stroke of genius, Shakespeare did not let his plot rest here, but swept the action on to the deaths of both father and daughter.[50]

Patience does not suffice.[51] A man may be patient unto death, and patient in dying, but afterward his patience is as if it had never been, if this life and this world are all. If this life and this world are all, what is the meaning of this life and this world? They have no meaning.[52] Their meaning, like all meanings, must be found in something that is not themselves, and hence in some supernatural and transcendent realm of being.[53] Throughout the last part of *King Lear* this realm begins to vouchsafe glimpses of itself. God, or the gods, intervene to show that man is more than a thing in nature.[54] The Myth of the Unknown Champion, who appears out of the blue to overcome triumphant evil, serves as refutation to Lear's third equation. Like Lohengrin from Monsalvat, like the many guileless fools of medieval legend who appear in blazonless or unfamiliar arms to upset or displace the acknowledged, but sin-stained, masters of the tourney, Edgar appears against Edmund to strike a blow for heavenly justice.[55] Thus the transcendent power of divinity is made manifest in human affairs. And yet these divine powers do not thereby rescue Cordelia and Lear and, so contradicting themselves, vindicate the merely natural order.[56] Father and daughter, having taken upon themselves "the mystery of things," are taken up into the mystery that is beyond all.[57]

King Lear ends with a question, the religious question of faith: Is there another life than this which gives meaning to this? Many a critic has answered no. Shakespeare permits them to do so, provided that they will face the full horror of meaninglessness that such an answer entails.[58] Yet one cannot help suspecting that he himself took a different road, the road that blind Gloucester took to Dover, with its wonderfully symbolic "leap in the dark," that proves to be a leap away from the fiends to blessedness, from despair to hope,[59] and that he intended to convey to his auditor, as Edgar assures his father, "Thy life's a miracle." The noblest answer of naturalism is not noble enough. So unreasonable are the conditions of man's life, so outrageous are the humiliations inflicted on him by an inexorable Nature, that they can be coped with only by a response equally outrageous and unreasonable: the response of love and faith.[60] A man must not merely be patient, but he must carry through the resolve of Lear: "No, I will be the pattern of all patience; / I will say nothing" (III.ii.37–38). The "pattern of all patience" is Christ himself, who said nothing at His trial; the Christlike figure of Cordelia likewise said "Nothing" in her ordeal: [61] yet in spite of Lear's and the naturalist's "Nothing can come from nothing," the spectator of this tragedy is left with the feeling that out of such "Nothings" as Christ's and Cordelia's comes nothing less than all.[62]

9
=

Eliot's MURDER IN THE CATHEDRAL

Myth and History

THERE are three possible human reactions to suffering: the natural, the stoical, and the saintly.[1]

The natural human reaction is one of simple avoidance. It is the outcome of human weakness, and has as its corollary that appetite for pleasure which is characteristic of the human creature at its most undeveloped. The First of the Tempters who appear to Becket in Act One of *Murder in the Cathedral* holds out the bait of pleasure (I.275–76):

> Clergy and laity may return to gaiety,
> Mirth and sportfulness need not walk warily.

And this Tempter goes on to paint the round of pleasure-seeking as a development concomitant with the circle of the seasons (I.279 ff.):

> Spring has come in winter. Snow in the branches
> Shall float as sweet as blossoms. Ice along the ditches
> Mirror the sunlight.

But Becket finds a temptation of this sort a particularly easy one to resist. Its strength of appeal depends upon the possession of lusty sensual urges; the Tempter has "come twenty years too late" (I.308).

> The natural vigor in the venial sin
> Is the way in which our lives begin (I.678–79),

but the Tempter is deceitful in proposing that to a man of Becket's maturity "the good times past" can "come again." The Archbishop is quick to point out to him that though the circularity of the generations of men, in its repetitiveness, may parallel the circularity of the seasonal succession, the life of one individual man cannot, strictly speaking, be such a circle. If it were so, the individual might equate his own career with the Wheel of Nature itself and suppose that its rotation is an expression of his own being, while actually the contrary is the case (289 ff.):

> Only
> The fool, fixed in his folly, may think
> He can turn the wheel on which he turns.[2]

Becket's reasons for rejecting this lowest order of temptation, the positive pursuit of pleasure, furnish a commentary on the lowest order of human reaction to pain. To take up the attitude that the proper way to deal with suffering is to dodge it, if one can, is to make an attempt at turning one's life into a meaningless circularity, a treadmill of routine in imitation of the seasons. To make such an attempt is the overmastering wish of the Chorus,[3] the old and poor Women of Canterbury, who, because they are poor, have never had the opportunities for sensual delight that Becket as Chancellor has enjoyed, and, because they are old, have lost such capacities for positive enjoyment as they once

pleasure

possessed. Like all good Epicureans, they have finally been reduced to a mere negativity, the avoidance of unusual suffering and the endurance of minimal pain. They are content if they are left alone (I.25), and wish to be like the laborer who "bends to his piece of earth, earth-colour, his own colour, / Preferring to pass unobserved" (I.28–29). *Lathe biosas,* said the Epicurean: "live the hidden life." Such "small folk who live among small things" (I.194) want to merge the routine of their existence with the round of the "quiet seasons" (I.30), not wishing "anything to happen" (I.153), except that (I.164 ff.)

> One year is a year of rain,
> Another a year of dryness,
> One year the apples are abundant,
> Another year the plums are lacking.

They are "living and partly living" (I.156), for "Human kind cannot bear very much reality" (II.232).[4]

Yet three facts of nature break in upon this comforting round and shatter its eventless perfection. One is the fact that much of pleasure's attractiveness is afforded by novelty; Becket may reject sensual temptation offhandedly because he has fully explored its domain, and when the Second Tempter appears to him with the not quite as obvious allurements of power over others, this being the pleasure peculiarly appealing to middle life, his satiety of experience enables him to resist that also. No particular credit is due him for such manifestations of virtue, nor does he accord himself any, since by the very nature of time such enticements are robbed of freshness, which is their greatest attraction. They can no longer satisfy curiosity, the natural human appetite for knowledge, which, as Aristotle says, affords us the greatest pleasure when its needs are served.

The second fact of nature that militates against the ordinary man's hedonistic system of happiness is the inevitability of pain in the progress of time. No dexterity in the avoidance of discomfort can be expected to succeed completely or permanently. The Chorus know this, and are willing to settle for an average amount of life's usual troubles; they are even willing to live hopelessly, so as to be spared the disappointments that hope unavoidably entails. "What tribulation" can there be, they ask (I.4–5), "With which we are not already familiar?" Familiarity, as it detracts from pleasure by eliminating novelty, likewise diminishes pain by lessening fear of the unknown. Yet the compromise offered by the Women of Canterbury, who are ready to offer their "private terrors" and "particular shadows" and "secret fears" (I.183–84) as sufficient expiation, is disallowed. Their supposition that a human being can get by with an amount of suffering that can be deemed moderate is an illusion. To live life through to the end costs "nothing less than all." Every man must share in the doom of the world (I.185 ff.):

But now a great fear is upon us, a fear not of one but of many,
A fear like birth and death, when we see birth and death alone
In a void apart.

These two inevitabilities, birth and death, our arrival out of the utterly unknowing and our procession into the utterly unknown, are of all things most common and most fearful. So the Chorus continue:

We

Are afraid in a fear which we cannot know, which we cannot
face, which none understands,
And our hearts are torn from us, our brains unskinned like the
layers of an onion, our selves are lost lost

In a final fear which none understands. O Thomas Archbishop,
O Thomas our Lord, leave us and leave us be, in our humble and
   tarnished frame of existence, leave us; do not ask us
To stand to the doom on the house, the doom on the Archbishop,
   the doom on the world.

But the clamor of the women for anonymity actually partakes of the very doom they fear; by wishing to be nothing they fall back in the direction of that very nothingness where their "selves are lost lost." Their claim is therefore disregarded, as has been said, and they are "drawn into the pattern of fate" (I.194) and forced to bear witness to a supposedly exceptional horror, which, however, like "the skull beneath the skin," is bound to emerge eventually through the surface of the everyday precisely because it lies at the foundations.

So the third fact is the fact of death, the incessancy of dying in time.[5] Time is itself a perpetual dying; this imminence of nothingness, of loss of being, is the "great fear" that renders trivial our lesser fears about the disappearance of pleasure or the advent of pain. To descend in the scale of being, even without a diminution of physical existence, is a step that the human mind cannot contemplate without horror. And if the laborer actually were to be faced with becoming as insentient as the earth whose protective covering he tries to assume, he would be smitten with that same frigid dread that the Women of Canterbury express at the scene of Becket's martyrdom. Not mere cessation of life, but diminution of being is to be shuddered at.

                  I have seen
      Rings of light coiling downwards, leading
        To the horror of the ape (II.195–97).

The ape, of course, is not horrid in itself, but only as representing a step downward from the human being, beneath whom is ranged all of life's absurd and often repulsive multiformity, the scaly-winged, the lunatic, the barely senti-ent, the putrid-fleshed—owl, jackal, rat, bird, beetle, viper, fish: with this swarming, self-devouring horde man can only acknowledge his material kinship in a sympathy that savors of disgust.[6]

> I have lain on the floor of the sea and breathed with the breath-ing of the sea-anemone, swallowed with ingurgitation of the sponge (II.192).

Such palingenetic recapitulation reminds man that the whole mass of living matter is one, pulsing according to the alternating principles of death and life, which at points are almost indistinguishable:

> I have eaten
> Smooth creatures still living, with the strong salt taste of living things under sea (II.187–88).

Beyond Death also there may lurk this reduction to minimal being, so much more repellent than a clean non-existence; this possibility is revealed in the next extended pronounce-ment of the Chorus:

> And behind the face of Death the Judgement
> And behind the Judgement the Void, more horrid than active shapes of hell;
> Emptiness, absence . . . (II.277–78)

> nothing with nothing,
> Not what we call death, but what beyond death is not death,
> We fear, we fear (286–88).

If such a passive hell should be, it would be, so to speak, a kind of freezing into eternity of a state representative of the death-in-life and life-in-death that is our pleasure-seek-

ing, pain-avoiding existence in time. So much, Eliot seems
to say, for the natural reaction.

The second reaction to suffering, the stoical, arises out of
the first.[7] Stoicism is not merely grim endurance of pain,
though this is all the word usually means in popular apprehension; but it must be admitted that a certain degree of
grimness is never absent from the stoic attitude. There is
certainly never any joy in this philosophy, which seems to
be logically resultant from the resignation that comes when
one realizes that suffering cannot be entirely avoided. Dr.
Johnson's former schoolfellow, who found it impossible to
become a philosopher because "cheerfulness kept breaking
in," must have been identifying all philosophy with stoicism. The stoic is obliged to perceive the grand design of
nature, which, in view of the historical Stoa's near-worship
of the heavenly bodies and admiration for their perfect
circularity of motion, one may well interpret as an end-
lessly circular design. And he is also obliged to perceive his
own particular position in this design and to fill this position
with full consciousness of duty discharged. (Small letters
and the present tense are in order throughout this discussion, since in our own culture most thinking people who
are not Christians are to all intents stoics, and in the unthinking popular mind there is much confusion between
the two.)

The stoic cultivates the classic natural virtues, justice,
prudence, temperance, and fortitude, and has no inkling of
the theological trinity, faith, hope, and charity. His justice
causes him to perform his duties in the political and social
worlds; his prudence leads him to demarcate the limitations
of his own nature and of his position in the scheme of nature as a whole; his temperance involves a retrenchment of
desires in conformity with these limitations; and his forti-

tude enables him to tolerate the niggardliness or disad-
vantages of his natural endowments and accidental circumstances. He prudently scales down his ideals within the
confines of practicality; of faith, with its advice to follow
through to the ideal in its pristine fullness and with its pro-
visional guarantee that the ideal and the practical are ultimately the same in essence, he takes no account. He
courageously accepts his fate, as it appears to be allotted by
Nature, but refuses to know charity, which is to love that
supernatural perfection of which one's own and others'
earthly destinies are only the indication. He anticipates
self-satisfaction by reducing the self which needs to be
satisfied, but of genuine hope, which is the desire to desire
what one ought to desire, he has not the slightest notion. It
will be seen that in spite of its vaunted outward-turning
contemplation of the vast cosmos, stoicism tends to end in
self-absorption, a kind of pulling-in of the skirts about the
self: self-obduration, self-satisfaction, self-pride are its besetting vices.

There is no overt representation of stoicism in *Murder in
the Cathedral;* nevertheless, the opposition between the
stoic sage in Becket and the Christian saint in Becket constitutes the basic conflict of the plot. Eliot recognizes that
stoicism is the only really dangerous opponent of Christianity in modern cultural life. Of course, the church-versus-
state controversy that furnishes the major part of the plot
complications is only the most spectacular and frequent
form of the clash between stoic and Christian attitudes.
The Chorus, like the ordinary man when cornered, rise to
the comparative height of philosophic endurance, with the
chill comfort that suffering has its limit in natural cessation
and the forgetfulness induced by routine (II.400 ff.):

The terror by night that ends in daily action,
The terror by day that ends in sleep;
But the talk in the market-place, the hand on the broom,
The nighttime heaping of the ashes,
The fuel laid on the fire at daybreak,
These acts marked a limit to our suffering.
Every horror had its definition,
Every sorrow had a kind of end:
In life there is not time to grieve long.

In these lines the Chorus obey the natural human impulse, so much elaborated in our own day, to degrade evil into a series of problems which can be solved by rational definition and appropriate action, action leading either to direct attack on the circumstances or merely to distraction. So stoicism, with its prudential, political approach, is inimical to the sense of mystery.

The Chorus, however, immediately thereafter recognize that there is a mysterious immensity of evil that knows no bounds:

But this, this is out of life, this is out of time,
An instant eternity of evil and wrong.
We are soiled by a filth that we cannot clean, united to supernatural vermin,
It is not we alone, it is not the house, it is not the city that is defiled,
But the world that is wholly foul.

Two of the Tempters also, the Second and the Third, base the strength of their appeals on the typically stoic virtue of justice, which finds expression in duty and patriotism. Unfortunately for them their claims cancel each other, since the Second Tempter locates patriotism in service of the king, whereas the Third locates it in the cause of

the rebellious barons. Moreover, the justice of the appeals
is specious. The Second Tempter's invitation to Becket to
resume the Chancellorship, though it is couched in terms of
"dispensing justice" (I.351 ff.):

> To set down the great, protect the poor,
> Beneath the throne of God can man do more?
> Disarm the ruffian, strengthen the laws,
> Rule for the good of the better cause,

is revealed at the outset as the naked attractiveness of
power. But this wielding of power, so much more sub-
stantial than the "two files of shadows," the shadowy chase
after pleasure and the shadowy longing for God, is in-
advertently, but logically, shown to end in what is "solid
substance" and a "permanent possession" indeed, namely
the "templed tomb, monument of marble." The Third
Tempter, too, cuts the ground from beneath his arguments
by offering a duty that is in actuality a revolt from duty; his
political system, the "rise of a new constellation," can appear only upon the setting of the old, and can only be as
impermanent. The proffered temptation and the whole
stoic attempt to remedy the defects of one political arrange-
ment merely by replacing it with another have already
been rejected by Becket (I.393 ff.):

> Those who put their faith in worldly order
> Not controlled by the order of God,
> In confident ignorance, but arrest disorder,
> Make it fast, breed fatal disease,
> Degrade what they exalt.

The Fourth, unexpected, Tempter is stoicism, the cultivation of the self, as it enters into the very sanctum of
Christianity, wearing the very robes of saintliness. But of
this later.

Finally, the murdering Knights themselves are stoic ex-
emplars.[8] In the semi-comic speeches which they address
to the audience after killing Becket, speeches which parody
the judicial and parliamentary procedures which were
eventually to be established as a result of this very struggle
of King, Church, and People,[9] they stake their case on fundamental stoic principles, and the fact that their case, in
the context, remains jarringly absurd points up the principles' inadequacy. Reginald Fitz Urse introduces the
other three with an evocation of the sense of justice implanted in mankind; William de Traci delineates the
murder as a disinterested discharge of duty, the unpleasant
consequences of which the quartet are prepared to face
manfully; Hugh de Morville underscores the primacy of patriotism, social justice, and secular order; and Richard Brito
explains the necessity of eliminating anything which threatens to transgress its limit in the natural and political cosmos. Their rebuttal and condemnation are pronounced by
the Third Priest (II.601 ff.): [10]

> In the small circle of pain within the skull
> You still shall tramp and tread one endless round
> Of thought, to justify your action to yourselves,
> Weaving a fiction which unravels as you weave,
> Pacing forever in the hell of make-believe
> Which never is belief. . . .

Here the Priest clearly shows that the insufficiency of the
Knights' pleas is no other than the insufficiency of the stoic
attitude, which in its preoccupation with self must ultimately be reduced to an unending, meaningless, treadmill
circularity, "the small circle of pain within the skull," and
by its rejection of faith and hope must finally divorce itself
from the all-embracing order that encompasses the order

of the natural cosmos and must make shift with a poor imitation of the supernatural virtues, namely the justice that has as its sole activity the justification of oneself, "the hell of make-believe which never is belief."

Now to consider the saint's approach to suffering, which differs from the hedonistic and the stoical because of the addition of these very supernatural virtues.[11] First, the saint adds faith. Faith is the virtue complementary of the intellect, being man's acknowledgment in humility of his own mental limitations. It is simply the assumption that life makes sense.[12] It transcends prudence, which is the taking into consideration of all that the individual perceives to exist, by positing further that this perceptible whole, in spite of its chaotic appearance, is actually only part of a pattern that moves in time, through time, and beyond time for its completion. Faith is therefore, from an intellectual standpoint, that "still point of the turning world" which engrossed Eliot's attention throughout the composition of *Murder in the Cathedral* and the nearly contemporary *Four Quartets*. We recall Becket's opening speech (I.209 ff.), which he delivers in pride, and which is retorted upon him, by the Fourth Tempter, as the Archbishop begins to grasp its true meaning in humility (I.600 ff.):

You know and do not know, what it is to act or suffer.
You know and do not know, that acting is suffering,
And suffering action. Neither does the actor suffer
Nor the patient act. But both are fixed
In an eternal action, an eternal patience
To which all must consent that it may be willed
And which all must suffer that they may will it,
That the pattern may subsist, that the wheel may turn and still
Be forever still.

Faith is simultaneously knowing and not-knowing, since it is to proceed on the basis of the unknown as though it were known already. The important point of the speech, of course, is the willing participation of the individual himself in the pattern, thus raising himself, while still in time, to the level of eternity. For the pattern, though each of its details appears in time and though orderly temporal succession of these details is of its very essence, exists as a pattern beyond time. Eliot is more explicit about this meaning of "eternity" in "Burnt Norton" (Section II):

> . . . at the still point, there the dance is,
> But neither arrest nor movement. And do not call it fixity
> Where past and future are gathered. Neither movement from
>   nor towards,
> Neither ascent nor decline. Except for the point, the still point,
> There would be no dance, and there is only the dance.[13]

This is to say: the movements of the dance take place in time, and must do so, yet the whole pattern of the dance is above time;[14] the first step is not taken for the sake of the last, in order to arrive at some destination, but rather the first movement has as much meaning as the last and all the intervening movements; and all these motions, from a superior vantage-point, constitute a motionless design.[15] So, again (in Section V), Eliot repeats his argument:

> Words move, music moves
> Only in time; but that which is only living
> Can only die. Words, after speech, reach
> Into the silence. Only by the form, the pattern,
> Can words or music reach
> The stillness, as a Chinese jar still
> Moves perpetually in its stillness.[16]

To have meaning, then, life must be looked upon as, so to speak, aestheticized, or rather ritualized, turned into a dance.[17] Therefore the trouble with the modern pragmatic conception of man's life is that it looks for a specific goal in time; such a goal, however, renders comparatively meaningless the time before and after its attainment. But in an aesthetic or ritual pattern, the beginning is quite as significant as the ending; as "East Coker" assures us in the first and the last lines: "In my beginning is my end" and "In my end is my beginning." And so only by means of such a pattern can time past and time future be given meaning: through the pattern time is redeemed.

Since the pattern may be repeated infinitely often at different intervals of time and still remain essentially the same, so the individual by his willing participation in the pattern may transport his temporary life to the plane of eternity. All this the saint and the savage know well; but modern pragmatic man has lost this knowledge. By entering into the ritual dance and acting out the primeval myth, the savage presents a model of this mystery of time and eternity; he harks back to "things as they were done at the first of the world"; by surrendering himself to the prescribed motions he renews action as it ought to be acted; he "creates the world"; he redeems time.[18] (Authorities seem fairly well agreed now that the old controversy, "Which came first, myth or ritual?," falls into the chicken-or-egg category. Ritual is the physical enactment of the mystery; myth is its verbal counterpart.) So by means of myth and ritual, "birth and copulation and death" are lifted above the animal level.

Modern pragmatic man is, by contrast, prideful, ambitious, oriented toward worldly success. His past is meaningless whether or not it leads him to the attainment of his goal; for, if it does not, it loses all point through failure; and, if it does, it goes into the discard because it was only a preliminary. And his future is equally meaningless, because it can only represent a decline from the height and a cancellation of the gain. Hence, as the Four Tempters say (1.613 ff.):

> Man's life is a cheat and a disappointment;
> All things are unreal,
> Unreal or disappointing.

Thomas accordingly rejects ambition, along with the enticements of pleasure (I.688 ff.):

> Ambition comes when early force is spent
> And when we find no longer all things possible.
> Ambition comes behind and unobservable,

and as he joins in the joyful eternal dance, he is fully aware that to the spectators his behavior is that of a madman (II.331 ff.):

> I give my life
> To the Law of God above the Law of Man.
> Those who do not the same
> How should they know what I do?

The pattern that Becket consents to have reiterated in his own career is, of course, the pattern of Christ.[19] No pains are spared to make clear the identification of Becket with the Christ-figure. He returns to England in "happy December," as a year-deity should, at the time of the low point of the sun, when "the Son of Man" is "born again in the litter of scorn" (cf. I.47–48). He makes his triumphal entry into Jerusalem (I.88 ff.):

> Assured, beyond doubt, of the devotion of the people,
> Who receive him with scenes of frenzied enthusiasm,

> Lining the road and throwing down their capes,
> Strewing the way with leaves and late flowers of the season.

He is spoken of by the Second Priest (I.126–27) in terms proper to the Messiah:

> Yet our Lord is returned. Our Lord has come back to his own again.
> We have had enough of waiting, from December to dismal December.

He is the Master, whom the Chorus aver they will not deny, as Peter denied Christ (I.15–17):

> . . . and who shall
> Stretch out his hand to the fire, and deny his master? who shall be warm
> By the fire, and deny his master?

And he is the slaughtered and eaten God, an identification made in jest by the First Knight (II.43–44):

> We will roast your pork
> First, and dine upon it after.

So Becket himself makes the identification explicit in death just before the murder (II.365 ff.):

> His blood given to buy my life,
> My blood given to pay for His death.
> My death for His death.

Yet, it may be objected, in this eternizing of oneself by identification with the divine pattern, is not the martyr concerned, to a monstrous degree, only with himself? Is there not in this ritualizing and aestheticizing of life a terrible danger of self-glorification and self-aggrandizement that would surpass the modest selfishness of the stoic? Of

course there is, and the play is well aware of the danger.[20]
Since "Sin grows with doing good" (I.691) and (I.698 ff.),

> Servant of God has chance of greater sin
> And sorrow, than the man who serves a king.
> For those who serve the greater cause may make
>   the cause serve them
> Still doing right,

it is possible that the would-be saint, by having faith and only faith, may subordinate the pattern to himself instead of himself to the pattern: this is the substance of the "last temptation." So the Last Tempter finds his opportunity to shake Becket's resolution from its very foundations by confirming Becket's faith in an eternal order, but pointing out that such a faith alone is compatible with such pride and selfish ambition as would throw into eclipse all ambition for earthly goods. For faith is the complementary virtue of the intellect only, and cannot supply motivations.[21] It may therefore lead man to "the greatest treason: / To do the right deed for the wrong reason" (I.676–77).

Faith, accordingly, must be supplemented by hope and love. Hope, in the Christian sense, is not the same as anticipating the pleasurable fulfillment of all human desires;[22] this sort of unredeemed hedonism is sure to end in the sin of despair and to bring the individual, as the crown of his lifetime's effort ("Little Gidding," Section II),

> The cold friction of expiring sense
> Without enchantment, offering no promise
> But bitter tastelessness of shadow fruit
> As body and soul begin to fall asunder.

Nor is faith the negativistic "reasoned" despair of the stoic, who, by a sort of perverted temperance, starves the appetites into submission;[23] as faith is the perfective virtue of the intellect, so hope is perfective of the free will, not disapproving of the passions in their essence, but reproving them for desiring too little rather than too much. Man, in his littleness, is fain to be content with something less than perfection. Hope demands that the self undergo the ultimate of unselfishness in that it must will to hand itself over entire in order to be constructed anew; it asks that the individual reduce himself to "A condition of complete simplicity / (Costing not less than everything)" ("Little Gidding," Section V).

In such a light can be understood the diabolism of the Fourth Tempter's assault; at the very brink of the saint's salvation he tries to substitute a redemption that redeems nothing.[24] He tempts Becket "with his own desires"—that is, with the prospect of prolonging his own self as it exists in imperfection—, and when Becket inquires (I.586), "What do you offer? what do you ask?," the Tempter replies, "I offer what you desire. I ask what you have to give": a proposal directly antithetical to that of Christ, who offers to make the individual capable of desiring that which he ought to desire, and who asks that he give his whole self. Becket's Tempter, as Becket recognizes in terror, offers him an ostensible Heaven which is really a Hell of triumphant selfishness, in which his old self is to be in no degree magnified and in no way improved.[25] The result of this is that Becket is faced with that despair that is inevitably attendant upon the soul's surrender of all that it is and all that it has known itself to be; a hymn to disillusion and disappointment is what the Four Tempters accordingly chant at this point (I.613 ff.), and the Chorus sing of the Dark Night of the Soul, the night of the Death of God, wherein (I.664 ff.)

God is leaving us, God is leaving us, more pang, more pain, than
   birth or death.
Sweet and cloying through the dark air
Falls the stifling scent of despair.[26]

This is the state of the soul that Eliot depicts so skillfully
in *Ash Wednesday,* for instance in Section II:

> At the first turning of the second stair
> I turned and saw below
> The same shape twisted on the banister
> Under the vapour in the fetid air
> Struggling with the devil of the stairs who wears
> The deceitful face of hope and of despair.

Here, however, it becomes clear that the despair that is the
consequence of loss of hope in the fulfillment of one's im-
perfect desires may, by the acquiescence of the will, pass
over into a despair that is an abandonment of the old
passions and a preparation for the advent of desires completely perfected and transformed.[27] For the individual
is here not merely going round and round on the treadmill
of nature's endless circle; here the image of circularity
unites with a vertical pattern of change:[28] the soul is
ascending a winding stair, and at a turning point looks
down upon its old self engaged in a struggle that is now
transcended. So Thomas Becket replies to the Chorus's cry
of desperation with a speech reviewing the stages of his
life, showing that he is beyond hope and despair as the
world understands them, and hence professing to wait for
his consummation in a state that is neither action nor
suffering (I.674 ff.).
This willingness to wait for the advent of perfection is
thematic throughout the play, from the reluctant Chorus's

first line: "Here let us stand, close by the cathedral. Here let us wait," to Thomas's consummate patience at the close, which is neither action, since the events are not of his own initiation, nor suffering, since the events are willed by him to occur as they do. He agrees in effect with his author in "East Coker," Section III:

I said to my soul, be still, and wait without hope
For hope would be hope for the wrong thing; wait without love
For love would be love of the wrong thing; there is yet faith
But the faith and the love and the hope are all in the waiting.
Wait without thought, for you are not ready for thought:
So the darkness shall be light, and the stillness the dancing.

A final objection remains to be countered: even with faith and hope, the career of Becket seems to be essentially negative, a thing without content. To supply this positive content is the task of the virtue of love.[29] Love, as has been explained, is the virtue perfective of the appetites and passions through the acquiescence of the free will in the will of God. By joyously accepting his own lot, the saint wills that which is to be. Hence his suffering is no longer "suffering" in the strict sense; it is no longer passive, but has become a matter of active choice.[30] He does not merely tolerate misery and pain which come to him from without, as the stoic does. (Still less does he derive pleasure from his own passivity, like a masochist, as I have heard suggested.) Rather he perceives the pattern of justice in this sequence of action and suffering and "consents to it that it may be willed." As long as the sufferers undergo their suffering unwillingly, the pattern is not complete, for their reluctance drives a new wedge of evil, so to speak, between the individual and the expiation. The suffering, being actual, may cancel out the actual overt consequences of the evil action, but the will, being still recalcitrant, cannot compensate for the original intentional evil. But when the victim wills his own fate, then the action and the suffering are "at one," and there is true atonement.[31]

Thanks also to the mystical oneness of all creation that Eliot has emphasized, the good will of one man may balance the evil will of another; the love of the saint is greater than that of any man and partakes of the divine, since he wills not merely to lay down his life for his friends, but to die for his enemies' sake. Therefore all the better if, as in Becket's case, the fate falls upon one who is largely innocent, for then he is freely able to identify himself with the guilty and to suffer, in a sense, in their behalf. In a sense only, for Christ's is the grand example that makes his own possible; he thus assimilates his own history to the history of Christ and becomes an active-passive participant in the Christ-myth.[32] He recognizes that the paradox of God as both efficient and final cause, the one from whom creation issues forth and into whom it is ultimately gathered, the Creator and Redeemer, is figured in miniature in the mystery of his own human situation, he being both caused by the world, as object, and the causer of the world, as percipient subject. His willing participation, both for himself and for others, brings the cosmic pattern of justice nearer completion.[33] He thus leads all of creation one step nearer to its consummation in the love of God.

So Becket consoles the frightened Chorus (II.221 ff.):

> These things had to come to you and you to accept them.
> This is your share of the eternal burden,
> The perpetual glory. This is one moment,
> But know that another
> Shall pierce you with a sudden painful joy
> When the figure of God's purpose is made complete.

It is, of course, this "painful joy" which the Chorus fear.
As Dante so subtly teaches, the love of God, which never
changes its all-consuming, all-demanding, and all-proffer-
ing quality, is the fire of Hell to those who are unprepared
to accept it. The Chorus acknowledge their unpreparedness
in their final prayer (II.633 ff.): [34]

Forgive us, O Lord, we acknowledge ourselves as type of the
     common man,
Of the men and women who shut the door and sit by the fire;
Who fear the blessing of God, the loneliness of the night of God,
     the surrender required, the deprivation inflicted;
Who fear the injustice of men less than the justice of God;
Who fear the hand at the window, the fire in the thatch, the fist
     in the tavern, the push into the canal,
Less than we fear the love of God.[35]

After all this has been said, it should not be necessary
to insist that the matter of *Murder in the Cathedral* is not
only drawn from history, but is equally molded into
myth.[36] This molding Eliot himself did not have to under-
take, for St. Thomas Becket had already done so in
shaping his own fate after the pattern of Christ. Christianity
is unique among religions in laying emphasis upon both
myth and history: it rejects the belief that time and causality are illusions to be escaped from, and it thereby differs
from all Manicheisms; [37] it differs from all forms of paganism in refusing to locate the mythic pattern in a primeval
time which can be renewed only in ritual imitation; it locates its myth in the center of history and finds its eternal
pattern in the causal series of events which unfold in time.[38]
Christianity can afford to forfeit neither its historicism nor
its mythicism.[39] At the juncture of myth and history, at the
still point of the turning wheel, is salvation.

10

Afterword: Tragedy and Mystery

ARISTOTLE'S famous Four Causes—the Material, the Formal, the Efficient, and the Final—are, it is generally agreed, perhaps best understood not so much as "causes" as "essential constituent factors." In line with the linguistic-analytic bent of modern philosophy, we might almost call them "approaches to definition." Literary critics are becoming more aware these days that some of their quarrels—not all—are due to different avenues of attack rather than to real differences of opinion; some of the controversies about the significance of tragedy may be shown to be needless if we keep the four "approaches to definition" in mind.[1]

Aristotle himself, notoriously a poor Aristotelian, somewhat muddied the waters at the source by confounding his own definitional principles in the *Poetics*. To be sure, he did all that could be done in the way of Material Definition. Such defining is arrived at through conceptual analysis, and Aristotle shows quite clearly in his opening chapters what tragedy is materially made up of. He differentiates the arts from other human activities, and literature from the other kinds of art, and drama from the other kinds of literature. And in the lost treatment of comedy he probably clarified the particular place of tragedy in the kinds of drama; in fact, in the *Poetics* as we have it, it might be said that he does so, Materially speaking, when he insists and expatiates on the dignified and elevated language proper to a tragic, but not to a comic, play.

Material definition, because it depends so much on analysis, is liable to draw the definer's attention to so many and so diverse particulars that he loses sight of generality and contents himself with an extreme nominalism; Aristotle flirts with this danger in Book One of his *Ethics* (ultimately evading it), but escapes it altogether in the *Poetics*. Nevertheless it has not been altogether avoided by others. Wilamowitz, the Big Bertha of German erudition, fired off a nominalistic salvo a few generations ago in his edition of *Heracles*, when he declared that the term "tragedy" must be taken to include any dramatic piece written by a Greek poet and produced before a Greek audience at a Greek festival—and called presumably by the Greeks a "tragedy." [2] The echoes have yet to die away. But we might as well be told that "Herodotean history" is something written by Herodotus and called by Herodotus "history." A definition of tragedy that includes *Iphigenia among the Taurians* but excludes *King Lear* is hardly worth the trouble of formulating. Nominalism is the besetting sin of common sense; Swift's Laputian nominalists, we may remember, were eventually reduced to carrying around large packs of objects and producing an object in lieu of a word, thus attaining perfect clarity of reference. This solution we recommend to some Neo-Korzybskian, and pass on.

Final Causes, explanations in terms of purpose, are perhaps of limited use in the criticism of literature; they may be subdivided into two classes, expressive theories or explanations from the author's point of view, and pragmatic theories or explanations from the point of view of the audience. Expressive theories, though they still appear to flourish in art criticism and music criticism, have been pretty well routed out of the literary field, at least for the time being; Aristotle in his day had nothing to say about them, and we might as well imitate his blissful ignorance. As for pragmatic theories, any tarrying in their neighborhood leads to premature shipwreck on the Rock of Catharsis.[3]

Efficient Causes, in an inquiry like this, necessarily become investigations of origins, and attempts to trace the origins of tragedy undoubtedly have some contributions to make to our fuller understanding. But here the trail back to the beginnings is particularly dark, and one might be allowed to register some doubt about the helpfulness of reblazing it even if it were clearer. For genetic investigations are always ringed around with terrible pitfalls.[4] There is William James's Genetic Fallacy itself, the temptation to evaluate something in terms of what it was originally. And there is its opposite number, the Evolutionary Fallacy, which is the temptation to evaluate something in terms of what it was to become. This latter is the delight of music critics, who never tire of pointing out how Mozart broke a path for Beethoven, Beethoven for Berlioz, Berlioz for the latest banalities, *et cetera:* this way madness, or Tin Pan Alley, lies. Worse still may be the fallacy of carrying an origin too far back; we return with an explanation that explains everything, and hence nothing. Here is the trouble with the theory of the myth-and-ritual origin of tragedy so stressed in the foregoing essays: if tragedy evolved from myth and ritual, so did comedy and the various forms between the two, satire, romance, melodrama. Efficient Causes fail to provide means of distinction.

As with myth, so with tragedy: one is driven finally to Formal Causes, the philosophical definition. And here the means of differentiating tragedy from other forms of literature is near to hand: Tragedy puts its stress on mystery; comedy and all the other intermediate forms are analogues of problem-solving. Comedy puts emphasis on the problems themselves; romance-melodrama emphasizes the solving process; satire points out the solution and deplores society's failure to take it. Satire may at times draw rather close to tragedy, but at best eventuates not in the tragic, but in the pathetic. In Ibsen's *The Wild Duck*, for instance—a great play, no doubt, but probably better not called a tragedy—, after Hedvig has shot herself, we are left with such thoughts as "If only Gregers had not interfered in the Ekdals' marriage! If only Gina had told Hialmar the truth to begin with!"; and these and similar reflections lead directly to the conclusions, which the author certainly does not deny us: "Well, at least Gina and Hialmar will get along better from now on. And perhaps Dr. Relling is right: human beings ought not to be robbed of their illusions." But this is, in the final analysis, contemptible. If we take a similar attitude toward *King Lear*, and wish that the old king had not resigned his crown or banished his daughter, we are ultimately reminded that those who look on life in such a piffling utilitarian light "Shall never see so much, nor live so long." The solution of problems is important only as it leads us to an intuition of mystery.

The Chain of Being has, by and large, become a specimen pickled in philosophers' laboratories, but it may just possibly afford more than a palaeontological interest. Plants do somehow seem to exist more fully than stones do, and animals do seem to move on more planes of awareness than plants. And, with all other men, "I, in my intricate image, stride on two levels," as Thomas says—at least two, we should agree. An ape seems to be able to solve such problems as how to put a counter of the right color into the right slot in order to get a banana. But an ape is presumably unaware of the problem whether it is right for him to have the banana at all; this later question is of a different order of being from anything the ape is acquainted with. Yet all human beings—yes, even scientists—move inescapably in this order, always. (Accuse the scientist who denies this of cooking up his experimental results!) And this order is the order of justice.[5] Now and then we have premonitions of a still higher plane, of the pattern of justice as it might be when viewed from above, and not horizontally in time as we are for the most part doomed to view it. According to how near the individual approaches that plane, he may be said to participate in tragic knowledge, tragic courage, or tragic triumph.[6]

Tragic knowledge is awareness of the pattern of justice; it differs from mere problem-solving in that the parts of the pattern are viewed as a whole. Looked at sequentially, from the problem-solving standpoint, the parts of the justice-pattern make no sense; we come to the intentional evil, and say, "This must be avoided"; we come to the expiatory suffering, and say, "This must be eliminated." And we decide, "Two wrongs do not make a right." But since neither interior nor exterior evil is ever wholly removable, we must finally conclude that nothing actually makes for right; this is the ultimate pessimism that always threatens to engulf the liberal befuddlement about justice. We should not listen to the notes of the melody in such isolation one from another. To be sure, temptations to evil ought to be reduced and sufferings ought to be alleviated, but our failure and negligence in both these tasks become themselves parts of the mysterious overarching design. In a work of literature awareness of this pattern may be almost non-existent or moderately obscure in the perceptions of the protagonists, as it is in Agamemnon's mind, or Orestes', or Lear's, or Hamlet's, but if it is implicit in the author's design the audience is led to agree that one facet, perhaps the simplest, of mystery has been illuminated.[7]

A more complex attitude is that of tragic courage, which, however, in the individual is nearly always consequent upon the attainment of tragic knowledge.[8] Tragic courage adds to the perception of the pattern the acceptance of its rightness, even as it involves oneself: "a terrible beauty is born," we may say with Yeats. Here the protagonist thinks: "This is the evil which I myself have created, and I must exhaust it by my own suffering. Looked at externally the chain of sin and expiation may appear to be merely two wrongs failing to make a right: but this is *my* chain; I must *not* look upon it from without, or I cut myself out of true being; looked at internally, the only way the prior wrong *can* be made into a right is through the subsequent wrong." This is the prospect of Charity that Hamlet seems to be blind to, but that Oedipus gains.

Lastly, the literary work may highlight the facet of tragic triumph, whereby suffering is chosen and thus becomes the sufferer's own deliberate action. Here the protagonist may not see the pattern as a whole clearly, but he has faith in its wholeness all the same; the suffering that comes to him he either assumes to be in expiation of his own sin or hopes to be a diversion from others.[9] Such is the attitude of Antigone and Thomas Becket, both of whom choose to purchase, at the cost of suffering, that which they trust to be right. Every eliminator of suffering, to whom the struggle for such elimination must entail suffering to himself, would have to acknowledge that his action-passion, far from disproving the mystery of justice, really only illustrates the ineluctable human situation of apparent disorderliness in a universe of order.[10]

With such takings as we may have from the foregoing brief "raid on the inarticulate" we may try to construct still another definition of tragedy, Formally considered:

A tragedy is a work of literature which has as its chief emphasis the revelation of mystery.[11]

As for the questions asked in the first essay, whether a tragedy may have a happy ending,[12] and whether a martyr's story may be a tragedy, we may conformably answer a yes to both. Such issues, and dozens of others like them, are insoluble problems only to the inveterately problem-solving.

Notes

CHAPTER 1: MYTH AND MYSTERY

1. Swift's satire was inspired by the pretensions of the newly-founded Royal Society; cf. Marjorie Nicolson, *Science and Imagination* (Ithaca, 1956) pp. 115–16, who adds that Swift may have derived his idea of the Struldbrugs from reports to the Royal Society about the Brahmins of India, among others. Cf. also William Barrett, *Irrational Man* (Garden City, N. Y., 1958) Ch. 6: "The Flight from Laputa."

2. From Part III of "New Year Letter (January 1, 1940)," p. 303 of *The Collected Poetry of W. H. Auden* (N. Y., 1945).

3. *Biographia Literaria* (Everyman Edition) p. 27 Note.

4. The entire discussion in Eric Voegelin, *Order and History*, Vol. One: *Israel and Revelation* (Baton Rouge, 1956) pp. 1–5, is relevant here.

5. Quoting himself on pp. 211–212 of his *The Mystery of Being*, Vol. One, tr. G. S. Fraser (Chicago, 1950).

6. Tr. Manya Harari (London, 1948) pp. 8–9.

7. Cf. Reinhold Niebuhr, "The Truth in Myths," in *Evolution and Religion*, ed. Gail Kennedy (Boston, 1957) p. 93: "It is because man can transcend nature and himself that he is able to conceive of himself as the center of all life and the clue to the meaning of existence. It is this monstrous pretension of his egoism, the root of all imperialism and human cruelty, which is the very essence of sin." Cf. also André Bonnard, *La Tragédie et l'Homme* (Neuchatel, 1951) pp. 191–92.

8. Cf. Mircea Eliade, *The Myth of the Eternal Return,* tr. Willard P. Trask (N. Y., 1954) pp. 81 ff., for a discussion of the attitude toward time of the mythopoeic mind; e. g., p. 81: "In all rites there is discovered the will to devaluate time."

9. *Ibid.,* pp. 91–92: the primitive desire to start all over again is not a longing for a lost animal paradise, so much as for a state of "spiritual plenitude"; it testifies to man's fear of losing himself in the meaninglessness of profane existence; it is "a desperate effort not to lose contact with *being.*"

10. Cf. Heinrich Weinstock, *Die Tragödie des Humanismus* (Heidelberg, 1953) p. 25: "It would seem then that the incomprehensibility of Being emerges in all its fullness only in man, since in him the contradictories that constitute the Incomprehensible clash, annihilate each other, and weigh him down with their uncontrolled conflict. . . ."

11. See Basil Willey, however, *The Seventeenth Century Background* (London, 1934) p. 5, for a discussion of why modern man rejected the medieval apprehension of mystery.

12. So Jacques Maritain, *The Dream of Descartes,* tr. Mabelle L. Andison (N. Y., 1944) p. 51, remarks, ". . . the suppression of intellectual habitus will cause us little by little to lose sight of the fact that science is something of a determined subject, something of man, the intrinsic perfecting of a being endowed with a certain nature and situated in certain conditions; the tendency is more and more to look upon it as an absolute which is sufficient to itself in the abstract. . . ."

13. E. O. James, *Myth and Ritual in the Ancient Near East* (N. Y., 1958) pp. 27–29, gives the usual pragmatic interpretation of "The Mimetic Sacred Dance," but includes among its motivations the desire to establish a "sacramental relationship between man and the supernatural source of his food-supply."

14. This is not even supposed by primitive men themselves, says E. O. James, *Prehistoric Religion* (N. Y., 1957) pp. 232–33.

15. Mario Untersteiner, *Le Origini della Tragedia e del Tragico* (1955, n. p.) pp. 58–60, discourses on the spirit of festival and ritual behavior (the festival exists "to create," as opposed to the "to do" of everyday life) and traces his theories back to Posidonius.

16. Since nowhere in English is the modern misunderstanding of myth and cult so well delineated as in Walter F. Otto, *Dionysos: Mythos und Kultus* (Frankfurt-am-Main, 1933), the following

points seem worth summarizing (from pp. 11–46): The two schools of thought about early religion, the folkloristic and the philological, both err in reducing the ancient gods to empty abstractions; though Wilamowitz pointed out that "No man prays to an idea," he was as guilty of this as anyone else. The truth is that the dynamic and pragmatic bent of our culture leads us astray into conceiving of the primitive gods as mere powers. Both schools of thought hold that myths about the gods are sheer poesy, and that the key to an understanding lies in the study of the *cultus*. But myth and *cultus* are inseparable: the true meaning of both is that with his whole person man must express his sense of the sublime and the divine. Modern thought, with its emphasis on purposiveness does not realize that *cultus* has as its purpose the apprehension of God's nearness; utilitarian considerations, though sometimes present, are always secondary. Our pragmatic bias has caused us to construct a theory of a "magical mode" of thought, but magic is a degeneration of myth: it deals with hidden powers, whereas myth and cult profess to serve an open, even if mysterious, reality. To understand myth it is necessary to understand creativity, and to the rationalist mind creative activity always seems paradoxical, since the artist always feels that his most characteristic effects are not his own at all: they spring from his innermost being, and yet are given to him from without. (In other words, creativity is most objective precisely when it is most subjective.)

17. This somewhat Frazerian solution might be varied with elements more up-to-date, but the elements would be equally pragmatic. (But this remark is not meant to indicate an alignment with the depreciators of Frazer; one can deplore the pragmaticism that led him to the over-emphasis on sympathetic magic, but still acknowledge that his single-hypothesis theory of the genesis of myth in fertility-rites is preferable to the multiple-hypothesis theories that have allegedly supplanted it.)

18. There are, of course, intermediate interpretations of ritual, such as that of Jane Ellen Harrison, *Ancient Art and Ritual* (Oxford, 1947), who retreats from a purely pragmatic to a psychological position (cf. pp. 26, 44, 47).

19. Cf. W. F. Otto, "Der Mythos," *Studium Generale* 8 (May, 1955) 263–68.

20. Gerhard Nebel, *Weltangst und Götterzorn: eine Deutung der Griechischen Tragödie* (Stuttgart, 1951) p. ii, gives it as his opinion that no one can appreciate the greatest Greek tragedies except

on the assumption of a fundamental rift in the human condition ("einer ursprünglichen Gebrochenheit der menschlichen Natur").

21. The attitude is common. For an example of it in a classicist, see Alan Little, *Myth and Society in Attic Drama* (N. Y., 1942) esp. Ch. 1; for an example in a theologian, cf. the psychological-need approach of Rudolf Bultmann, as outlined in George W. Davis, *Existentialism and Theology* (N. Y., 1957) esp. pp. 25 ff.

22. Ernst Cassirer's view; cf. *The Philosophy of Symbolic Forms*, Vol. Two: *Mythical Thought*, tr. Ralph Manheim (New Haven, 1955), esp. Chs. 1 and 2. For a critique of Cassirer see David Bidney, "Myth, Symbolism, and Truth," pp. 1-14 of *Myth: A Symposium*, ed. Thomas A. Sebeok (Philadelphia, 1955; Bloomington, Ind., 1958).

23. Cf. Herbert Weisinger, "Some Meanings of Myth," pp. 1-10 of *Comparative Literature, Proceedings of the ICLA Congress in Chapel Hill, N. C.*, ed. W. P. Friederich (Chapel Hill, 1959). For an eclectic view of myth in a classicist, see Martin P. Nilsson, *A History of Greek Religion*, 2nd ed., tr. F. J. Fielden (Oxford, 1949), esp. p. 48 and Ch. 2 *passim*.

24. Cf. Otto, "Der Mythos," p. 266; Weisinger, *Tragedy and the Paradox of the Fortunate Fall* (East Lansing, Mich., 1953) pp. 16-17.

25. This view is all the easier to hold if one takes myth to include any kind of primitive tale, as apparently Stith Thompson does, p. 106, *Myth: A Symposium*, ed. Sebeok.

26. This theory is not to be confused with those of Alfred Weber or Mario Untersteiner, who, while occasionally speaking as though myth arose from the radical contradictions in man's existential position, ultimately trace its origin back to a clash between a mystical "Mediterraneanism" and an invading superior culture. (Aryanism perhaps? The shade of Hitler seems to be flitting in the background here.) Cf. Weber's *Das Tragische und die Geschichte* (Hamburg, 1943) pp. 69-71, 77, 83-89, *et passim*; and Untersteiner's *La Fisiologia del Mito* (Milan, 1946) pp. 23-24, 68, etc.; *The Sophists*, tr. Kathleen Freeman (N. Y., 1954) pp. 102, 111-12; *Le Origini della Tragedia e del Tragico*, pp. 128 ff.: criticized by Albin Lesky, *Die Tragische Dichtung der Hellenen* (Göttingen, 1956) pp. 14-15.

27. Cf. Weisinger, *Tragedy and the Paradox of the Fortunate Fall*, pp. 193-94.

28. Cf. Voegelin, *Order and History*, Vol. One, p. 3; Edwin Bevan, *Symbolism and Belief* (London, 1938).

29. Richard Chase, *The Quest for Myth* (Baton Rouge, 1949) apparently ends his quest with this identification: ". . . poetry is a primitive, a fundamental product of man's mind and . . . wherever it has appeared it has striven against human bias and exclusiveness to transfigure itself into myth" (p. 131).

30. Though Northrop Frye almost makes out his case for so considering it, by taking *mythos* in the sense of "plot" and extending myth far beyond its primitive signification; see his suggestive "Archetypal Criticism: Theory of Myths," pp. 131–239 of *Anatomy of Criticism* (Princeton, 1957).

31. For an evaluation of myth directly opposed to the one sketched here, see H. and H. A. Frankfort, "Myth and Reality," pp. 11–36 of H. and H. A. Frankfort *et al., Before Philosophy: The Intellectual Adventure of Ancient Man* (Chicago, 1946). The Frankforts profess to take myth seriously, but indicate as characteristics (and implied defects) of ancient thought the following beliefs: (1) Man is part of society; society is imbedded in nature and dependent upon cosmic forces. (2) Man stands in an I-and-Thou relationship toward the universe rather than an I-and-It relationship. (3) Whatever is capable of affecting mind, feeling, or will is real. (4) Causality functions in a personal way, not in a mechanical way. (5) An event cannot be looked at in isolation, and therefore there is no one single explanation which will hold good under all conditions. (6) Time and space are conceived of qualitatively and concretely, not quantitatively and abstractly. And so on. The authors' judgment on these beliefs is shown by the title of the final chapter: "The Emancipation of Thought from Myth." Cf. Wilhelm Nestle, *Von Mythos zum Logos,* 2nd ed. (Stuttgart, 1942), who after conceding that rational thinking cannot explain everything (p. 3), proceeds to declare Logos the winner in the struggle with Mythos (p. 19). For a dissenting, but still pragmatical view, cf. Paul Radin, *Primitive Man As a Philosopher* (N. Y., 1927, 1957) esp. Ch. 3.

32. *Poetics* 1453a.

33. Cf. W. Macneile Dixon, *Tragedy* (London, 1925) p. 137.

34. For a well-reasoned discussion of the relationship between myth and Greek tragedy, cf. G. M. Kirkwood, *A Study of Sophoclean Drama* (Ithaca, 1958) pp. 11–29, though I am at a loss to understand why the "power of myth" is called (p. 24) an "unusable datum" for literary criticism.

35. Even the evolution from ritual to drama meant a lessening of participation in the mystery and therefore indicated a need for its discursive presentation; cf. Bruno Snell, *The Discovery of the Mind,* tr. T. G. Rosenmeyer (Cambridge, Mass., 1953) pp. 97-98.

36. Untersteiner, *The Sophists,* p. 102 and esp. pp. 111-12: ". . . the tragic genius of the Greeks had discerned at the heart of the myth the radical contradictions of existence. . . ."

37. Cf. Gertrude R. Levy, *The Gate of Horn* (London, 1948) pp. 329-30.

38. And to do so, of course, he had to universalize his story and deliberately refrain from appealing to his audience's limited prejudices; hence the fatuity of such questions as, "What did Sophocles' Athenian auditor think? What was the Elizabethan groundling's reaction to a Shakespeare play?" Bonnard, *La Tragédie et L'Homme,* p. 15, calls the latter sort of criticism treason to the poet.

39. Cf. Gerald F. Else, *Aristotle's Poetics: the Argument* (Cambridge, Mass., 1957) pp. 378 ff.

40. For another close analysis of what Aristotle meant by *hamartia,* see Kurt von Fritz, "Tragische Schuld und Poetische Gerechtigkeit in der Griechischen Tragödie," *Studium Generale* 8 (April, May, 1955) 194-237.

41. The expression, "Cosmic Toryism," is the title of a chapter in Basil Willey, *The Eighteenth Century Background* (London, 1940).

CHAPTER 2: AESCHYLUS' "ORESTEIA":
THE MARRIAGE OF HEAVEN AND EARTH

1. Among the most suggestive commentators on the *Oresteia* are John H. Finley, *Pindar and Aeschylus* (Cambridge, Mass., 1955); Antonio Maddalena, *Interpretazioni Eschilee* (Turin, 1953); Heinrich Weinstock, *Die Tragödie des Humanismus* (Heidelberg, 1953); H. D. F. Kitto, *Form and Meaning in Drama* (N. Y., n. d.); Gerhard Nebel, *Weltangst und Götterzorn* (Stuttgart, 1951); and Dieter Kaufmann-Bühler, *Begriff und Funktion der Dike in den Tragödien des Aischylos* (Dissert., Heidelberg, 1951). Of the learned editions of Aeschylus, as far as imaginative interpretation is concerned one can only say, with Cardinal Newman (*The Scope and Nature of University Education,* Discourse V): "How many commentators are there on the

Classics, how many on Holy Scripture, from whom we rise up, wondering at the learning which has passed before us, and wondering why it passed!"

2. Cf. Maurice P. Cunningham, "Didactic Purpose in the *Oresteia*," *Classical Philology* 45 (1950) 183-85.

3. The phrasing is my own. But see Denys Page's Introduction to his and J. D. Denniston's edition of *Agamemnon* (Oxford, 1957) esp. pp. xiii f. (quoting W. Kranz, *Stasimon*) and xv f. Cf. also Kranz, "Zwei Lieder des Agamemnon," *Hermes* 54 (1919) 301-320, where a warning is given against trying to reconcile the "contradictions" in Aeschylus' thought: "they are marks of a primitive man!"

4. Cf. Nebel, *Weltangst und Götterzorn*, p. 101, and Hans Jürgen Baden, *Das Tragische*, 2nd ed. (Berlin, 1948) pp. 32 ff., for speculation on the meaning of this fact.

5. Richmond Lattimore, p. 16 of the Introduction to his translation of the *Oresteia* (Chicago, 1953), identifies some of the imagery that expresses this "idea of entanglement."

6. Cf. E. R. Dodds, *The Greeks and the Irrational* (Berkeley, 1951) pp. 39-40, where he develops the thought: "In the *Agamemnon* we meet . . . interpretation on two levels. Where the poet, speaking through his Chorus, is able to detect the overmastering will of Zeus . . . working itself out through an inexorable moral law, his characters see only a daemonic world, haunted by malignant forces."

7. In the *Republic*, of course, in so many words. Cf. Books IV, VIII-X.

8. Dodds, *The Greeks and the Irrational*, p. 38, calls this "the consciousness of a mysterious dynamic nexus . . . binding together crime and punishment," conceived by Aeschylus as the *ménos áte·s:* "all the elements of that sinister unity are in a wide sense *ate.*" (Cf. also Dodds' note on this, p. 57.) Mario Untersteiner, *Le Origini della Tragedia e del Tragico* (1955, n.p.) pp. 526, 531 ff., discusses *Dike* as a "cosmic power": "truth and reality as opposed to appearance," citing *Ag.* 788-89 and *Cho.* 61-69. Kaufmann-Bühler, *Begriff und Funktion*, pp. 9 ff., has a summary of previous theories, mostly German, about the Aeschylean doctrine of *Dike:* Pohlenz, *Die Griechische Tragödie*, Vol. Two (Göttingen, 1954), sees in Aeschylus the proclaimer of a world-immanent justice which with inner necessity causes suffering to follow every offense, taking *Dike* to be an ethicized fate-concept standing near or over Zeus in some undefined relation; this is approximately the view of Porzig,

Aischylos: die Attische Tragödie (Leipzig, 1926), and Wilhelm Schmid, with the additional recognition that the divine power personified by Zeus is identical with Moira, Aisa, and fate in general. *Dike* is the real order of the world, the ability of the cosmos to regain its balance after every disturbance, and Zeus guarantees and safeguards *Dike*'s workings. Kaufmann-Bühler objects (in the following list the objections are re-arranged):

(1) The view rests on an identification of *Dike* with a cosmic conception of *lex talionis,* whereas *talio* appears to be only one mode of the action of *Dike.*

(2) *Dike* does not stand above the action, but seems interwoven in the action; right opposes right, and all characters believe themselves to be in the right.

(3) The term *Dike* has all shades of meaning, from a personification of Justice, Daughter of Zeus, to mere social convention.

It ought to be said in reply to Nos. 1 and 2 that they are not really objections at all: no one minds that the term "Justice" should indicate a wider range of equilibria than the balance of the *lex talionis,* provided that the latter constitutes its basis; and No. 2 seems a clear case of confusing the sentiments of the characters with the over-all theme of the author. Objection 3 stems from Alfred Weber, *Das Tragische und die Geschichte* (Hamburg, 1943) pp. 239 ff. (cf. esp. pp. 243, 250), who was much in favor of a simple-minded, fatalistic Aeschylus, a yea-sayer to the decrees of Zeus, and from H. W. Smyth, *Aeschylean Tragedy* (Berkeley, 1923). Objection No. 2 arises also from Kaufmann-Bühler's thesis (cf. *Begriff und Funktion,* pp. 11, 113–14) that Aeschylus centered his drama on the conflict between human rights and man's obligations to the divine. But these latter, chiefly the traditional commandments to reverence the gods, one's parents, and strangers, can hardly be looked on as antithetical to human rights. No, the antithesis is precisely between the human delusion that there exists such a conflict between rights and the divine certainty, unavailable to mankind, except through faith, that cosmic order is ineluctable.

9. The quality of Aeschylus' faith has been much discussed. We know that he was an initiate into the Eleusinian Mysteries; Albin Lesky, *Die Tragische Dichtung der Hellenen* (Göttingen, 1956) p. 15, lists the literature on the subject, but thinks that there was a vast chasm between the Mysteries and the "logosbestimmte" world of Tragedy.

10. Cf. Kaufmann-Bühler, *Begriff und Funktion,* p. 59.

11. *Ibid.*, p. 87.

12. To Maddalena, *Interpretazioni Eschilee* (cf. esp. pp. 3, 8, 13, 35), one of the chief themes of the *Oresteia* is that of "unjust justice" (cf. Finley, *Pindar and Aeschylus*, p. 10): punishment is just with reference to the guilty one who receives it, but often unjust with reference to the one who inflicts it. Agamemnon sees only the justice of his vengeance; Clytemnestra sees only the injustice of his actions. The Trojan War itself, because it brings on sufferings disproportionate to the original offense, constitutes a new crime. So is it always with justice. (Scarcely a criminal can be punished without inflicting the pain of disgrace at least on his innocent family: should we therefore abolish all penalties?)

13. Cf. Kitto, *Form and Meaning*, pp. 5-6, and also p. 36: ". . . to achieve Dike Zeus avails himself of guilty human passions."

14. E. T. Owen, *The Harmony of Aeschylus* (Toronto, 1952) p. 7, observes that Zeus for Aeschylus is no more metaphor, but that in the trilogy is depicted "the hand of God shaping out of the evil of men, both the evil they do and the evil they suffer, his righteousness."

15. *Ibid.*, p. 119, where Croiset's *Éschyle* is quoted to the effect that the trilogy is ended with the acquittal of Orestes and a second denouement is engrafted on to the first; Croiset hesitates to call this a serious flaw, but feels the second ending has less appeal for us today than the first.

16. Georges Méautis, *Éschyle et la Trilogie* (Paris, 1936) p. 251, thinks that the "expulsion of the human element upon the irruption of the divine" is prefigured early in the *Eumenides* by the flight of the Pythia at the sight of the Furies.

17. Any political state is therefore an institution that participates in, or is modeled after, the divine order; cf. Karl Reinhardt, *Aischylos als Regisseur und Theologe* (Bern, 1949) p. 160; Walter Porzig, *Aischylos*, p. 148; and Eric Voegelin, *Order and History*, Vol. Two: *The World of the Polis* (Baton Rouge, 1957) p. 255: "It was the greatness of Aeschylus that he understood the order of Dike in society as a precarious incarnation of divine order, as a passing realization wrung from the forces of disorder through tragic action by sacrifices and risks, and—even if momentarily successful—under the shadow that ultimately will envelop it." Cf. also pp. 256-57.

18. Kitto, *Sophocles, Dramatist and Philosopher* (London, 1958) pp. 47-49, tries to make a distinction between "Justice," a moral word,

and *Dike,* a neutral word, and quotes Anaximander's remark, "Things are always exacting retribution from each other, and paying it, for their injustice (*adikia*)." But Kitto seems to miss the point of the Greeks' wisdom: "Fundamentally, *dike* is the principle of order, regularity, balance . . . the Greeks made the mistake of extending the general laws of the physical universe to that other universe, the world of human action and passion." A mistake? Kitto himself does not seem clear why he thinks so, or even sure that he thinks so.

19. Walter Nestle, *Menschliche Existenz und Politische Erziehung in der Tragödie des Aischylos* (Stuttgart-Berlin, 1934) p. 49, says that the problem of justice is eventually passed on by man to the gods: "die Entlastung des Menschen belastet den Gott," and, p. 58, connects this with the *theòs sullé·pto·r* theme. For this latter theme of "God as Coadjutor with Man," see the references in Mario Untersteiner, *The Sophists,* tr. Kathleen Freeman (N. Y., 1954) p. 36 Note, and *Le Origini della Tragedia,* p. 506.

20. In his famous review of Soame Jenyns' *Free Enquiry into the Nature and Origin of Evil.*

21. Porzig, *Aischylos,* esp. pp. 144 ff., and Weinstock, *Die Tragödie des Humanismus,* pp. 28 ff., have perhaps the fullest discussions of the roles played by the different gods.

22. Cf. Kitto, *Form and Meaning,* pp. 80 ff.; Nebel, *Weltangst und Götterzorn,* p. 158.

23. Cf. F. Vian, "Le Conflit entre Zeus et la Destinée dans Éschyle," *Revue des Études Grecques* 55 (1942) 190–216.

24. Compare the interview with an American Indian in Paul Radin, *Primitive Man As a Philosopher* (N. Y., 1927, 1957) pp. xxxiii f Hans Baden, *Das Tragische,* pp. 146–48, believes that the important consequence of the change from polytheism to monotheism was that the former offered only heroism as a means of overcoming man's tragic situation, whereas the latter, while it does not mitigate the tragedy, affords the possibility of fitting the "Threatening Unknown" into an over-all plan.

25. For two examples of this theory, out of many, see Kitto, *Form and Meaning,* pp. 69 ff., 82; and Gilbert Murray, *Aeschylus: the Creator of Tragedy* (Oxford, 1940) pp. 200–201.

26. Cf. Weber, *Das Tragische und die Geschichte,* p. 241.

27. Bernard M. W. Knox, "The Lion in the House," *Classical Philology* 47 (1952) 17–25, calls attention (p. 23) to the significance

of time in the plays: ". . . 'in time' is the characteristic cry of all characters of the trilogy. . . ." But this does not mean that the gods undergo development in time.

28. Cf. Finley, *Pindar and Aeschylus*, pp. 192–93.

29. Friedrich Solmsen, *Hesiod and Aeschylus* (Ithaca, 1949) p. 217, draws a parallel between the development of justice on earth and "progress among the gods."

30. Nestle, *Menschliche Existenz*, pp. 74 ff., makes an elaborate distinction between *theoi* and *daimones*, but emphasizes their final reconciliation.

31. Cf. Karl Deichgräber, *Der Listensinnende Trug des Gottes* (Göttingen, 1952) p. 129.

32. Cf. Edwin Bevan, *Symbolism and Belief* (London, 1938) pp. 217 ff.

33. This is the point from which, Weinstock, *Die Tragödie des Humanismus*, p. 65, thinks, Aeschylus took his world-view: (1) Ignorant man can only learn responsibility by the trial-and-error method of guilt and suffering. (2) Since the individual breaks under this burden, only in the Polis is life possible. (3) But the existence of the Polis depends on the citizens' wholesome fear of the gods. (4) Hence the Polis, to keep this fear alive, must foster tragedy, which reminds the people of their tragically conditioned existence.

34. Cf. Untersteiner, *Le Origini della Tragedia*, p. 547. To assert the lack of a theodicy in Aeschylus is not to agree with Reinhardt, *Aischylos*, pp. 12–13, that such a theodicy was attempted, but spoiled by the retention of the old "Envy of the Gods" idea; or with Weber, *Das Tragische und die Geschichte*, p. 250, that Aeschylus was too primitively pious to think of such matters at all.

35. Cf. Nebel, *Weltangst und Götterzorn* pp. 116–117.

36. Cf. Carlo del Grande, *Hybris* (Naples, 1947) p. 110; and Goffredo Quadri, *I Tragici Greci e l'Estetica della Giustizia* (Florence, 1936) p. 84.

37. The theory of Denys Page, pp. xxiv ff., Introduction to the edition of *Agamemnon*, to the effect that Artemis demanded Iphigenia's death in requital for the destruction of the mother hare by the two eagles, cannot be countenanced. "That is what is in the text," Page says; but surely it only adds to the confusion to mistake a portent for the event that it is portentous of. We might as well understand the opening lines of the Chorus to mean that the Trojan War was brought on by the kidnapping of a vulture's young. (Which is just about what

Nebel does in *Weltangst und Götterzorn,* p. 113.) For full discussions of the choral ode, see Kaufmann-Bühler, *Begriff und Funktion,* pp. 67 ff.; Kitto, *Form and Meaning,* pp. 2 ff.; Charles H. Reeves, "The Parodos of the *Agamemnon,*" *Classical Journal* 55 (1960) 165–171; and cf. Maddalena, *Interpretazioni Eschilee,* p. 8.

38. Reinhardt, *Aeschylos,* p. 140, classifies prevalent interpretations of the *Oresteia* along three lines: (1) "rechtsgeschichtliche," (2) "religionsgeschichtliche," and (3) "staatsethische," all three of which proceed on the assumption that the Erinyes are essentially transformed from their original evil nature.

39. Wilamowitz, in *Heracles,* was perhaps the most prominent and insistent advocate of a transformation in the nature of the Erinyes; cf. Kaufmann-Bühler, *Begriff und Funktion,* pp. 106–107.

40. Untersteiner, *The Sophists,* pp. 21–23, supposes that there is a clash between Mediterranean-primitive and Indo-European-enlightened concepts of justice, for which Aeschylus provides an "irrational" resolution.

41. Cf. Murray, *Aeschylus,* p. 203.

42. Cf. Maddalena, *Interpretazioni Eschilee,* pp. 3, 6.

43. On this most of the commentators agree: best expressed perhaps by Finley, *Pindar and Aeschylus,* p. 273: "By admitting the evil with the necessity of his act, Orestes at last shows a moral awareness of what he is doing, a freedom from the automatism of hurt and counterhurt."

44. But Maddalena, *Interpretazioni Eschilee,* p. 63, considers this circumstance a piece of incoherence on Aeschylus' part.

45. Cf. Untersteiner, *Le Origini della Tragedia,* pp. 531 ff., and Quadri, *I Tragici greci,* p. 93. Why Page, Introduction to edition of *Agamemnon,* p. xx, asserts that Orestes knows no doubts and shows almost no hesitation is not clear.

46. This is the usual view. But W. Schadewaldt, "Der Kommos in Aischylos' Choephoren," *Hermes* 67 (1932) 312–354, disagrees.

47. Kaufmann-Bühler, *Begriff und Funktion,* p. 96, and esp. p. 99, sums up the case for Orestes in so many words: (1) His justice is not a personal justification. (2) The others do not realize that in asserting their own right they clash with a higher right, whereas Orestes is fully conscious of the horror of his task. (3) Intellectual confusion precedes their deeds as cause, leading to moral ruthlessness; whereas madness follows his deed as effect, leading to humility.

48. Cf. Maddalena, *Interpretazioni Eschylee,* pp. 29, 35, 50.

236 NOTES TO PAGES 57-59

49. *Ibid.*, p. 77: the "new Justice" at the end of the trilogy is compounded of the old justice of revenge plus the grief and pain of such as Orestes, since only out of such suffering come consciousness and compassion to complete the older system. This is similar to Murray's idea in *Aeschylus* that forgiveness is superadded to the automatic workings of justice (pp. 199–201, 207); cf. Finley's discussion of Orestes' "atonement" in *Pindar and Aeschylus*, pp. 248–49, 268–69.

50. Weinstock, *Die Tragödie des Humanismus*, p. 23: Orestes, when he takes on the guilty responsibility of action, comes face to face with "that splendid and pernicious distinction which is at once the glory and bane of humankind: Freedom, which cannot exist apart from guilt. He becomes aware of himself as a tragic being."

51. *Ibid.*, p. 46: Clytemnestra's approach to the powers above mankind is through the way of magic, which is perverted ritual; Orestes' reaction is reverent and religious.

52. Murray, *Aeschylus* (cf. p. 199), intimates that Orestes' acquittal brings to an end the chain of evil, but this can be true only in a transcendent sense; in time, the court-system is established to deal with an unending series of crimes.

53. Nebel, *Weltangst und Götterzorn*, p. 165, explains why the *Eumenides* is still a tragedy, in spite of its "happy ending": "Der tragische Gott besteht nicht unbedingt auf dem Tod des Menschens, sondern darauf, als Grenze gefühlt und geehrt zu werden."

54. But Owen, *The Harmony of Aeschylus*, p. 129, would have it that Peitho also is transformed at the end, from Peitho-"Temptation," thanks to whom Clytemnestra was able to bring Agamemnon to walk over the crimson tapestry to his doom (cf. pp. 126 ff. of Robert F. Goheen, "Aspects of Dramatic Symbolism: Three Studies in the *Oresteia*," *American Journal of Philology* 76 [April, 1955] 113–137), to Peitho-"Persuasion," who effects the conversion of the Erinyes. Cf. Quadri, I *Tragici Greci*, p. 80.

55. Cf. Pearl C. Wilson, "Note on *Eumenides* 881–91," *Classical Philology* 42 (1947) 122–23, who also believes that the Erinyes suddenly pay attention to Athena here because they are confronted with a heretofore unfamiliar concern with everlasting good, as revealed in the goddess's words, "I shall not grow weary of telling you what is good": their better nature, their genuine concern for justice, is appealed to successfully. A. C. Verrall, in his edition of the *Eumenides* (London, 1908) Introduction pp. xxxii f. and Note to vv. 882–892,

supposes that there is a break between verses 887 and 888 ("But if the majesty of Peitho is revered by you. . . . So then you will stay!"), during which Athena communes with the Erinyes in silence. But silence is a strange way to demonstrate the powers of "Persuasion," especially at such a climax.

56. Solmsen, *Hesiod and Aeschylus*, p. 209, in good modern Rousseauistic fashion, regrets that "Aeschylus cannot establish Justice on its own intrinsic value; it must rest on a feeling of fear." But what human being knows its "intrinsic value"? Weinstock, *Die Tragödie des Humanismus*, throughout his first chapter, "The Birth of the Polis from the Tragic Spirit," shows that such fear, or *Angst*, can be a humanizing force.

57. Finley, *Pindar and Aeschylus*, pp. 273, 276, 277, takes the emphasis given to marriage throughout the *Eumenides* to be symbolic of the union of freedom and necessity, "creativity with heritage, scope with commitment": "freedom is the inresidence of potentiality in the fixed" (p. 277).

58. *Ibid.*, pp. 278–280; cf. Solmsen, *Hesiod and Aeschylus*, p. 224.

59. For a recent discussion of the Sacred Marriage, see E. O. James, *Myth and Ritual in the Ancient Near East* (N. Y., 1958) Ch. 4.

60. Méautis, *Éschyle et la Trilogie*, p. 200, understands this line to show why Agamemnon was compared to a spring for a thirsty traveler in v. 901.

61. Cf. Philip Wheelwright, *The Burning Fountain* (Bloomington, 1954) pp. 232–267: "Thematic Patterns in the *Oresteia*," esp. pp. 235 ff., "The Blood Bath"; and Goheen, "Aspects of Dramatic Symbolism," p. 119.

62. Cf. Weinstock, *Die Tragödie des Humanismus*, p. 17.

63. *Ibid.*, pp. 14–15, and Ch. 1 *passim*.

64. Cf. R. P. Winnington-Ingram, "Clytemnestra and the Vote of Athena," *Journal of Hellenic Studies* 68 (1948) 130–147, esp. pp. 132, 134, 144.

65. And Athena may equally well be a Great Mother figure also, as Maud Bodkin, *Archetypal Patterns in Poetry* (London, 1934) pp. 183–85, would have it, and thus a double of Clytemnestra herself, to follow Porzig, *Aischylos*, pp. 214–15.

66. Winnington-Ingram, *Euripides and Dionysus* (Cambridge, 1948) p. 145, thinks that the struggle between Apollo and the Furies represents a tension between the marriage-tie and the mother-child

238

238

relationship; Athena, as a virgin sprung from Zeus, casts her vote for the male: theologically, she expresses the will of Zeus; sociologically, she asserts the dominance of the male sex.

67. Cf. Nebel, *Weltangst und Götterzorn*, p. 105. Kenneth Burke, "Form and Persecution in the *Oresteia*," *Sewanee Review* 60 (1952) 377–396, believes, pp. 383–34, that women, because of their subordinate position in Athens, could serve to symbolize all kinds of submerged motives.

CHAPTER 3: SOPHOCLES' "ANTIGONE": EROS IN POLITICS

1. So think C. M. Bowra, *Sophoclean Tragedy* (Oxford, 1944) p. 64, and Cedric H. Whitman, *Sophocles* (Cambridge, Mass., 1951) pp. 263–64.

2. *Hypothesis* to Sophocles' *Antigone*, attributed, probably erroneously, to Aristophanes the Grammarian.

3. *Phoenissae*, 1588 ff.

4. So went a dithyramb of Ion of Chios, referred to in Sallustius' *hypothesis* to the play.

5. *Fabulae 72*.

6. "Erigone" was taken to mean "Child of Strife"; "Antigone" might mean the same.

7. See Sir James Frazer's references in Vol. Two, pp. 96–97, of his translation of Apollodorus (Loeb Classical Library); and cf. the various discussions of Erigone in Robert Graves' outrageously speculative and delightfully suggestive *The Greek Myths* (Baltimore, 1955).

8. Cf. Gertrude R. Levy, *The Gate of Horn* (London, 1948) pp. 52 ff.; Mircea Eliade, *Birth and Rebirth*, tr. Willard Trask (N. Y., 1958) p. 58; W. F. Jackson Knight, *Cumaean Gates* (Oxford, 1936) Chs. 1 and 2.

9. Cf. Robert F. Goheen, *The Imagery of Sophocles' Antigone* (Princeton, 1951) pp. 37–41. This grisly turn of the marriage-motif may be responsible for the idea of Antigone's "uncanniness" so emphasized by Gerhard Nebel, *Weltangst und Götterzorn* (Stuttgart, 1951), in his discussion, "Antigone und die wilde Welt der Toten," esp. pp. 189 ff., where he goes too far, however, when he calls her "a representative of the feminine principle of the underworld" (p. 189), "a pathological example" (p. 191), and "a sister of Clytemnestra and Cassandra" (p. 193), finally confessing that he cannot understand her.

10. The idea of H. D. F. Kitto, *Form and Meaning in Drama* (N. Y., n. d.) p. 172, that in this stasimon Sophocles leaves the final judgment on Antigone to be made by the audience, is attractive, and owes much to Bowra, *Sophoclean Tragedy*, pp. 104–105; cf. Goheen, *Imagery*, pp. 64–74.

11. Cf. Jane Ellen Harrison, *Ancient Art and Ritual* (Oxford, 1947) pp. 65–66.

12. Aristotle accordingly reduces the classes of goods to two in his discussion of Plato in *Ethics* 1096b.

13. 1096b; cf. 1100a–1101a.

14. Cicero says that he is following Panaetius, or rather completing a discussion which Panaetius had promised, but had not carried through; Posidonius, however, had treated the subject: see W. C. Greene, *Moira* (Cambridge, Mass., 1944) p. 353.

15. But Mario Untersteiner, *Sofocle* (Florence, 1935) p. 528, tries to show that Sophocles shared in the movement of which the Sophists were a part—a movement toward individualism.

16. According to Eric Voegelin, *Order and History*, Vol. Two: *The World of the Polis* (Baton Rouge, 1957) p. 216, Parmenides grappled with precisely the issue that is central in *Antigone:* "The conflict occurs between two types of experience. Truth is the philosophy of the realissimum that we experience if we follow the way of immortalization in the soul; Delusion is the philosophy of the reality that we experience as men who live and die in a world that itself is distended in time with a beginning and an end. The characterization of this philosophy of reality as a Delusion derives its justification from the experience of a superior reality, of an immortal ground of the mortal world."

17. Heinrich Weinstock, *Sophokles,* 2nd ed. (Berlin, 1937) p. 124, objects even to Hegel's famous analysis of *Antigone* on the ground that in it "the most profound poet of the human condition is reduced to the status of a preacher of practical common-sense."

18. *Ibid.,* p. 142.

19. Hans Jürgen Baden, *Das Tragische,* 2nd ed. (Berlin, 1948) pp. 68–76, has reflections on the relationship between Eros and Death.

20. Cf. Gabriel Marcel, *The Mystery of Being*, Vol. Two: *Faith and Reality,* tr. G. S. Fraser (Chicago, 1951) pp. 62, 82–83.

21. Cf. Kitto, *Form and Meaning*, pp. 147–48.

22. For a brief summary of views see Whitman, *Sophocles*, pp. 263–64, who votes for an "actor's interpolation" theory. But Antigone here,

it seems rather, is deliberately lowering herself to the level of reasoning of Creon, a man who could console his son for the loss of his betrothed by reminding him that "there are other fields to plow" (569). And she is showing that even so such reasoning will not work.

23. Goethe's stigmatization of her farewell speech as a "dialektischer Kalkül" is often referred to. But in it, as shown above (preceding note), she is not reasoning on her usual level.

24. Aside from a few common-sense observations, such as that she would die anyway, whether Creon had anything to do with it or not (460–61).

25. There is nothing in the play, however, to justify the view of Untersteiner, pp. 93–98, or of Max Pohlenz, *Die Griechische Tragödie,* 2nd ed. (Göttingen, 1954) p. 195, that Antigone's true Ego will somehow find its completion in death.

26. For their contrasting "wisdoms" see Goffredo Quadri, *I Tragici Greci e l'Estetica della Giustizia* (Florence, 1936) pp. 136–37.

27. Albin Lesky, "Forschungsbericht über Griechische Tragödie, 3: Sophokles," *Anzeiger für die Altertumswissenschaft* 2 (1949) 1–11, discusses with disapproval several commentators who make out Antigone herself to be of the irrational, impulsive, intuitive type.

28. Cf. S. M. Adams, *Sophocles the Playwright* (Toronto, 1957) p. 51.

29. See Weinstock's excursus, in *Sophokles,* "Scherz und Ernst," pp. 151–57.

30. Walter Jens, "Antigone-Interpretationen," in *Satura: Früchte aus der Antiken Welt* (Baden-Baden, 1952) p. 47, makes this point.

31. Victor Ehrenberg, *Sophocles and Pericles* (Oxford, 1954) p. 31, wishes rather perversely to limit the meaning of Eros in the play to *philía,* eliminating any suggestion of *agápe·* or of Eros in the usual sense.

32. Compare 295 ff. with 781 ff.

33. Cf. André Bonnard, *La Tragédie et l'Homme* (Neuchatel, 1951) p. 61.

34. Cf. Weinstock, *Sophokles,* pp. 142 ff.

35. Cf. Kitto, *Form and Meaning,* p. 237.

36. The "diptych" charge is answered by S. M. Adams, "The *Antigone* of Sophocles," *Phoenix* 9 (1955) 47–62.

37. Extreme examples of such misreading are afforded by Gennaro Perrotta, *Sofocle* (Messina-Milano, 1935) pp. 59 ff., and A. J. A.

Waldock, *Sophocles the Dramatist* (Cambridge, 1951); the latter criticizes the drama for a "hidden shift from one theme to another" (p. 52), but immediately reveals (p. 53) that he is not really speaking of "theme" at all, but merely of which character holds the center of the stage.

38. E. g., W. N. Bates, *Sophocles, Poet and Dramatist* (Philadelphia, 1940); T. D. Goodell, *Athenian Tragedy* (New Haven, 1920); G. M. Kirkwood, *A Study of Sophoclean Drama* (Ithaca, 1958); T. B. L. Webster, *An Introduction to Sophocles* (Oxford, 1936); Gilbert Norwood, *Greek Tragedy* (London, 1928); and J. T. Sheppard, *Greek Tragedy* (Cambridge, 1934).

39. The *O.E.D.* indicates that the signification reprobated here was not in existence before the Eighteenth Century, and not at all common till the Nineteenth.

40. From Richmond Y. Hathorn, "Homer As a Literary Psychologist," *Kentucky Foreign Language Quarterly* 3 (1956) 3–4.

41. Karl Reinhardt, *Sophokles,* 3rd ed. (Frankfurt-am-Main, 1947) p. 85, emphatically denies that Antigone is saint or martyr, on the ground that she has knowledge. Though what knowledge she is supposed to have is scarcely clear. Cf. Laura Jepsen, *Ethical Aspects of Tragedy* (Gainesville, Fla., 1953) p. 68, and Georges Méautis, *Sophocle* (Paris, 1957) p. 218.

42. Hence her play is a test-case for those who do not believe it possible that tragedy and religious faith can coexist; the problem here is strictly analogous to that in the controversy over the possibility of Christian tragedy. See, among numerous treatments of the theme, Albin Lesky, "Zwei Sophokles-Interpretationen," *Hermes* 80 (1952) 96; Nebel, *Weltangst und Götterzorn* pp. 175–231; Heinrich Weinstock, *Die Tragödie des Humanismus* (Heidelberg, 1953) pp. 344 ff. These are negative views; I incline to Herbert Weisinger, *Tragedy and the Paradox of the Fortunate Fall* (East Lansing, Mich., 1953), when he says (pp. 267–68): "Tragedy, therefore, cannot exist where there is no faith; conversely, it cannot exist where there is no doubt; it can only exist in an atmosphere of sceptical faith." Provocative indeed is the question raised by Baden, *Das Tragische,* p. 130: "Hier erhebt sich jene letzte unbeantwortbare Frage: ob nicht alle menschliche Tragödie nur der Widerschein himmlischer Tragödie ist—ein Abbild also metaphysischer Konflikte, die uns verborgen bleiben und deren Vorhandenheit wir nur ahnen auf Grund ihrer Spiegelung innerhalb des vergänglichen Seins."

43. But just as Socrates' words have no effect on Crito in the *Phaedo,* so none of Antigone's fine sentiments carries the slightest weight with Enrico Turolla, *Saggio sulla Poesia di Sofocle* (Bari, 1934) p. 78, who equates both Antigone's and Creon's careers with zero.

44. For a survey of the *kérdos*-motif in the play, see Goheen, *Imagery,* pp. 14–19. Cf. Jens, "Antigone-Interpretationen," p. 57.

45. Weinstock's analysis of the Eros-Chorus concludes (*Sophokles,* p. 149): "Das Menschliche nur bestehen [kann], wenn es im Göttlichen sich birgt." Cf. Walter F. Otto, *Dionysos: Mythos und Kultus* (Frankfurt-am-Main, 1933) pp. 38 ff., where modern misinterpretations of the *pharmakos*-rituals are discussed and where it is emphasized that the ritual was really an attempt to respond to the awful presence of the supernatural with a human activity equally awful; in sum, the ritual was a bringing to light of the terrible presence behind reality, and, as with any creative act, the creation freed the creator from the anxieties and compulsions which motivated him.

46. Reinhold Niebuhr, "The Truth in Myths," *Evolution and Religion,* ed. Gail Kennedy (Boston, 1957) p. 96, discusses Love as the fulfillment of political justice. Cf. also Marcel, *The Mystery of Being,* Vol. One, p. 165.

47. Yet Henri W. van Pesch, *De Idee van de Menselijke Beperktheid bij Sophocles* (Wageningen, 1953) p. 291, can say that Sophocles "considered love a necessary evil rather than a blessing for man." S. M. Adams, "The *Antigone* of Sophocles," p. 57, is more discerning: "Most fitly, then, and with strong irony, do the Chorus describe Eros as 'an assessor in office by the side of the Great Laws.'"

48. But see the view of Antigone in Alan M. G. Little, *Myth and Society in Attic Drama* (N. Y., 1942) p. 44.

49. Cf. J. T. Sheppard, *The Wisdom of Sophocles* (London, 1947) pp. 52–53.

50. Sophocles was not crudely anti-Sophistic, as is shown by the well-recognized fact that his *Antigone* is a contribution to the *nómos-phúsis* controversy on the side of *phúsis* more or less, a side to which the Sophists generally adhered. Yet he must have been opposed to their ultimate relativism, and from this charge not even Untersteiner in *The Sophists,* tr. Kathleen Freeman (N. Y., 1954), can acquit such men as Protagoras and Gorgias, however much profundity he may have discovered in them. See Voegelin, *Order and History,* Vol. Two, pp. 267–331, esp. 274–75, where it is shown that the Sophists, like the Enlighteners of the Eighteenth Century, substituted a *homo-mensura*

view of the world for a *deus-mensura* view, a change that was sure to mean "the destruction of philosophy." And (*pace* Whitman, *Sophocles*) Sophocles was indubitably a *deus-mensura* man.

51. Cf. John A. Moore, *Sophocles and Arete* (Cambridge, Mass., 1938) p. 65 and Webster, *An Introduction to Sophocles*, p. 39. To Albrecht von Blumenthal, *Sophokles* (Stuttgart, 1936), Antigone is representative of "das Schöne Mass" as opposed to "das Unmass des Hasses," which was the chief danger to Greece in Sophocles' day (pp. 156 ff.). Cf. also Kitto, *Sophocles, Dramatist and Philosopher* (London, 1958) p. 63.

52. Cf. the Parodos, esp. 148 ff.

CHAPTER 4: THE EXISTENTIAL OEDIPUS

1. Treatments of Sophoclean drama from an existentialist standpoint are nothing new; well-known are Heinrich Weinstock, *Sophokles*, 3rd ed. (Wuppertal, 1948) and Karl Reinhardt, *Sophokles*, 3rd ed. (Frankfurt, 1947). Weinstock's suggestive theory about *Oedipus Rex*, that man's limited knowledge, in contrast to the omniscience of the gods, inevitably involves every human action in guilt and evil ("Wer unwissend handelt, muss schuldig werden"), thus leading to a state of existential "Angst," which is best converted by the individual into a reverence strictly religious—this theory has been justly criticized, on the grounds that Weinstock's Original Sin (the "Allverschuldung" and "Allverantwortung" of every human being) is only glancingly treated by Sophocles, whereas Oedipus' anxieties and fears arise from quite definite occasions and are by no means identical with the "Daseinsangst" or "Weltangst" of existentialism. Reinhardt, in a discussion equally suggestive, if rather rhapsodical, develops the implications of the "Schein-Sein" antithesis in the play—an issue by no means peculiarly existentialist—while having much also to say about "Angst."

2. Even scientific studies in ancient times were pursued for ethical ends: cf. F. M. Cornford, "Greek Natural Philosophy and Modern Science," pp. 81–94 of *The Unwritten Philosophy and Other Essays* (Cambridge, 1950).

3. Cf. William Barrett, *Irrational Man* (Garden City, N. Y., 1958) Ch. 1: "The Present Age."

4. For a discussion of the difficulties involved in defining existentialism and of the inadequacy of Jean-Paul Sartre's widely quoted definition, "Existentialism is the philosophy which declares as its first principle that existence is prior to essence," see Marjorie Grene, *Dreadful Freedom: A Critique of Existentialism* (Chicago, 1948) pp. 1–4. Actually the Sartrean definition smuggles in Sartre's peculiar doctrine of freedom: cf. Wilfrid Desan, *The Tragic Finale* (Cambridge, Mass., 1954) pp. 162 ff.

5. Cf. Gabriel Marcel, *The Mystery of Being*, Vol. One, tr. G. S. Fraser (Chicago, 1950) p. 54.

6. Concise characterizations of existentialism may be found in H. J. Blackham, *Six Existentialist Thinkers* (London, 1952) esp. pp. 149–65, and in Jean Wahl, *A Short History of Existentialism*, tr. Forrest Williams and Stanley Maron (N. Y., 1949).

7. Max Pohlenz, *Die Griechische Tragödie*, 2nd ed., Vol. Two (Göttingen, 1954) p. 6, remarks of the existentialist approach to Sophocles (specifically that of Weinstock in *Sophokles*): "Es war gewiss eine zeitgebundene Illusion, wenn Schillers Humanismus sich die Griechen als ein seliges Geschlecht vorstellte, das von den Göttern an der Freude leichtem Gängelbände geführt wurde; aber ebenso einseitig und verfehlt ist es, wenn man heute eine nicht minder zeitgebundene Daseinssicht in das Griechentum hineinträgt." (Cf. also Vol. One, pp. 9–11.) There is some justice in this, yet Pohlenz himself is victim of an illusion equally "zeitgebundene," namely the Hegelian notion that cultures develop in the direction of greater freedom for the individual.

8. For the development of the myth see Carl Robert, *Oidipos* (Berlin, 1915); J. C. Opstelten, *Sophocles and Greek Pessimism*, tr. J. A. Ross (Amsterdam, 1952) pp. 102–103; Lord Raglan, *Jocasta's Crime* (London, 1933) Chs. 22, 23, 26. But Martin P. Nilsson, "Der Oidipusmythus," pp. 335–348 of *Opuscula Selecta*, Vol. One (Lund, 1951), in accordance with his usual rejection of comparative mythology, denies that Oedipus was a cult-figure, as Robert thinks.

9. L. W. Daly, however, in the article "Oidipos" in *Pauly-Wissowa* (p. 2109), says that to take Jocasta for a goddess is "ein bedauerlicher Irrgang der vergleichenden Mythologie."

10. Cf. Claude Lévi-Strauss, "The Structural Study of Myth," in *Myth: A Symposium*, ed. A. Sebeok (Philadelphia, 1955) pp. 54–58, for an analysis of the parallelisms in the Oedipus myth.

11. This is not to say, of course, that it explains nothing. Scholars have an ancestral rite of their own, which consists of making straw-figures of theories they oppose, sticking pins into them, and repeating the incantation: "You are dead! Everyone knows you are dead!" So we are told that the ghosts of Frazer and the Cambridge Mythologists are not yet laid. But perhaps they refuse to die because they still have secrets to impart to mankind. Granted that their theories have lost their neatness and patness under the pressure of criticism, yet no later unified explanations have even been proposed, much less accepted. We might as well go back to believing that fossils are only rocks curiously shaped by wind and water as suppose that all the astounding parallels in myth and all the ritualistic features of Greek tragedy are there by coincidence.

12. Cf. Francis Fergusson, *The Idea of a Theater* (Garden City N. Y., 1953) p. 28, where a suggestion is mentioned to the effect that the medieval method of fourfold interpretation might be applicable to the understanding of myth.

13. See, among many, John A. Moore, *Sophocles and Arete* (Cambridge, Mass., 1938) esp. Chs. 2 and 3; Victor Ehrenberg, *Sophocles and Pericles* (Oxford, 1954) Ch. 7; and Enrico Turolla, *Saggio sulla Poesia di Sofocle*, 2nd ed. (Bari, 1948).

14. See Cedric Whitman, *Sophocles: A Study in Heroic Humanism* (Cambridge, Mass., 1951) p. 228. Whitman's "heroic humanism," incidentally, might also very properly be described as existentialist, in spite of his explicit rejection of Weinstock's (*Sophokles*) and Reinhardt's (*Sophokles*, pp. 26–27) approach, and aside from his advancement of a dubiously Sophoclean teaching about the possibility of apotheosis (Ch. 11).

15. Cf. Georges Méautis, *Sophocle: Essai sur le Héros Tragique* (Paris, 1957) p. 111: "Non, précisément parce que les Grecs furent la race intelligente par excellence, elle sut comprendre aussi les limites de l'intelligence, l'incliner humblement devant le suréminent, le sacré."

16. Pp. 32–33. Whitman, *Sophocles,* discusses the chief rival theories fully. It will be seen that the present treatment is not so much a contradiction as a reconciliation of these.

17. Though it becomes so, of course, if the individual, on being apprised of his condition, refuses to acknowledge the truth.

18. Philip W. Harsh, "Implicit and Explicit in the *Oedipus Tyran-*

nus," *American Journal of Philology* 79 (July, 1958) 243–58, would charge Oedipus with manslaughter, at least, and with excessive ambition in marrying an old woman in order to gain position and power. (But Jocasta was not so old as not to be able to present him with four children.)

19. Cf. Weinstock, *Sophokles,* 2nd ed. (Berlin, 1937) p. 181.

20. Cf. Hans Jürgen Baden, *Das Tragische,* 2nd ed. (Berlin, 1948) p. 51, for an analysis of this kind of hybris.

21. Worth quoting is H. T. Wade-Gery, *The Poet of the Iliad* (Cambridge, 1952) p. 45: "With the death of Patroklos, or of Mercutio, we are suddenly, in General Mihailovich's phrase, caught in the gale of the world: no contrivance now will work, all contrivances are now insignificant. This is what we recognize as tragedy: it was the pattern of thought of Shakespeare's and Homer's mind. The greatness of life, to these two, is when intrigue, the moral or hedonistic calculus, is caught in the gale."

22. Cf. Hans Diller, *Göttliches und Menschliches Wissen bei Sophokles* (Kiel, 1950) esp. pp. 18 ff., where there is developed a very suggestive opposition between the analytic habits of human thought, "das seiner Natur nach trennende, isolierende menschliche Denken" (p. 22) and the unitary nature of reality, "die Eindeutigkeit der göttlichen Antwort." Cf. also p. 30: "Auch im sophokleischen Oedipus erscheint der Mensch als der Rätsellöser, der das Rätsel seines Daseins nicht lösen kann, solange er in Gegensätzlichkeit isoliert sieht, was doch zusammengehört. Ihm erscheint als fremd, was in Wahrheit seine eigenste Sache ist. . . ." All the way through the play there is a contrast between what is theoretically known and what is personally known—between what is perceived with the intellect alone and what has penetrated to the depth of the soul—between knowledge, in short, and wisdom: e. g., the interplay between Oedipus and Teiresias, 359 ff.

23. Many commentators have remarked on this, e. g., Whitman, *Sophocles,* p. 125, and Gennaro Perrotta, *Sofocle* (Messina-Milan, 1935) p. 199.

24. Most influential of these is Tycho von Wilamowitz, *Die Dramatische Technik des Sophokles* (Berlin, 1917), with his insistence on the essential disunity of the plays; most entertaining is A. J. A. Waldock, *Sophocles the Dramatist* (Cambridge, 1951), with some excellent demolitions of others' interpretations; most typically Romantic is Perrotta, *Sofocle,* who vehemently denies that any of the

plays is a "dramma a tesi" or any of the poetry "poesia di Pensiero," affirming rather that all is "soltanto poesia" and Sophocles himself "sopratutto poeta," whatever that may mean; most recent perhaps is Herbert Musurillo, "Sunken Imagery in Sophocles' 'Oedipus,'" *American Journal of Philology* 78 (1957) 36–51, who, after an analysis of the dominant images in the play—interesting, but rather pointless unless shown to be illustrative of an underlying theme—concludes surprisingly, "And thus it may be said that the *Oedipus*, in a sense, has no interpretation." Harsh, "Implicit and Explicit" (cf. Note 18) takes issue with Musurillo.

25. *The Figure of Beatrice* (London, 1943) p. 100.

26. Cf. Gabriel Marcel, *The Philosophy of Existence*, tr. Manya Harari (London, 1948) p. 68.

27. Compare Heidegger's doctrine of the "Entwurf," and see Jean-Paul Sartre, *Being and Nothingness*, tr. Hazel E. Barnes (N. Y., 1956) esp. pp. 34–35, 39, 40–43, 367–71, 433–556 *passim*. It must be admitted, however, that the Sartrean "project" has very little in common with Oedipus' project in regard to nobility and altruism.

28. Throughout the Prologue, beginning with the first line, Oedipus addresses the Thebans as "children."

29. Imagery based on the idea of equation is scattered throughout and is fully discussed by Bernard M. W. Knox, *Oedipus at Thebes* (New Haven, 1957) pp. 147–58.

30. *xénos . . . toû lógou . . . xénos toû prachthéntos.*

31. Note the irony in 141: "Therefore, by doing my duty to him, I aid myself."

32. That Oedipus' suspicions of Creon begin quite early in the play is noticed by J. T. Sheppard, *The Oedipus Tyrannus of Sophocles* (Cambridge, 1920) p. 111. Probably the suspicions are first aroused by Creon's desire to report the oracular response in private (91 ff.).

33. Oedipus is not merely passive in the last scene, as is amply shown by Knox, *Oedipus at Thebes*, pp. 185 ff. This scene, far from being the protracted piece of sentimentality some critics have found it, is the *raison d'être* of the play. Cf. Wolfgang Schadewaldt, *Sophokles und das Leid* (Potsdam, 1947) esp. pp. 28–29, for a discussion of the meaning of tragic suffering in Sophocles.

34. *The Myth of Sisyphus and Other Essays*, tr. Justin O'Brien (N. Y., 1955) p. 128. Camus disavowed being an existentialist, but his so-called "Absurdism" was obviously Kierkegaardian in origin.

35. Cf. Marcel, *The Mystery of Being*, Vol. One, pp. 68–69.

36. Kurt von Fritz, "Tragische Schuld und Poetische Gerechtigkeit in der Griechischen Tragödie," *Studium Generale* 8 (April, May, 1955) 194–237, maintains that Oedipus' moral suffering consists precisely in the fact that he learns he has done something objectively repulsive while subjectively innocent, but that the possibility of this is fundamental to the human condition.

37. Which is not to deny that every man is similarly singled out in the gods' own time and way; otherwise Oedipus could not truly serve as a *parádeigma*. This lack of universal application seems to be the weakness of C. M. Bowra's theory in *Sophoclean Tragedy* (Oxford, 1944) pp. 209–11, that Oedipus' fate is something essentially unusual, that his catastrophe is a warning from gods to men, and that by taking heed the latter may somehow escape.

38. He even proclaims that no other mortal could endure the suffering he endures (1414–15); cf. Méautis, *Sophocle*, p. 129.

39. Baden, *Das Tragische*, p. 18, characterizes him as "ein Schulbeispiel existentieller Fehlbarkeit."

40. Cf. Blackham, *Six Existentialist Thinkers*, pp. 92–98, and Wahl, *A Short History of Existentialism*, pp. 12–13.

41. The fullest discussion of this whole problem is Opstelten's in *Sophocles and Greek Pessimism*. Cf. also Schadewaldt, *Sophokles und das Leid*, p. 26 *et passim*, who proposes an interesting theory about the necessity of suffering to effect the emergence of the self. But Turolla, *Saggio sulla Poesia di Sofocle*, pp. 110, 214–15, 221, supposes that Sophocles brings a message of utter despair.

42. Whitman's interpretation in *Sophocles* is marred by vagueness in the use of the word. Does "irrational" mean "non-rational, subrational, or super-rational"? Whitman is aware that the question is important, but he fails to observe the distinction always. This confusion carries over into his discussions of Sophocles' religious beliefs (cf. pp. 235, 245 for example). If Sophocles believed at all that evil, though god-sent, was "irrational" in the third sense, he was *ipso facto* committing himself to a theodicy and eschewing the utter pessimism that Whitman supposes he fell into in *Oedipus Rex* and the *Trachiniae*. (Of irrational evil as a mystery Whitman has no hint.) Fergusson, *The Idea of a Theater*, p. 29, is similarly unclear: "For the peculiar virtue of Sophocles' presentation of the myth is that it preserves the ultimate mystery by focusing upon the tragic human at a level beneath, or prior to any rationalization whatever."

43. Cf. Marcel, *The Mystery of Being*, Vol. Two, pp. 7–8.

44. Cf. Méautis, *Sophocle,* p. 120.

45. Cf. Gerhard Nebel, *Weltangst und Götterzorn* (Stuttgart, 1951), "König Ödipus und der Zornige Gott," esp. pp. 215, 227–231.

46. Baden, *Das Tragische,* pp. 83–86, points out that the tragic elements of human life are the inescapability of egoism and the deification of success, with all its consequences.

47. The significance of the answer to the riddle is remarked upon only, to my knowledge, by Erich Fromm, *The Forgotten Language* (N. Y., 1951) p. 212.

48. Compare Kierkegaard's theory that truth depends upon one's own *appropriation* of it; cf. Barrett, *Irrational Man,* p. 152.

49. Cf. Weinstock, *Die Tragödie des Humanismus* (Heidelberg, 1953) p. 333: "Das tragische Drama der Griechen . . . stellt die Personen auf der Bühne dem Zuschauer so dar, wie der Mensch sich vor den Göttern darstellt. . . ."

50. All of this seems implied in the phrase *pánta no · mô · n.*

51. There also is a bare possibility here that Sophocles is bringing to life the espression *téle · lúein* with the implication: "How terrible is wisdom if it does not give man a solution to his ultimate goals!"

52. Cf. 707–710, 857–58, 964 ff., 977 ff.

53. Hence the frequent references to journeying and wandering. For the play on the word *poús* see Knox, *Oedipus at Thebes,* pp. 182–84. (I venture the suggestion that *Oidípous,* "Swollen Foot," may originally have been a euphemism for the ithyphallos or its wearer in a fertility rite.)

54. For the translation of *homósporos* here, see Knox, *Oedipus at Thebes,* p. 115.

55. Admittedly the last phrase is not a translation, but a paraphrase. The "cutting down" idea is imported in order to complete the "sowing" imagery.

CHAPTER 5: THE GATEWAY OF "HIPPOLYTUS"

1. Cedric Whitman, *Sophocles: A Study of Heroic Humanism* (Cambridge, Mass., 1951) p. 122, believes that this is substantially the message of Sophocles' middle plays.

2. Even Verrall's disciple, Gilbert Norwood, retreated from the position that Euripides deliberately represented his gods as "trans-

parent impostures": see his *Essays on Euripidean Drama* (Berkeley, 1954). But that Euripides was some sort of agnostic has become the orthodox view, actually dating back at least as far as A. W. Schlegel.

3. G. M. A. Grube, *The Drama of Euripides* (London, 1941) pp. 195–96, sums up the failings of the chief characters in *Hippolytus*. Grube also catches many of the verbal echoes that are so significant in a play as complex as this.

4. Commentators have variously located the source of the play's action either in the gods or in the human beings. Norwood, *Essays* p. 106, gives a brief historical summary of the controversy. Norwood himself promises in the beginning of his essay, p. 74, to gain a clearer view by postponing consideration of the theological side, but in effect he postpones theology quite out of the play. For a recent view that Hippolytus and Phaedra are not real characters, but simply sacrifices to the gods, see Hans Strohm, *Euripides: Interpretationen zur Dramatischen Form* (Munich, 1957) p. 105.

5. It is, in short, the story of the death and resurrection of a fertility-spirit, the subject of Frazer's *Golden Bough*. The latter work takes its start, of course, from the Grove of Nemi, where Hippolytus was thought to have dwelt after being dismembered by his horses and revived by Diana.

6. Yet there are still classicists, distinguished scholars, who would throw the study of mythology back to where it was in the days of Bulfinch: so C. M. Bowra, reviewing Robert Graves' *The Greek Myths* in the *Sewanee Review* 64 (1956) 502, expresses doubt that the story of Hippolytus is a myth at all, since it has nothing to do with ritual or "primitive perplexities."

7. Cf. Theodor H. Gaster, *Thespis: Ritual, Myth, and Drama in the Ancient Near East* (N. Y., 1950) pp. 257 ff.

8. The original has *thaumastós*, an odd word to use for "to be worshiped"; it connotes rather "to be looked on with admiration," and hence is quite applicable to a Moon-Goddess.

9. Norwood, *Essays*, p. 37, considers the introduction of this idea "crazily incongruous."

10. Carlo del Grande, "Il Problema delle Baccanti," *Dioniso* 10 (1947) 27–28, comparing this play to the *Bacchae*, likens Aphrodite's vengeance against Artemis through Hippolytus to Dionysus' vengeance against Hera through Pentheus. But traces of a theomachy in the *Bacchae* are practically invisible.

11. 1327 ff.; cf. also 1400 ff. André Rivier, *Essai sur le Tragique d'Euripide* (Lausanne, 1944) pp. 74–75, would locate the mystery of the play in the clash between the two goddesses.

12. Artemis forgets her explanation at once, adding (1339–41) that the gods do not rejoice when the reverent die, but destroy the wicked: i. e., either Aphrodite does not rejoice at Hippolytus' death, or Hippolytus is irreverent.

13. Few modern critics would agree with L. A. Post, *From Homer to Menander* (Berkeley, 1951) that Hippolytus is an innocent victim. As Post makes clear, Hippolytus is certainly not an invert (which he becomes in Robinson Jeffers' modernization of the play, "The Cretan Woman," pp. 25–91 in *Hungerfield and Other Poems* [N. Y., 1951]), but he is none the less unnatural in the deepest sense of the word, since he is opposed to the whole natural order. His "rudeness"—Post's term—to Phaedra is certainly more than a "mistake" (Note, pp. 292–95).

14. Cf. L. H. G. Greenwood, *Aspects of Euripidean Tragedy* (Cambridge, 1953) pp. 32 ff., esp. 42–44, for criticism of the symbolist theory. But Greenwood's determination to attend only to the "surface meaning" of the plays brings up the old questions: What is the meaning of "surface meaning"? Surface meaning for whom? Is surface meaning different from superficial meaning? If so, how? If not, wherein lies the greatness of these plays? And so forth.

15. Though desire may occasionally do so, which is just another instance of the passions-will-intellect mystery treated herein.

16. Cf. David Grene, "The Interpretation of the *Hippolytus* of Euripides," *Classical Philology* 34 (1939) 45–58, esp. 54–55.

17. The argument of R. P. Winnington-Ingram, *Euripides and Dionysus* (Cambridge, 1948) p. 28, seems self-contradictory: after calling the gods symbols of impersonal forces, beyond good and evil, he concludes the paragraph with the implication that Euripides considered them evil.

18. André Bonnard, *La Tragédie et l'Homme* (Neuchatel, 1951) p. 155, thinks that the theme of the play is that a repressed or flouted passion becomes an instrument of death.

19. Cf. Greenwood, *Aspects of Euripidean Tragedy*, p. 34.

20. See Bernard M. W. Knox, "The Hippolytus of Euripides," *Yale Classical Studies* 13 (1952) 3–31, for discussion of the problem in *Oedipus Rex, Agamemnon,* and *Hippolytus.*

21. This obsolescent word is used advisedly, since it is the only term wide enough to comprise, among the other psychic components, the will, that *terra deserta* of modern psychology.

22. E. M. Blaiklock, *The Male Characters of Euripides* (Wellington, New Zealand, 1952) p. 39, is typical of those commentators who think that no one in the play is intended to be culpable, the play has no moral, Euripides is a realist giving us a slice of life, etc.

23. But see Gabriel Marcel, *The Mystery of Being*, Vol. One, tr. G. S. Fraser (Chicago, 1950) p. 212, for a distinction between the mysterious and the unknowable.

24. The argument of Carlo del Grande, *Hybris* (Naples, 1947) p. 161, that both Phaedra and Hippolytus are presented as guilty of *hybris hereditaria*, is hardly convincing.

25. Cf. Laura Jepsen, *Ethical Aspects of Tragedy* (Gainesville, Fla., 1953) p. 82.

26. Cf. Hans Jürgen Baden, *Das Tragische*, 2nd ed. (Berlin, 1948) p. 13: *Hippolytus* represents the surrender of understanding and prudence before the forces of anarchy.

27. As noted by Grube, *The Drama of Euripides*, p. 189.

28. Grube, *The Drama of Euripides*, seems to feel that Hippolytus' language is priggish only in the presence of others, but sincere and beautiful when he is alone. My impression is that he is conceited and misguided from his first word to his last.

29. And one is tempted to add the rendering, "Embarrassment," considering the trouble the word seems to have given translators and commentators.

30. Baden, pp. 9–10, thinks that Hippolytus shows the hybris of excessive virtue.

31. Cf. Bonnard, *La Tragédie et l'Homme*, pp. 183–84.

32. As though women were strangers from that Land of Night which is Aphrodite's dwelling-place (106) and which hides what may be dearer than life (191–92).

33. Rivier, *Essai*, p. 69, points out that the innocence of Hippolytus is not destroyed, but preserved, by death.

34. A. R. Bellinger, "The Bacchae and Hippolytus," *Yale Classical Studies* 6 (1939) 17–27, counters criticism of the play which would have it a blemish that Phaedra disappears at mid-point.

35. Cf. Bonnard, *La Tragédie et l'Homme*, p. 156.

36. Yet Plutarch quotes the passage in *De Virt. Mor.* 448F.

37. By E. R. Dodds, "The *Aidos* of Phaedra and the Meaning of the *Hippolytus*," *Classical Review* 39 (1925) 102–104.

38. Cf. Rivier, *Essai*, p. 70.

39. For this apt quotation I am indebted to B. M. W. Knox, "The Hippolytus of Euripides," who, however, reaches the conclusion that the play shows the meaninglessness of moral choice and of human speech, its medium (cf. pp. 15–16).

40. "Are you our daughter?" Lear asks Goneril in Act One, Scene Four, obviously baffled by the discrepancy between "a female descendant" and "one who behaves as a female descendant ought to behave." See Robert Heilman, *This Great Stage* (Baton Rouge, 1948) for a discussion of Lear's puzzlement about "*natural*—what nature is" and "*natural*—what nature ought to be."

41. But D. W. Lucas, *The Greek Tragic Poets* (Boston, 1952) pp. 162–63, finds the use of myth responsible for the play's supposed defects; Lucas makes a fundamental mistake in applying common-sense logic to myth, which is always translogical and plurisignative. (These terms come from Philip Wheelwright, *The Burning Fountain: A Study in the Language of Symbolism* [Bloomington, 1954].) Norman J. DeWitt points out, p. xiv of "Tragedy and Personal Humanism," an introduction to Eugen H. Falk, *Renunciation As a Tragic Focus* (Minneapolis, 1954), that Greek tragedy deals, if anything, with the super-rational.

42. Cf. Guy Soury, "Euripide Rationaliste et Mystique d'après Hippolyte," *Revue des Études Grecques* 56 (1943) 29–52, esp. 52.

43. Cf. Hans Herter, "Theseus und Hippolytos," *Rheinisches Museum* 89 (1940) 276.

44. As suggested by Bruno Snell, *The Discovery of the Mind*, tr. T. G. Rosenmeyer (Cambridge, Mass., 1953) p. 127. By referring to the statues as "visible symbolism" I do not mean to conclude, as Snell does, that the goddesses themselves are "all but reduced to the function of symbols, illustrating a variety of psychological types" (pp. 127–28). They are parts of what Robert F. Goheen, "Three Studies in the Oresteia," *American Journal of Philology* 86 (1955) 113–37, calls "the imagery of action, and imagery of scene" (p. 114).

45. But not as bright and innocent as she has seemed to many commentators on the play. Cf. Walter F. Otto, *The Homeric Gods*, tr. Moses Hadas (N. Y., 1954) pp. 98–99, and for a general view of the gods, esp. pp. 11, 29, 161.

46. Or "words," or, better, both "myths" and "words," since the play is concerned with the fact that words themselves, in their plurisignativeness, partake of the mythopoeic function. Cf. Ernst Cassirer, *Language and Myth*, tr. Susanne K. Langer (N. Y., 1946), who says, p. 98: "Myth, language, and art begin as a concrete, undivided unity, which is only gradually resolved into a triad of independent modes of spiritual creativity." But it is doubtful whether the independence of art and language from myth could ever be as complete, or whether it would be as desirable, as Cassirer seems to think.

CHAPTER 6: EURIPIDES' "BACCHAE":
THE STRANGER WITHIN US

1. But A. R. Bellinger, "The Bacchae and Hippolytus," *Yale Classical Studies* 6 (1939) 27, remarks that in the worship of wine, one must expect to find blood as well as milk and honey.

2. Even Hans Jürgen Baden, *Das Tragische*, 2nd ed. (Berlin, 1948) pp. 91–94, takes the *Bacchae* to be a refutation of Dionysus and thinks that Euripides leaves it an open question whether there really is such a god. Similarly Carlo del Grande, "Il Problema delle Baccanti," *Dioniso* 10 (1947) 29.

3. This is the general attitude of R. P. Winnington-Ingram in his book-length treatment of the play, *Euripides and Dionysus* (Cambridge, 1948); cf. esp. pp. viii, 163, 175, 178–79.

4. For summaries of many of their views, see V. Mogni, "De Baccharum aenigmate, quod ita appellatur," *Antiquitas* 2 (1947) 50–64; and del Grande, "Il Problema delle Baccanti," 24–25.

5. Cf. e. g. the approach of Max Pohlenz, *Die Griechische Tragödie*, 2nd ed. (Göttingen, 1954) p. 456.

6. Insistent on the play's not taking sides is Felix M. Wassermann, "Man and God in the *Bacchae* and in the *Oedipus at Colonus*," from *Studies Presented to David Moore Robinson*, Vol. Two (St. Louis, 1953) pp. 559–69.

7. This idea, welcomed by several critics, seems to have originated with G. M. A. Grube, "Dionysus in the *Bacchae*," *T. A. P. A.* 66 (1935) 37–54.

8. Bruno Snell, *The Discovery of the Mind*, tr. T. G. Rosenmeyer (Cambridge, Mass., 1953) p. 111, thinks that by Euripides' time myth had come to an end, and the only way to recapture its essence was to

analyze its psychological motivation. Cf. E. M. Blaiklock, *The Male Characters of Euripides* (Wellington, New Zealand, 1952) p. 208.

9. But Gilbert Norwood, *The Riddle of the Bacchae* (Manchester, 1908) p. 17, thinks that Euripides used myth only in order to laugh at it and throw it aside.

10. The best-known treatment of the *Bacchae* from the myth-and-ritual standpoint is probably Gilbert Murray's in *Euripides and His Age* (N. Y., 1913) pp. 179–89. For an ingenious application of the *agon-pathos-sparagmos-anagnorisis* formula, the basic formula of the *Bacchae*, see Northrop Frye, *Anatomy of Criticism* (Princeton, 1957) p. 192.

11. Theocritus, *Idyl* 26; cf. Propertius III.17.24.

12. Oppian, *Cynegetica* iv.281 ff.

13. Pausanias II.2.6–8.

14. Hyginus, *Fabulae* 184 and 240.

15. A. G. Bather, "The Problem of the *Bacchae*," *Journal of Hellenic Studies* 14 (1894) 244–63, was the first to make a systematic study of this play from the ritual point of view.

16. That the Bacchic religion is at once traditional and newly introduced is made much of in the *Bacchae* (Pentheus calls it new; Teiresias defends it as old), and this fact has long puzzled commentators. The only explanation is the one given here, that the religion was indeed age-old, but that every manifestation of it seemed a novel eruption. Cf. Bather, "The Problem of the Bacchae," pp. 244–49, who shows that the whole importation and invasion idea is merely the bringing-back of the fertility-god after having carried him out. Robert Briffault, *The Mothers*, Vol. Three (N. Y., 1927) p. 123 (cf. also Note, pp. 122–23), contends that Dionysus is a typical specimen of the culture-gods who always come as strangers to dwell among men. Cf. Walter F. Otto, *Dionysos: Mythos und Kultus* (Frankfurt-am-Main, 1933) pp. 71 ff. E. R. Dodds, whose edition of the *Bacchae* (Oxford, 1944) has contributed heavily to the present chapter, seems to blow hot and cold on the matter.

17. It does not seem to have occurred to those who interpret historically the "resistance to Dionysianism" that Herodotus' (II.49) story of Melampus' "recent" introduction of the Dionysian rites into Greece may be a bit of rationalistic analysis of the myths on the part of Herodotus himself, who was as great a euhemerist as Euhemerus.

18. See W. K. C. Guthrie, *The Greeks and Their Gods* (Boston, 1954) Ch. 6, "Dionysos," esp. pp. 153–73. After giving every reason

for rejecting the historical explanation of the myth, Guthrie neverthe-less accepts it (cf. p. 173). Cf. Mario Untersteiner, *Le Origini della Tragedia e del Tragico* (1955, n. p.) pp. 89 ff. Briffault, *The Mothers,* Vol. Three, p. 122, is probably right: "Rather than say that Dionysos was a late importation into Olympian religion, it would probably be nearer the truth to say that Olympian religion was a comparatively late importation into Dionysian cults." Henry D Ephron, in a paper read to the American Philological Association in 1960, gave evidence for reading the Phrygian name of Dionysus (Diounsis) on the Phaistos Disk in Mycenaean Greek text; this would place Dionysus in a Mycenaean Greek setting some twelve hundred years before Euripi-des.

19. Cf. Otto, *Dionysos,* pp. 187 ff., and Winnington-Ingram, *Euripides and Dionysos,* p. 36.

20. H. W. Parke and D. E. W. Wormell, *The Delphic Oracle,* Vol. One (Oxford, 1956) pp. 330 ff., give evidence that certain Greek city-states were instructed to institute Dionysus-worship. But this does not prove opposition.

21. Cf. E. R. Dodds, *The Greeks and the Irrational* (Berkeley, 1951) Appendix 1, "Maenadism," pp. 270-82.

22. Cf. Dodds' edition of the *Bacchae,* "Introduction," pp. ix-xxxv, *et passim.*

23. C. Kerényi, *The Gods of the Greeks,* tr. Norman Cameron (London-New York, 1951) p. 251, discusses Dionysus as a "second Zeus."

24. Cf. Briffault, *The Mothers,* Vol. Three, p. 125 Note. But Ludolf Malten, *Kyrene* (Berlin, 1911) pp. 85-93, takes Actaeon to be a sea-demon and his metamorphosis to be the last element of the story to develop. This seems unlikely.

25. Cf. Dodds, *The Greeks and the Irrational,* pp. 276-78.

26. The "Ah!" that the Stranger utters at this point has been variously interpreted. Dodds in his edition of the *Bacchae,* p. 166, takes it to mean, "Stop!" But it may be only incantatory and hyp-notic. Cf. Dodds' note, p. 166, and Grube, "Dionysus in the *Bacchae,*" p. 48.

27. And this has the further symbolic significance that Pentheus, in order to see into the heart of the Bacchanals' mysteries, must become one of them: an emotion can never be understood from without. Cf. Dodds' note to 854-55 (pp. 171-72 of his edition of the *Bacchae*); Briffault, *The Mothers,* Vol. Three, pp. 129 ff.; Mircea Eliade, *Birth*

and Rebirth: The Religious Meanings of Initiation in Human Culture,
tr. Willard Trask (N. Y., 1958) pp. 25–26.

28. At 508 Dionysus says to Pentheus, "Your name shows you fit
for misfortune"; cf. 367–68.

29. Cf. H. Jeanmaire, *Dionysos* (Paris, 1951) p. 145, where the
sufferings of Dionysus (but not of Pentheus) are hesitantly compared
to the Passion of Christ; cf. also pp. 372 ff.

30. Compare the effect of the broken dialogue, 966–70, with its
emphasis on softness and luxuriousness. For the Return to the Womb,
see Eliade, *Birth and Rebirth,* pp. 51 ff.

31. Cf. Untersteiner, *Le Origini della Tragedia,* pp. 111 ff., for the
function of *theoria* in Pythagoreanism and the Mysteries.

32. There may have been games and competitions in conjunction
with Theban Dionysiac festivals: cf. Bather, "The Problem of the
Bacchae," pp. 260–61.

33. Climbing a tree or pole has frequently symbolized an initiate's
Ascent to Heaven; cf. Eliade, *Birth and Rebirth,* Ch. 4, pp. 61–80,
"Individual Initiations and Secret Societies," and also pp. 93–94.

34. Cf. Dodds' note to 1114 (p. 203 of his edition of the *Bacchae*).

35. Dodds, in his edition of the *Bacchae,* thinks the reading is
"probably corrupt."

36. A. W. Verrall, *The Bacchants of Euripides and Other Essays*
(Cambridge, 1910) p. 19, on the basis of this expression and with a
translation of *pistós* as "potable," composes a scene of the drugging
of Pentheus and foists it off on Euripides.

37. Cf. Dodds' note to 1157–58 (pp. 207–208 of his edition of the
Bacchae).

38. Ivan M. Linforth, "Corybantic Rites in Plato," *U. of California
Publications in Classical Philology* 13 (Berkeley 1950) 160, suggests
that "The common translation of the Greek *teleîn* by the English
'initiate' is fundamentally misleading." (Was there perhaps in *teleîn,*
"to come to an end," a meaning analogous to that of "coming through"
in Southern "holy-rolling" orgies, wherein the celebrant attains complete ecstatic union with the "spirit"?)

39. Gilbert Murray's myth-and-ritual theory of Greek Tragedy,
presented on pp. 341–63 of Jane Ellen Harrison's *Themis* (Cambridge,
1912), though often referred to as exploded, still has much to
recommend it. It was perhaps too rigid and over-schematic in its
original form; Murray's chief errors were to insist that in every play
the scheme appeared in its entirety and to confuse aetiological with

genetic considerations. Yet the objections of, for instance, A. W. Pickard-Cambridge, *Dithyramb, Tragedy, and Comedy* (Oxford, 1927) pp. 185 ff., seem to miss the point. It is Miss Harrison's main contention throughout *Themis*, and it is Murray's in his Excursus, that in the rites god and man, Pentheus and Dionysus, are the same: Pickard-Cambridge, without giving his reasons for rejecting this, says that the fact that they are not the same is "a very serious difficulty" (p. 188). Other objections are perhaps more serious, yet to throw out the theory *in toto* is to leave dozens of astounding coincidences unexplained. It is as if we were told to disbelieve in the common origin of the Indo-European languages on the ground that not a scrap of Indo-European has been preserved. T. B. L. Webster, "Some Thoughts on the Pre-History of Greek Drama," *U. of London, Institute of Classical Studies, Bulletin* 5 (1958) 43, sums up as follows: "It seems to me that the essential truth which Gilbert Murray saw was that both tragedy and comedy have a certain shape and rhythm, which can ultimately be derived from vegetation ritual and appears most clearly in those plays like the *Bacchae* in which the story is itself a Year-god Story."

40. Cf. the remarks of Kurt Goldhammer, "Die Entmythologisierung des Mythus," *Studium Generale* 8 (June, 1955) 378–93.

41. Cf. Martin P. Nilsson, *A History of Greek Religion,* 2nd ed., tr. F. J. Fielden (Oxford, 1949) pp. 94–95; Winnington-Ingram, *Euripides and Dionysus,* p. 156 Note, does not believe Euripides was aware of the implications of omophagy.

42. Cf. Martin P. Nilsson, *The Dionysiac Mysteries of the Hellenistic and Roman Age* (Lund, 1957). Most evidence for Bacchic mysteries is late, but something of the sort may be assumed to have come under Euripides' observation. Cf. also Jeanmaire, *Dionysos,* pp. 372 ff.

43. William Arrowsmith, pp. 152–53 of the introduction to his translation of the play, in *Euripides V,* ed. David Grene and Richmond Lattimore (Chicago, 1959), takes this scene to signify a discovery of compassion, leading to a sort of anti-divine humanism.

44. Cf. Dodds' edition of the *Bacchae,* pp. 56–58, 220–21, 229–31.

45. *Ibid.*

46. At precisely this point in most Greek tragedies the lamentations assume a formal cast and the dramatic action becomes less realistic than ever.

47. In *The Riddle of the Bacchae*. The theory, a *reductio ad absurdum* of the realistic approach, was largely retracted by Norwood in *Essays on Euripidean Drama* (Berkeley, 1954), Ch. 2, "The *Bacchae* and Its Riddle."

48. In *The Bacchants of Euripides and Other Essays*, pp. 1–163. But that the Stranger "is, as Pentheus calls him, a conjuror and master of spells, a fanatic, but also upon occasion an impostor" (p. 71), represents an indefensible position, and Verrall does not avail himself of much convincing evidence as to the non-identity of Stranger and God.

49. Cf. 45–46: Pentheus and Dionysus had previously been fighting a "truceless" war.

50. The Stranger disappears immediately before the Voice, "presumably the Voice of Dionysus" is heard from heaven (1077–79).

51. But cf. Norwood, *Riddle of the Bacchae*, Ch. 8, esp. pp. 82 ff., where the speeches in the Prologue and the Epilogue are also assigned to the Stranger—which involves some difficulties. There is no reason to assume that Euripides did not intend these to be delivered by the god *in propria persona*.

52. *Met.* iii.571 ff. Acoetes means "the husband." Hence he leads Pentheus attired as a bride. The Second Vatican Mythographer (in *Scriptores Rerum Mythicarum*, ed. G. H. Bode, Vol. One, p. 103) has Liber take the form of "his comrade, Acetes."

53. Cf. Harrison, *Themis*, esp. Chs. 1 and 2; and Dodds' edition of the *Bacchae*, note to 115.

54. Cf. Dodds' edition of the *Bacchae*, note to 300.

55. Cf. G. M. A. Grube, *The Drama of Euripides* (London, 1941) p. 404.

56. Cf. Jeanmaire, *Dionysos*, pp. 138 ff.; and Erwin Rohde, *Psyche*, 8th ed., tr. W. B. Hillis (London, 1925) p. 258.

57. Plutarch, *De Iside et Osiride* 365A; cf. Otto, *Dionysos*, pp. 148 ff.

58. A common opinion: cf., as examples, Walter F. Otto, *The Homeric Gods*, tr. Moses Hadas (N. Y., 1954) pp. 153–54, 158–59; and Verrall, *The Bacchants*, pp. 2–3.

59. So André Rivier, *Essai sur le Tragique d'Euripide* (Lausanne, 1944) p. 98, sees the *Bacchae* as an affirmation of the terrifying personal relationship between man and god.

60. Cf. Dodds, *The Greeks and the Irrational*, Ch. 1, "Agamemnon's Apology." Dodds denies (p. 10) that there is a real "blurring of the sharp line that separates humanity from deity," but in the light of his own argument it is hard to agree.

61. For a contrary view, see Guthrie, *The Greeks and Their Gods*, p. 181.

62. P. 41; cf. also pp. 2–17 for a full discussion of "psychic intervention."

63. Snell, *The Discovery of the Mind*, p. 31, seems nearer the truth when he says "what was later known as the 'life of the soul' was at first understood as the intervention of a god." Cf. also Otto, *Homeric Gods*, pp. 173 ff.; and John H. Finley, *Pindar and Aeschylus* (Cambridge, Mass., 1955) p. 186.

64. The *O. E. D.* defines the word "reaction" only in its physiological and political senses. Cf. Leo Spitzer, "Language—The Basis of Science, Philosophy and Poetry," in George Boas *et al.*, *Studies in Intellectual History* (Baltimore, 1953) p. 84: it seems to be characteristic of "primitive" thinking to use the " 'happening' type of expression for inner experiences."

65. See Linforth, "The Corybantic Rites in Plato," pp. 121–162, and "Telestic Madness in Plato, Phaedrus 244DE," *U. of California Publications in Classical Philology* 13 (Berkeley, 1950) 163–72; and Dodds, *Greeks and the Irrational*, Ch. 3, "The Blessings of Madness," pp. 64–101, esp. 76 ff.

66. Cf. Grube, *Drama of Euripides*, p. 419; and H. D. F. Kitto, *Greek Tragedy* (London, 1950) p. 382.

67. Cf. Blaiklock, *The Male Characters of Euripides*, Ch. 11, "The Natural Man," pp. 209–230, esp. 213, 217.

CHAPTER 7: HAMLET AND THE STRUMPET FORTUNE

1. This is pretty much what is stated or hinted at by Geoffrey Bush, *Shakespeare and the Natural Condition* (Cambridge, Mass., 1956) esp. pp. 5, 80 ff., 127 (one of the profoundest studies of *Hamlet*); Maynard Mack, "The World of Hamlet," pp. 237–57 of *Shakespeare: Modern Essays in Criticism*, ed. Leonard F. Dean (N. Y., 1957), who says that this mysteriousness is built into the play; and Roy Walker, *The Time Is Out of Joint* (London, 1948), who

also, pp. 3-4, quotes Wilson Knight's *Principles of Shakespearian Production* to the same effect.

2. Cf. Walker, p. 42; R. A. Foakes, *"Hamlet* and the Court of Elsinore," *Shakespeare Survey* 9 (1956) 35-43; and S. L. Bethell, *Shakespeare and the Popular Dramatic Tradition* (London, 1944) pp. 39-40.

3. Cf. Harry Levin, "An Explication of the Player's Speech," *Kenyon Review* 12 (1950) 273-296, esp. pp. 290 ff. William Empson, *"Hamlet* When New," *Sewanee Review* 61 (1953) 15-42, 185-205, discusses how *Hamlet* deliberately calls attention to the fact that it *is* a play (cf. esp. pp. 22 ff.).

4. Cf. Bush, *Shakespeare,* p. 127; Walker, *The Time Is Out of Joint,* p. 38.

5. Cf. John E. Hankins, *The Character of Hamlet and Other Essays* (Chapel Hill, N. C., 1941) pp. 91 ff. Why M. D. H. Parker, *The Slave of Life* (London, 1955) p. 94, insists that the play is a study in corruption rather than of either salvation or damnation is not clear, unless he means that Hamlet ought not to be judged as either saved or damned.

6. The question, "Regenerated or not regenerated?", seems to be displacing in critical popularity the disagreements about the hero's hesitation or madness. Taking the Affirmative side, among others, are Theodore Spencer, *Shakespeare and the Nature of Man* (N. Y., 1942) p. 108; S. F. Johnson, "The Regeneration of Hamlet," *Shakespeare Quarterly* 3 (1952) 187-207; Paul N. Siegel, *Shakespearean Tragedy and the Elizabethan Compromise* (N. Y., 1957) p. 116; Kurt Schilling, *Shakespeare: Die Idee des Menschseins in Seinen Werken* (Munich, 1953) pp. 161 ff.; Fredson Bowers, "Hamlet as Minister and Scourge," *PMLA* 70 (1955) 740-49; and Bush, *Shakespeare,* p. 127. Upholding the Negative are H. B. Charlton, *Shakespearian Tragedy* (Cambridge, 1948) p. 103; Roy Battenhouse, "Hamlet's Apostrophe on Man: Clue to the Tragedy," *PMLA* 66 (1951) 1073-1113; and L. C. Knights, *Explorations* (N. Y., 1947) pp. 82-93. Many critics consider Hamlet justified from the beginning, of course. Others show dissatisfaction that Shakespeare does not make his own verdict clearer; but J. Max Patrick, "The Problem of Ophelia," *Studies in Shakespeare,* ed. Arthur Matthews and Clark Emery (Coral Gables, Fla., 1953) pp. 139-44, and Empson, *"Hamlet* When New," 15-42, 185-205, and pp. 194 ff., think that Shakespeare advisedly left many questions undecided in the play.

7. For the origins of the Hamlet-story see Israel Gollancz, *The Sources of Hamlet* (London, 1926); and Kemp Malone, *The Literary History of Hamlet* (Heidelberg, 1923) esp. Ch. 1.

8. In *The Classical Tradition in Poetry* (Cambridge, Mass., 1927) Ch. 8, pp. 180–210—originally delivered as the 1914 Annual Shakespeare Lecture of the British Academy. Following Murray, *Euripides and His Age* (N. Y. 1913), the parallel has been developed by Percy Allen, *Shakespeare and Chapman as Topical Dramatists* (London, 1929) pp. 50–62, and Bush, *Shakespeare*, pp. 114–15.

9. By Nicholas Rowe in 1709 and by Addison in No. 44 of *The Spectator:* see Paul S. Conklin, *A History of Hamlet Criticism, 1601–1821* (N. Y., 1957) p. 51.

10. *Hamlet and Oedipus* (N. Y., 1949). Others have treated the Hamlet-Orestes, Hamlet-Oedipus comparison more philosophically, e. g. Margarete Susman, *Gestalten und Kreise* (Zürich, 1954) pp. 42 ff.

11. "The Combat between Summer and Winter" survived in folk-festivals and in the Mummers' plays, common enough in Shakespeare's time and later; cf. E. K. Chambers, *The Medieval Stage*, Vol. One (Oxford, 1903) pp. 187–88 *et passim;* Murray, *Classical Tradition in Poetry*, pp. 200 ff.; Gollancz, *The Sources of Hamlet*, pp. 33–34, 36; and William Montgomerie, "Folk Play and Ritual in *Hamlet*," *Folk-Lore* 67 (1956) 214–27.

12. Hamlet and Lear are compared to the Fool-Scapegoat by Siegel, *Shakespearean Tragedy*, p. 219 Note; cf. also pp. 95–98.

13. In Saxo, Bk. III, by his soothsaying abilities Hamlethus wins the daughter of the King of Britain; in Bk. IV he weds Hermutrude, Queen of the Scots, who loathes union with old men and desires only the embraces of youths; many of her suitors have suffered death in wooing her, and when Hamlethus is killed in turn by Wiglek in Jutland, she yields herself to the slayer. Cf. Murray, *Classical Tradition*, pp. 196–97; Gollancz, *The Sources of Hamlet*, p. 48.

14. Cf. Allen, *Shakespeare and Chapman*, p. 57.

15. Examples of this myth are collected from far and wide by J. Schick, *Corpus Hamleticum*, Vol. One: *Das Glückskind mit dem Todesbrief* (Berlin, 1912).

16. Principally Wilson Knight, *The Wheel of Fire* (N. Y., 1949) Ch. 2, "The Embassy of Death: an Essay on *Hamlet*," and *The Imperial Theme* (London, 1931) Ch. 4, "Rose of May: an Essay on Life-Themes in *Hamlet*."

17. In addition, Walker, *The Time Is Out of Joint,* p. 94 Note, compares the Hamlet-story to the Hercules-myth.

18. The Player's Speech is generally either ignored, or discussed merely from the standpoint of its odd style, or regarded only as the occasion for the following soliloquy. Exceptions to this are H. D. F. Kitto, *Form and Meaning in Drama* (N. Y., n. d.) pp. 298 ff.; Levin, "An Explication of the Player's Speech;" Susman, *Gestalten und Kreise,* pp. 43 ff.

19. To my knowledge, no one has put forward this identification, though it probably is extent somewhere in the enormous *Hamlet*-literature. Walker, *The Time Is Out of Joint,* p. 97, compares the atmosphere of the Speech to Hamlet's own inner hell.

20. This is the idea of Levin, "An Explication of the Player's Speech," p. 281.

21. And Peter Alexander, *Hamlet Father and Son* (Oxford, 1955) p. 165, finds traces of the medieval Chivalric Hero even in Saxo's Hamlethus.

22. Most emphasized, perhaps excessively, by Salvador de Madariaga, *On Hamlet* (London, 1948). Cf. also Bertram Joseph, *Conscience and the King* (London, 1953) Ch. 1; Spencer, *Shakespeare,* p. 94; Battenhouse, "Hamlet's Apostrophe on Man," pp. 1082–83 (connecting *Hamlet* with the Renaissance "Literature of Courtesy").

23. Cf. Bowers, "Hamlet as Minister and Scourge," pp. 746–48.

24. Most critics seem to agree with Hamlet. Polonius is admittedly innocent; of Rosencrantz and Guildenstern, there is nothing at all in the text that would run counter to their original wish, "Heavens make our presence and our practices / Pleasant and helpful to him!" But, we are told, all three are boring. Strange that literary critics should approve the death penalty for that crime!

25. There has been much disputation about a possible reference to *hamartia* here; for recent opinions see Joseph, *Conscience and the King,* pp. 14 ff., and Alexander, *Hamlet,* pp. 44 ff.

26. See J. Dover Wilson, *What Happens in Hamlet,* 3rd ed. (Cambridge, 1951) Ch. 3; I. J. Semper, *Hamlet without Tears* (Dubuque, Iowa, 1946) Ch. 2.

27. Cf. Knight, *Imperial Theme,* p. 107.

28. Some have been troubled or misled by the fact that Hamlet does not explicitly question the ethics of revenge. But that such a moral conflict is implicitly present is shown by J. J. Lawlor, "The

Tragic Conflict in *Hamlet*," *Review of English Studies* 1, New Series, No. 2 (April, 1950) 97–113, and J. C. Maxwell, "Shakespeare: The Middle Plays," pp. 201–227 of *The Age of Shakespeare*, Vol. Two of *A Guide to English Literature*, ed. Boris Ford (Baltimore, 1956).

29. The significance of this is noticed by Harold C. Goddard, *The Meaning of Shakespeare* (Chicago, 1951) p. 349, and Siegel, *Shakespearean Tragedy*, p. 103.

30. These were among the lines that aroused the ire of Dryden, Preface to *Troilus and Cressida*, who could only excuse Shakespeare by attributing them to "some other Poet": "What a pudder is here kept in raising the expression of trifling thoughts. Would not a man have thought that the Poet had been bound Prentice to a Wheelwright, for his first Rant . . . Fortune is painted on a wheel; and therefore the writer in a rage, will have Poetical Justice done upon every member of that Engin: after this execution, he bowls the Nave downhill, from Heaven, to the Fiends. . . . Wise men would be glad to find a little sense couch'd under all those pompous words. . . ."

31. Wheels were rolled downhill at seasonal folk-festivals, as in the still surviving Easter egg-rollings; cf. Chambers, *The Medieval Stage*, pp. 127–28.

32. See Howard R. Patch, *The Goddess Fortuna* (Cambridge, 1927) *passim*.

33. Cf. Willard Farnham, *The Medieval Heritage of Elizabethan Tragedy* (Berkeley, 1936) p. 446 *et passim*. The Wheel of Fortune was of course a favorite image with Shakespeare: Raymond Chapman, "The Wheel of Fortune in Shakespeare's Historical Plays," *Review of English Studies* 1, New Series (Jan., 1950) 1–7.

34. Cf. Joseph, *Conscience and the King*, pp. 132 ff.

35. Francis G. Schoff, "Horatio: a Shakespearian Confidant," *Shakespeare Quarterly* 7 (1956) 53–57, insists on the ineffectiveness of Horatio as a dramatic personage: all the more reason to think, then, that his function is largely symbolic. Joseph, *Conscience and the King*, p. 166, tries to make Horatio more of a Christian than a Stoic.

36. In this speech and elsewhere in *Hamlet* there are curious verbal reminiscences of Anthony Copley's *A Fig for Fortune* (which appeared in 1596); parts of the poem are paraphrased or quoted in Farnham, *The Medieval Heritage*, pp. 347–49.

37. Farnham, *The Medieval Heritage*, pp. 337 ff., attributes the third way of dealing with Fortune (distinct from Stoic fortitude and

Christian charity), namely entering Fortune's realm and striving to take it away from her, to the influence of Machiavellianism. And the Elizabethan abhorrence of the latter is well-known.

38. G. R. Elliott, *Scourge and Minister* (Durham, N. C., 1951) p. xxix, briefly notes the theme of charity in the play. Parker, *Slave of Life*, p. 74, remarks that in the Comedies, the solution is always "Charity fulfils the law."

39. But so concludes Irving T. Richards, "The Meaning of Hamlet's Soliloquy," *PMLA* 48 (1933) 741–66, who sums up much previous controversy.

40. Cf. Semper, *Hamlet Without Tears*, p. 60.

41. Cf. John Middleton Murry, *Shakespeare* (N. Y., 1936) pp. 202–203.

42. Cf. Henri Fluchère, *Shakespeare*, tr. Guy Hamilton (London, 1953) pp. 209 ff.

43. Semper, *Hamlet Without Tears*, p. 21, quotes St. Thomas Aquinas to the effect that private vengeance, if not directed toward the victim's good, is a sin against charity.

44. L. C. Knights, *Explorations*, pp. 83 ff., believes that Hamlet's harsh judgments on others are informed by self-righteousness; cf. Kitto, *Form and Meaning*, pp. 314 ff.

45. But perhaps one should prefer the reading "a God kissing carrion," which Parker, *The Slave of Life*, p. 88, takes to be symbolic of the human condition. The idea of Man as the critical link in the Chain of Being is fully treated by Battenhouse, "Hamlet's Apostrophe on Man," who, however, is over-anxious to establish a pagan conception versus a Christian one.

46. For the subject of repentance in *Hamlet* see Hankins, *The Character of Hamlet*, pp. 192 ff., 209, 215.

47. Harley Granville-Barker, *Preface to Hamlet* (Princeton, 1946) pp. 238–39, objects to Claudius' lines as irrelevant, saying of the speech (p. 239 Note): "nothing legitimately leads up to it or away from it." Of course, The Soliloquy had shifted position in the different versions of the play, but presumably Shakespeare placed it finally where we now have it.

48. Cf. Robert Speaight, *Nature in Shakespearian Tragedy* (London, 1955) p. 42.

49. Benjamin Boyce, "The Stoic *Consolatio* and Shakespeare," *PMLA* 64 (1949) 771–80, calls this speech a "formal and splendid *consolatio*" (p. 776), containing both Stoic and Christian elements.

50. Cf. Spencer, *Shakespeare*, pp. 102–104.

51. Schilling, *Shakespeare*, p. 160, compares Hamlet's task of purging the state to that of Oedipus, but seems to think Hamlet quite successful in the end.

52. Cf. Siegel, *Shakespearean Tragedy*, p. 108, who, p. 110, concludes that Denmark is eventually regenerated. But an Elizabethan audience would hardly so view the entrance of a foreign prince with his army.

53. See the summary of the religious issues in Knight, *Imperial Theme*, p. 124.

CHAPTER 8: LEAR'S EQUATIONS

1. For possible Lucretian influence on Shakespeare, see L. C. Martin, "Shakespeare, Lucretius, and the Commonplaces," *Review of English Studies* 21 (July, 1945) 174–82.

2. General indebtedness throughout this chapter should be expressed to Robert B. Heilman, *This Great Stage* (Baton Rouge, 1948).

3. Cf. Geoffrey L. Bickersteth, "The Golden World of 'King Lear,'" *Proceedings of the British Academy* 32 (1946) 147–71, esp. 151.

4. Coleridge's complaint is referred to in Kenneth Muir's Arden Edition of *Lear* (Cambridge, Mass., 1952) p. lxiii. According to Richard H. Perkinson, "Shakespeare's Revision of the Lear Story and the Structure of *King Lear*," *Philological Quarterly* 22 (1943) 315–29, Shakespeare must have deliberately increased the improbability when he chose to compress the first four scenes of the earlier *King Leir* into one (p. 317).

5. Cf. L. C. Knights, "*King Lear* and the Great Tragedies," in *The Age of Shakespeare*, Vol. Two of *A Guide to English Literature*, ed. Boris Ford (Baltimore, 1956) p. 233. Cf. also H. B. Charlton, *Shakespearian Tragedy* (Cambridge, 1948) pp. 189, 218 ff.; and D. G. James, *The Dream of Learning* (Oxford, 1951) Ch. 4, for fuller discussions.

6. Cf. Robert Speaight, *Nature in Shakespearian Tragedy* (London, 1955) p. 90. For fuller discussions see W. C. Curry, *Shakespeare's Philosophical Patterns* (Baton Rouge, 1937) Chs. 1 and 5; M. D. H. Parker, *The Slave of Life* (London, 1955) Ch. 1; Patrick Cruttwell, *The Shakespearean Moment* (N. Y., 1955) Ch. 6; and S. L. Bethell,

The Cultural Revolution of the Seventeenth Century (N. Y., 1951) *passim,* esp. pp. 118–19.

7. For Lipsius see J. L. Saunders, *Justus Lipsius: The Philosophy of Renaissance Stoicism* (N. Y., 1955); for Chapman, Ennis Rees, *The Tragedies of George Chapman* (Cambridge, Mass., 1954).

8. Cf. Bethell, *The Cultural Revolution,* pp. 56 ff.; James, *The Dream of Learning,* Ch. 1; L. C. Knights, *Explorations* (N. Y., 1947) Ch. 5, "Bacon and the Seventeenth-Century Dissociation of Sensibility"; John F. Danby, *Shakespeare's Doctrine of Nature: A Study of King Lear* (London, 1949) p. 36.

9. The setting-in of Jacobean disillusionment after Elizabethan exuberance had its effect also: cf. Henri Fluchère, *Shakespeare,* tr. Guy Hamilton (London, 1953) pp. 31 ff.

10. For a summary of the debate see Paul N. Siegel, *Shakespearean Tragedy and the Elizabethan Compromise* (N. Y., 1957) p. 213. The view presented in this chapter is now most generally adhered to: cf. James, *The Dream of Learning,* pp. 119 ff.; J. C. Maxwell, "The Technique of Invocation in 'King Lear,'" *Modern Language Review* 45 (1950) 142–47; James L. Rosier, "The Lex Aeterna and *King Lear,*" *Journal of English and Germanic Philology* 53 (1954) 574–80; Enid Welsford, *The Fool* (London, 1935) p. 268; Theodore Spencer, *Shakespeare and the Nature of Man* (N. Y., 1942) pp. 147–48, quoting Dowden, *Shakespeare, His Mind and Art* (N. Y., 1903), p. 240. Oscar J. Campbell, "The Salvation of Lear," *Journal of English Literary History* 15 (1948) 93–109; and S. L. Bethell, *Shakespeare and the Popular Dramatic Tradition* (London, 1944) pp. 54 ff., 61.

11. Edwin Muir, *Essays on Literature and Society* (London, 1949) pp. 31–48, "The Politics of *King Lear,*" believes that in performing this logical reduction Shakespeare forecast future developments and composed a "mythical drama of the transmutation of civilisation" (p. 33).

12. Called Lear's "motto" by Siegel, *Shakespearean Tragedy,* p. 179. Its significance is also underscored by Parker, *The Slave of Life,* pp. 131–32; cf. also William Empson, *The Structure of Complex Words* (Norfolk, Conn., n. d.) pp. 138–39: and the note in K. Muir's Arden Edition of *Lear,* p. 9.

13. Cf. Herbert Weisinger, "The Myth and Ritual Approach to Shakespearean Tragedy," *Centennial Review* 1 (1957) 142–66; the difficulties of this approach were summarized by Weisinger himself in a paper read to the Modern Language Association convention in

Dec., 1958 (kindly loaned to me in MS); nevertheless he sees its value. Cf. also Douglas Hewitt, "The Very Pompes of the Divell—Popular and Folk Elements in Elizabethan and Jacobean Drama," *Review of English Studies* 25 (1949) 10-23; and Siegel, *Shakespearean Tragedy,* pp. 95-98. For other approaches to Shakespeare's use of myth (the term being somewhat loosely used) see *English Institute Essays, 1948:* Leslie A. Fiedler, "The Defense of the Illusion and the Creation of Myth," pp. 74-94; and Edward Hubler, "Three Shakespearean Myths: Mutability, Plenitude, and Reputation," pp. 95-119.

14. In *The Aim and Structure of Physical Reality,* excerpted, pp. 26-28, in *Readings in the Philosophy of Science,* ed. Philip P. Wiener (N. Y., 1953).

15. Winifred M. T. Nowottny, "Lear's Questions," *Shakespeare Survey* 10 (1957) 90-97, points out that Lear's subsequent questions are as willful as this first one.

16. *Ibid.,* p. 93, where Shakespeare's deliberate exploitation of linguistic ambivalence is discussed, especially the use of the term "flesh" and related terms.

17. The ambiguity may have been helped along by the two meanings of "love": "feel affection for" and "set a value on"; cf. Terry Hawkes, " 'Love' in *King Lear,*" *Review of English Studies* 10 (1959) 178-81. These two distinct verbs, from OE *lofian* "praise" and *lufian* "love" were further confused by the similarly coalescing OF *aimer* (L *amare*) and *esmer* (L *aestimare*); see John Orr, *Words and Sounds in English and French* (Oxford, 1953) pp. 114-15; and the confusion lent point to what seems to have been a punning proverb, "Tant as, tant vals, e jo tant t'aim," which Wace gives as Cordelia's reply to Lear in his version of the story in *Brut.*

18. John M. Lothian, *King Lear: A Tragic Reading of Life* (Toronto, 1949) p. 93, calls the speech "the triumph of moral nihilism."

19. The story is fully analyzed by Giuseppe Cocchiara, *La Leggenda di Re Lear* (Torino, 1932), who gives many variant versions and traces the motif, "Sacrifice of the Younger Son," back to initiation rites and seasonal festivals. Wilfrid Perrett, *The Story of King Lear* (Berlin, 1904) is still of value: see esp. pp. 9-26.

20. The Gloucester-Edgar plot is essentially the same myth; it contains the elements of estrangement between father and son, the hint of the father's supersession by the son, the wandering of the son

in the wilderness, the meeting with a "wild man" or spirit in the wilderness, the abasement of the father, and the final reconciliation: all these are relics of initiation-myths, as shown by Cocchiara.

21. See W. Schultz's article, "Rätsel," in *Pauly-Wissowa*, and the article on "Riddles" in *The Encyclopedia of Religion and Ethics.* Cf. also Reidar T. Christiansen, "Myth, Metaphor, and Simile," pp. 39–49 of *Myth: A Symposium*, ed. Thomas A. Sebeok (Philadelphia, 1955), and Johan Huizinga, "Playing and Knowing," pp. 105–118 of *Homo Ludens* (Boston, 1955).

22. Cf. Gabriel Marcel, *The Mystery of Being*, Vol. Two (Chicago, 1951) p. 122.

23. Shakespeare's mere use of the symbolic-dramatic method was an implied refutation of this; a dramatic symbol is both itself and more than itself: see Alan S. Downer, "The Life of Our Design: The Function of Imagery in the Poetic Drama," pp. 19–36 of *Shakespeare: Modern Essays in Criticism*, ed. Leonard F. Dean (N. Y., 1957).

24. Cf. G. Wilson Knight, *The Wheel of Fire* (N. Y., 1949) Chs. 8 and 9. Danby, *Shakespeare's Doctrine of Nature*, pp. 104–106, uses the symbol of the wheel to explain much of the Fool's imagery. E. K. Chambers, *The Medieval Stage*, Vol. One (Oxford, 1903) pp. 127–28, mentions that a burning wheel, a common solar emblem, was often rolled downhill from the festival bonfires among the vineyards. This would fit in with the pattern of Lear as a *pharmakos*-figure.

25. The phrase is Lothian's in *King Lear*, p. 98.

26. Hence the prevalence of animal imagery: see Heilman, *This Great Stage*, pp. 93 ff. Edwin Muir, *Essays*, p. 40, has an analysis of Goneril's and Regan's equational thinking; cf. also pp. 34, 35, 42.

27. Hence evil cannot be explained by reason, and Edmund, like Iago, has something of The Vice in the Morality Plays in him: see Bernard Spivack, *Shakespeare and the Allegory of Evil* (N. Y., 1958) pp. 413–14.

28. Cf. Geoffrey Bush, *Shakespeare and the Natural Condition* (Cambridge, Mass., 1956) p. 91.

29. Therefore, in the play, goodness has to hide, as pointed out by Spencer, *Shakespeare*, p. 152.

30. Cf. Marcel, *The Mystery of Being*, pp. 13, 16–17.

31. Cf. Philip Wheelwright, "The Semantic Approach to Myth," p. 101, from *Myth: A Symposium.*

32. *The Fool*, pp. 253–70. See also Hewitt, "The Very Pompes of the Divell," pp. 17–20; Siegel, *Shakespearean Tragedy*, p. 219 Note;

and Maud Bodkin, *Archetypal Patterns in Poetry* (London, 1934) pp. 16 ff., 280 ff.

33. As one expelled from human society, Lear can criticize it from the outside, as Hewitt points out, "The Very Pompes of the Divell," pp. 19–20.

34. Cf. Welsford, *The Fool*, pp. 262–63.

35. See E. K. Chambers, *The Medieval Stage:* pp. 117, 137, 327, 348, for the garlands; 325–26 for the inversion of status; 316, 325 for the granting of indulgences; 325 for the preaching. It was at such a Feast at Gray's Inn in 1594 that *The Comedy of Errors* was performed (see p. 417). For the chasing of the king compare the *Regifugium* in J. G. Frazer, *The Golden Bough: The Dying God* (N. Y., 1935) pp. 213–14. Of course, Lear's speeches contain elements of distorted truth: cf. Nowottny, "Lear's Questions," pp. 94–96; and Harold C. Goddard, *The Meaning of Shakespeare* (Chicago, 1951) pp. 528, 538–39.

36. Cf. E. K. Chambers, *The English Folk-Play* (Oxford, 1933) pp. 50 ff. *et passim.*

37. Cf. Goddard, *The Meaning of Shakespeare*, p. 539.

38. Compare "The Phoenix and Turtle": "Number there in love was slain."

39. Not much of the horror of *Lear* would be mitigated if the play were only a mechanical demonstration of justice or "moral education": cf. R. W. Chambers, *King Lear* (Glasgow, 1940) pp. 49 ff.; and Clifford Leech, *Shakespeare's Tragedies* (N. Y., 1950) pp. 14 ff.

40. Campbell, "The Salvation of Lear," pp. 96 ff., is most insistent on a Stoic interpretation of *Lear*, but even he, p. 103, recognizes its inadequacy.

41. Danby, *Shakespeare's Doctrine of Nature*, p. 33, discusses the contrary view that Nature has "a *nisus* toward the topmost point of the pyramid."

42. Cf. Bickersteth, "The Golden World of 'King Lear,'" pp. 163 ff.; Leech, *Shakespeare's Tragedies*, p. 105.

43. According to Lothian, *King Lear*, p. 84, Lear "seeks a centre of stoic indifference."

44. This point is made by E. M. M. Taylor, "Lear's Philosopher," *Shakespeare Quarterly* 6 (1955) 364–65. Cf. Nowottny, "Lear's Questions," p. 93; Knights, *Age of Shakespeare*, p. 232.

45. Danby, *Shakespeare's Doctrine of Nature*, pp. 181 ff., discusses the Thunder-symbolism. The cause of thunder is treated by Lucretius,

VI.96 ff. Such questions were of common concern to both Epicurean and Stoic, who agreed in advocating the simple life and such contemplation of Nature as would conduce to inner tranquillity.

46. Campbell, "The Salvation of Lear," p. 102, also describes Kent and the Fool as Cynic-Stoic commentators in this scene.

47. K. Muir, p. lxi of the Arden Edition of *Lear*, connects the animal imagery with the Chain of Being, and furnishes further references.

48. Arthur Sewell, "Tragedy and the 'Kingdom of Ends,' " pp. 311–32 of *Shakespeare: Modern Essays in Criticism*, discusses *Lear* as a revelation of the insufficiency of reason.

49. Bethell, *Cultural Revolution*, p. 83: ". . . *Lear* is a dramatic study of an enquiry proposed by Montaigne and a refutation of his sceptical-fideistic conclusions."

50. But it is not accurate to say that Shakespeare invented Cordelia's unhappy fate: according to R. W. Chambers, *King Lear*, p. 20, Shakespeare actually mitigated the story in the chronicles, where she commits suicide in prison. Perrett, *The Story of King Lear*, pp. 25 ff., points out that such sad endings were traditional in the Celtic parallels to the Cordelia-story. (In the Kreiddylad story, perhaps analogous, she is the prize fought over by Gwythyr and Gwynn "every first of May till Doomsday," i. e. she is a priestess of the Earth-Goddess: cf. Perrett, p. 17.)

51. Cf. Bush, *Shakespeare*, pp. 88 ff.

52. But cf. Nowottny, "Lear's Questions," p. 97, for a contrary view.

53. Which comprehends Nature, but does not negate it: cf. Bush, *Shakespeare*, pp. 5–6.

54. The weakening of this conception meant the loss of tragic feeling: cf. Bethell, *Shakespeare and the Popular Dramatic Tradition*, p. 83.

55. If the immediate source of the Gloucester sub-plot was the story of the Paphlagonian King in Book Two of Sidney's *Arcadia*, then from the same work Shakespeare may have had suggested to him many other details with regard to the Edmund-Edgar duel, e.g. the "ill-appareled knight's" challenge to Phalanthus in Book One, and the challenges of the Knight of the Tomb and the Forsaken Knight to Amphialus in Book Three. For a possible Spring-versus-Winter mythical origin of such stories see R. S. Loomis, *Celtic Myth and Arthurian Romance* (N. Y., 1927) esp. Ch. 31, "Knights of the

272   NOTES TO PAGES 193-196

Swan." The outlines of the Defeat of Winter ritual itself were still to be discerned in the Mummers' Play in Shakespeare's time.

56. Cf. Knights, *Age of Shakespeare*, pp. 236 ff.; Danby, *Shakespeare's Doctrine of Nature*, pp. 181 ff., comments that Lear's wish, "Let's away to prison," is thwarted because goodness cannot isolate itself from life. The wish is, in fact, only another form of that shirking of responsibility with which the play begins; it is a form of Epicurean escapism, but, like much else in the play, is resonant of Christian overtones.

57. K. Muir, Arden Edition of *Lear*, p. lviii, compares Cordelia to the pure and innocent victims who "were chosen to propitiate the dragon, and . . . in ancient Mexico . . . were slain on the bloody alter of Tezcatlipoca." Cf. G. Wilson Knight, *The Crown of Life* (London, 1947) p. 12.

58. Cf. James, *The Dream of Learning*, p. 121.

59. R. W. Chambers, *King Lear*, p. 48, thinks that Gloucester is climbing the Mountain of Purgatory; Bickersteth, p. 153, calls the episode of the leap an "acted 'morality' in miniature." Roland M. Smith, "King Lear and the Merlin Tradition," *Modern Language Quarterly* 7 (1946) 167, suggests that the incident was copied from Suibhne's leap in the Irish *Buile Suibhne*, citing many other parallels.

60. Cf. Bush, *Shakespeare*, pp. 128-29; Paul N. Siegel, "Adversity and the Miracle of Love in *King Lear*," *Shakespeare Quarterly* 6 (1955) 325-36.

61. Bethell, *Shakespeare and the Popular Dramatic Tradition*, pp. 59-61, lists passages that liken Cordelia to Christ.

62. Cf. Bickersteth, "The Golden World of 'King Lear,'" p. 169; Goddard, *The Meaning of Shakespeare*, p. 533.

CHAPTER 9: ELIOT'S "MURDER IN THE CATHEDRAL":
MYTH AND HISTORY

1. These three reactions may perhaps show some correspondence to Pascal's "three orders," an analysis admired by Eliot: cf. Francis Fergusson, *The Idea of a Theater* (Princeton, 1949) pp. 229-30.

2. Peter Kline, "The Spiritual Center in Eliot's Plays," *Kenyon Review* 21 (1959) 457-72, thinks that Eliot may have derived his symbol of the Wheel from T. E. Hulme (pp. 463 ff.); the symbol is age-old, however. The image "lies at the heart of Eliot's poetry," says Louis L. Martz, p. 446, "The Wheel and the Point: Aspects of

Imagery and Theme in Eliot's Later Poetry," pp. 444–62 of *T. S. Eliot: A Selected Critique,* ed. Leonard Unger (N. Y., 1948).

3. That the Chorus represent some kind of commonplace attitude is generally observed; there are differences of opinion concerning to what degree they develop in the course of the play: cf. Grover Smith, Jr., *T. S. Eliot's Poetry and Plays* (Chicago, 1959) p. 185, referring to Theodore Spencer; Martz, "The Wheel and the Point," p. 461; John Peter, "Murder in the Cathedral," *Sewanee Review* 61 (1953) 362–83.

4. Echoed in "Burnt Norton," Section I; cf. George Williamson, *A Reader's Guide to T. S. Eliot* (N. Y., 1953) p. 212.

5. One of the themes of *Four Quartets;* see Philip Wheelwright, "Eliot's Philosophical Themes," pp. 96–106 of *T. S. Eliot: A Study of His Writings by Several Hands,* ed. B. Rajan (London, 1947).

6. This chorus has been extensively analysed; cf., e. g., Smith, *T. S. Eliot's Poetry and Plays,* p. 192; Martz, "The Wheel and the Point," pp. 457 ff.

7. Cf. "Ash Wednesday," Sec. III.

8. A parallel between Tempters and Knights is often drawn (cf. Fergusson, *The Idea of a Theater,* p. 225), and the roles are often taken by the same actors. Kline, "The Spiritual Center," p. 469, elaborates such a parallel. Cf. also F. O. Matthiessen, *The Achievement of T. S. Eliot* (N. Y., 1947) p. 164.

9. Cf. Martz, "The Wheel and the Point," p. 461.

10. Frank Wilson, *Six Essays on the Development of T. S. Eliot* (London, 1948) p. 49, ranks the Priests even below the Old Women in apprehension of reality, but he fails to distinguish between the individual Priests.

11. One is reminded of F. R. Leavis' warning, in *The Common Pursuit* (N. Y., 1952) p. 287, against the religious-dogmatic approach to Eliot, on the ground that it tends to "abet the reader's desire to arrive without having travelled." But surely that is a danger in any kind of expository criticism.

12. See Williamson's discussion, *A Reader's Guide,* pp. 209 ff., of Eliot's use of the Logos-doctrine.

13. *Ibid.,* pp. 213 ff.

14. See Nathan A. Scott, Jr., *Rehearsals of Discomposure* (N. Y., 1952) p. 211, for a discussion, derived from Tillich, on the difference between *chronos,* mere duration, and *kairos,* the fulfilled moment when the eternal breaks into the temporal.

15. For the connection of this idea with free-will and determinism, see Gabriel Marcel, *The Mystery of Being*, Vol. Two (Chicago, 1951) p. 112, where the point is made that the sequential pattern of the notes in a melody has nothing to do with causation.

16. Perhaps a reminiscence of Keats's "Grecian Urn."

17. The point is often made that this play is successful chiefly because of its "close connection with church ritual": cf., e. g., Raymond Williams, *Drama from Ibsen to Eliot* (London, 1954) pp. 227–31. Eliot himself modestly agrees, in *Poetry and Drama* (Cambridge, Mass., 1951) p. 29. Yet the ritual is not merely *donné*, but is fully integrated into the play's ultimate meaning.

18. A leading theme of *Four Quartets;* cf. Williamson, *A Reader's Guide*, pp. 205 ff. For the primitive view of time, see Mircea Eliade, *The Myth of the Eternal Return*, tr. Willard Trask (N. Y., 1954) *passim*.

19. And consequently of Dionysus, too. Cf. Fergusson, *The Idea of a Theater*, pp. 223, 225.

20. And Eliot's resolute avoidance of the danger seems to have given rise to the objection that the characters, Becket especially, lack "personality"; cf. Wilson, *Six Essays*, p. 48. So, one might retort, do all the characters in Greek Tragedy lack personality. Helen Gardner, *The Art of T. S. Eliot* (London, 1949) p. 135, asserts that "there is in the play an almost Gnostic contempt for personality. . . ." But Eliot is consistently anti-Gnostic; his well-known disdain for personality stems from a Christian exasperation at the modern substitution of "development, cultivation, or integration of the personality" for a concern with the soul's salvation. Miss Gardner's further criticism of the play is based on her assertion that "we have to take it for granted that Thomas dies with a pure will' (p. 134), since the play does not, in fact cannot, prove this to us. To be sure, we have to take for granted whatever the text of a play affirms; for all their soliloquies and actions, we have to "take it for granted" that Antigone and Hamlet die "with a pure will" also.

21. Cf. Eliot, *Poetry and Drama*, pp. 43–44: "For it is ultimately the function of art, in imposing a credible order upon ordinary reality, and thereby eliciting some perception of an order *in* reality, to bring us to a condition of serenity, stillness, and reconciliation; and then leave us, as Virgil left Dante, to proceed toward a region where that guide can avail us no further."

22. See Marcel, *The Mystery of Being*, p. 162, for further contrast between hope and desire.

23. Cf. Marcel, *The Philosophy of Existence* (London, 1948) pp. 19–20.

24. Peter, "Murder in the Cathedral," pp. 378–79 Note, warns that if the parallel between the Fourth Tempter and Fourth Knight is pressed too far, Becket's death will really seem to be a suicide. Yet probably Eliot intends us to press it pretty far: the death is a "suicide" in the sense of being a complete abnegation of the natural self; Peter is right, of course, in showing that it is not so in the Knight's sense of the word.

25. *Ibid.*, p. 373.

26. *Ibid.*: Thomas is saved when he perceives that involved in his struggle is the spiritual well-being of the Church. Cf. also Brother George Every, "The Way of Rejections," pp. 181–88 of *T. S. Eliot,* ed. Richard March and Tambimuttu (Chicago, 1949).

27. Cf. Marcel, *Philosophy of Existence,* pp. 16–17.

28. Cf. E. E. Duncan Jones, "Ash Wednesday," pp. 37–56 (esp. p. 40) of *T. S. Eliot: A Study of His Writings by Several Hands.* Leonard Unger, "Ash Wednesday," pp. 349–94, of *T. S. Eliot: A Selected Critique,* compares this movement to that of the souls up Dante's Mount of Purgatory (p. 352). The movement differs from both the Greek conception of time as circular and the Lockean-modern as rectilinear: cf. Williamson, p. 236.

29. The relations of love and desire to the movements of time are contrasted in "Burnt Norton": cf. Williamson, *A Reader's Guide,* p. 217.

30. The frequently urged objection that the play lacks dramatic action shows a failure to grasp what Eliot is doing; both action and passion, in their ordinary senses, are here transcended: cf. Smith, *T. S. Eliot's Poetry and Plays,* pp. 188 ff.; Martz, "The Wheel and the Point," pp. 445 ff.

31. Only, of course by becoming "at one" with Christ's atonement; cf. Smith, *T. S. Eliot's Poetry and Plays,* pp. 186–87. For the Aquinan doctrine of suffering as atonement, see M. D. H. Parker, *The Slave of Life* (London, 1955) p. 226.

32. For the sense in which another Eliot character (Harcourt-Reilly in *The Cocktail Party*) plays a Christ-role, see John Edward Hardy, "An Antic Disposition," *Sewanee Review* 65 (1957) 1–11.

33. But it is going rather far to assert that the play is therefore a comedy, as Smith does, p. 184; such a classification comes from a too rigid application of the *hamartia*-theory: cf. Louis L. Martz, "The Saint as Tragic Hero: *Saint Joan* and *Murder in the Cathedral*," pp. 150–78 of *Tragic Themes in Western Literature*, ed. Cleanth Brooks (New Haven, 1955).

34. Cf. Martz, "The Wheel and the Point," pp. 455–56.

35. Cf. Scott, *Rehearsals*, p. 217.

36. An attempt has been made, by Hugh Ross Williamson, *The Arrow and the Sword* (London, 1947), to prove that the historical Becket's death was a ritual Catharist sacrifice, rather than an orthodox Christian martyrdom.

37. Scott, *Rehearsals*, p. 244, says that some Christian interpreters of Eliot have felt that he leans too much toward Platonist speculations about time and eternity. But however else Eliot may err, he certainly has no patience with Platonic Manicheism; his antagonism is manifest in *Four Quartets*: cf. B. Rajan, "The Unity of the Quartets," pp. 78–79 of *T. S. Eliot: A Study of His Writings by Several Hands*.

38. Cf. Williamson, *A Reader's Guide*, pp. 233 ff.

39. Rudolf Bultmann's *Entmythologisierung* seems to forfeit both, and thus to fall directly into Gnosticism.

CHAPTER 10: AFTERWORD: TRAGEDY AND MYSTERY

1. For a recent review of the components of tragedy see T. R. Henn, *The Harvest of Tragedy* (London, 1956) esp. Ch. 2.

2. This is perhaps not entirely fair to Wilamowitz, *Heracles*, but the fact that he attempted to define only "Attic tragedy" shows his nominalistic bias. His definition is, in full: "An Attic tragedy is a portion of heroic saga, complete in itself, which has undergone poetic treatment in elevated style so as to be performed by a citizen-chorus and two or three actors and so as to be presented as part of the official religious celebrations in the sanctuary of Dionysus." This no-nonsense approach wins approval from many German critics, and apparently also from Richmond Lattimore, *The Poetry of Greek Tragedy* (Baltimore, 1958) pp. 3 ff.

3. Several of these terms are drawn from M. H. Abrams, *The Mirror and the Lamp* (N. Y., 1953) Ch. 1.

4. Including nominalism: cf. George Boas, "Some Problems of

Intellectual History," pp. 3–21 (esp. 17–18) of George Boas *et al.*, *Studies in Intellectual History* (Baltimore, 1953).

5. For another view of the relation of tragedy to the concept of justice, see Carlo del Grande, *Trago·idía: Essenza e Genesi della Tragedia* (Naples, 1952) pp. 114–17.

6. Cf. Herbert Weisinger, *Tragedy and the Paradox of the Fortunate Fall* (East Lansing, Mich., 1953) pp. 266 ff.

7. Cf. Henry A. Myers, *Tragedy: A View of Life* (Ithaca, 1956) pp. 6, 26.

8. This would be to disagree with Murray Krieger, "Tragedy and the Tragic Vision," *Kenyon Review* 20 (1958) 281–99, who maintains that the truly "tragic vision" is one of despair and is a "facing up to nothingness."

9. This is in contrast to Nietzsche's "mystery doctrine of tragedy" in which individuation is considered as the prime basis of evil and oneness is to be attained in tragedy through breaking the spell of individuation: needless to say, this is not what is meant in these essays by the word "mystery." Cf. W. Macneile Dixon, *Tragedy* (London, 1925) p. 214, and Hans Bogner, *Der Tragische Gegensatz* (Heidelberg, 1947) pp. 15 ff.

10. For a different triple classification of tragedies see E. M. W. Tillyard, *Shakespeare's Problem Plays* (Toronto, 1949) pp. 14 ff.

11. Cf. André Bonnard, *La Tragédie et l'Homme* (Neuchatel, 1951) pp. 191–92.

12. Cf. Gerhard Nebel, *Weltangst und Götterzorn* (Stuttgart, 1951) p. 165, relative to the *Oresteia*.

Index